Economic
Vulnerability
in International
Relations

Economic Vulnerability in International Relations:

*The Case of
East-West Trade,
Investment,
and Finance*

Beverly Crawford

*Columbia University Press
New York*

Columbia University Press
New York   Chichester, West Sussex
Copyright © 1993 Columbia University Press
All rights reserved

Library of Congress Cataloging-in-Publication Data

Crawford, Beverly.
  Economic vulnerability in international relations : the case of
East-West trade, investment, and finance. 1970–1990 / Beverly
Crawford.
      p.   cm.
  Includes bibliographical references and index.
  ISBN 0–231–08296–7. — ISBN 0–231–08297–5 (pbk.)
  1. East-West trade. 2. International economic relations.
  3. Post-communism. I. Title
HF4050.C73 1993
382'.09171'301717—dc20   93–35563
                                                               CIP

♾

Casebound editions of Columbia University Press books are printed
on permanent and durable acid-free paper.
Printed in the United States of America
c 10 9 8 7 6 5 4 3 2 1

This book is dedicated to my Mom

Contents

Preface

The themes of this book intersect with a number of issues that have long puzzled me. From the time I first decided to study political science I have been interested in how foreign policy is made in the United States. How do knowledge, policy analysis, policy evaluation, and politics interact in the making of foreign policy? To what extent and under what conditions will decision makers ignore policy analysis in favor of formulating policies that fit ideological proclivities and political agendas? Second, I have been caught up with trying to understand the relationship between security and economics in international relations. The logic of behavior in each issue area is so different, the two logics clash so harshly, and the policy implications are so thorny that it is little wonder that the relationship has, until recently, been neglected in the literature on international interdependence and international relations more generally. To what extent, for example, will the international political economy be "militarized" as the focus on economic security increases? Third, I am concerned with the role that foreign technology can play in a nation's industrial development and growth: the Soviet Union was a "hard case" to examine because there was relatively little imported technology, and its institutional structure mitigated against technological diffusion. Nonetheless, the foreign-policy community in the United States seemed to believe that Western technology would have an important effect on Soviet economic as well as military strength, so I was determined to try and find out what that effect might have been and how the Soviet case might be generalized. Finally, I was interested in how Cold War was waged and how it ended. What did economic relationships between adversaries have to do with the "war" itself, with who "won," and with the collapse of the Soviet Union? Are there lessons we can learn from this episode for future policy?

This project has allowed me to explore these issues and address these questions. Although I am entirely responsible for what is written here, the issues of concern to me were sufficiently broad and complex that I could not have tackled them entirely alone. With gratitude, therefore, I acknowledge the institutions and people who helped to make this book possible: the University of Pittsburgh Institute for Strategic Economics and Industrial Vulnerability provided the initial grant to get it started; the Hoover Institution, Stanford University gave me a year free from teaching and access to a wonderful library; the University of California Center for German and European Studies and its director, Richard Buxbaum, provided essential support; and International and Area Studies under Dean Albert Fishlow was most helpful in countless ways. I am also grateful to the U.S. Department of State's Title VIII Program in Soviet-Eastern European Research and Training for a generous grant that enabled me to complete much of the research for this book.

Many people read all or parts of the manuscript and offered helpful comments and criticism as well as support and encouragement. It is a pleasure to acknowledge the help I received from Janet Chapman, Jeff Frieden, John Hardt, Dan Kevin, Tim McKeown, Stuart Macdonald, Syd Mintzer, Bill Root, Dennis Quinn, Harry Rowen, and Steve Van Evera. Sally Fifer read and offered helpful criticism on early drafts and Mike Mastanduno carefully read the entire manuscript; his sharp insights sent me back to the drawing board more than once and I very much appreciate his thoughtful comments and questions. John Leslie, James Martel, Syd Mintzer, and Susan Overdorf provided valuable research assistance. Syd Mintzer constructed the tables for chapters 5 and 6 and offered valuable comments on the argument as it related to energy and finance; I am especially grateful to him. James Martel proofread the entire manuscript. All not only offered valuable help but were fun to work with as well.

I also want to thank Peggy Phillips and Patricia La Hay for all of the administrative support that have given me during the writing of this book. Their help, though indirect, was invaluable and their good cheer brightened many days of hard work. I also thank Kate Wittenberg and

Jonathan Director at Columbia University Press for taking on this project and shepherding it through the process of publication.

I am most grateful, of course, to Sal and Erin for their support, inspiration, encouragement, and understanding, and for the privilege of a strong family. Thanks to my parents, Vincent and Sammy Utter, and especially to my mother, who often sacrificed to support the things I wanted to do in life, whether she agreed or not. This book is dedicated to her with much love and appreciation.

1

The Unresolved Question

Introduction

As the former Soviet bloc entered the international economy, the industrialized world embarked on its most radical reorganization of trade in postwar history. The crumbling of Cold War walls, the death of the Soviet Union, the birth of fragile democracies, the halting introduction of the market, and the spread of ethnic conflict and economic crisis throughout the region set the conditions under which the United States and Western Europe would do business with the "postcommunist" world. Business hesitated before it rushed eastward with new capital, and Western governments and multilateral lending institutions debated over whether and how to aid ailing economies and states of the former USSR and Eastern Europe.

The demise of Soviet Communism, and the Soviet Union, itself marked the beginning of a radical transformation of U.S. and Western strategic trade restriction policies, as policymakers began to reexamine the very foundations of the constraints within which a new global economic order was to evolve. The central aim of export control and other strategic trade restrictions has been to limit economic relations with adversaries or potential adversaries. Until the end of the Cold War the policy was directed at the Communist World in general, and the Warsaw Pact in particular.

That policy's basic assumption is that the industrialized world makes itself vulnerable when it trades with military rivals, or even potential economic competitors, who can quickly translate economic strength into military power. In the post-Soviet international environment, the dominance of that assumption has led many policymakers in the U.S. to begin to lift controls on former adversaries, but argue for increased controls on Third World nations as well as present allies, such as Japan.[1] These changing arguments have led to increasing policy confusion and incoherence.

An important reason for that confusion is that the central vulnerability assumption guiding policy was never specified and systematically tested. Throughout the Cold War, vulnerability *beliefs*—often tied to specific political interests—guided policy, but the beliefs were never specified and vulnerability *facts* were rarely examined. Therefore, assumptions about Western trade vulnerability (or lack thereof) were (and continue to be) simply symbolic currency in debates over appropriate trade policy goals toward rival nations. Because vulnerability assumptions were unsubstantiated but nonetheless became the rationale for coercive U.S. policies toward its allies, opposing beliefs tied to specific political and economic interests became equally powerful in the policy debate. Throughout the Cold War, while U.S. decision makers warned of the vulnerability effects of expanded East-West trade, Europeans minimized Western vulnerability in their assessments of the role of foreign technology in Soviet economic development and military power, the role of energy trade as an instrument of Soviet foreign policy, and the role that loans and credits to the East played in national economic development and in international political negotiations.

In fact, few other issues aroused such passionate dispute between the United States and its Cold War allies, signaling so clearly or so early Europe's emerging self-assertion and drift from the preferences of the United States. The decade of the 1980s witnessed acrimonious debate between the United States and its European allies over Europe's "dependence" on the Soviet Union for its energy supplies, conflict over the definition of strategic dual-use technologies, conflict over extending credits in international lending, and general allied disgust over America's extension of extraterritorial export controls. And Toshiba Corporation's illegal sale of submarine quieting technology to the Soviet Union became an important issue in ongoing trade disputes between the United States and Japan.

Debates also emerged within the U.S. policy community about the value of trade controls in reducing economic and military vulnerability and the damage those controls could do to the innovative capability of

American industry—damage that business argued could lead to more vulnerability than technology trade. American manufacturing and trading interests claimed that strategic trade restrictions to protect security actually weakened the defense industrial base by restricting markets that were open to other industrial nations, thus reducing revenue that could have been plowed back into research and development.

These disputes emerged in part because the arguments for and against trade vulnerability were not clearly spelled out and the evidence to support them was not forthcoming. This is not to say that had the evidence been available, disputes would have been entirely resolved; as we shall see, other foreign-policy objectives and interests were also at stake in these debates, and often claims for and against vulnerability served wider political objectives.

Nonetheless, it is incumbent upon those who formulate public policy to base their recommendations on the best knowledge available.[2] Clear and judicious assessment of policy arguments helps to avoid debased public discourse and political demagoguery. If assumptions go untested and facts are assumed without proof, those who would purvey disinformation to enhance their own interests can gain the upper hand in the policy debate. In a larger sense, the lack of policy evaluation can lead to national misperceptions that can in turn distort foreign policy goals.[3]

Throughout the Cold War, the effects of trade on relative capabilities among rival nations were never carefully assessed; vulnerability assumptions were therefore often used carelessly in the political debate. Clarification and testing of those assumptions about the kind and degree of vulnerability industrialized nations risk when they trade with adversaries, with those who pose potential military threats—and even with states who may become economic competitors—can enable policymakers to formulate more effective policies in the future.

It is my purpose here to subject assumptions about economic vulnerability in international economic relations to a rigorous analysis that will have significance for the formulation of policies focusing on reducing new vulnerabilities in familiar places (the Soviet Union and Eastern Europe) and old vulnerabilities in new places (the Third World). It can also contribute to emerging theoretical debates about the relationship between global economic relations and national security.

The policy relevance of this study is straightforward. The central issue policymakers face when they reconstruct strategic trade restrictions or decide how far to dismantle them is an assessment of their vulnerability in trade with adversaries or potential adversaries, or with countries that have the capability to become fierce economic competitors or inflict economic harm—whether intentional or unintentional. Do Western nations trade away their security when they sell commercial "dual-use" high technology to nations that may pose military threats? Will they create powerful competitors on world markets with the transfer of state-of-the-art production technology? As the 1990s opened, many in the United States were reluctant to pour aid into the rebuilding of the former Soviet economy. That reluctance stems from forty-five years of defending the West against a perceived nuclear threat and the uncertain direction of the post-Soviet political future in the region.

If, for example, Russian economic reforms succeed, will Russia then be capable of presenting an even more formidable military threat than the Soviet Union ever did? Under what conditions could the states of the former Soviet Union use trade as a tool to exert subtle or even direct political influence over their Western trading partners in the event of future crises? As the West reaches out to help rebuild the former Soviet-bloc economies, will there be danger of another debt crisis? Will former Soviet-bloc debtors be in a position to extract bargaining concessions in negotiations with creditors? And, as the West is now learning, its pressure for privatization in former Communist nations is not only a precondition for markets and democracy but can also help an entrenched elite survive.[4] As the former Soviet bloc lurches toward an uncertain future in which states may be either too strong or too weak, what kinds of trade vulnerability is the West likely to face? How can we know?

The Gulf War raised similar questions with regard to the West's economic relations with the South. Except for its possession of the "oil weapon," most of the "South" has been considered too poor and too weak to constitute a threat to the industrialized West. But the Gulf War revealed that Western nations sold Iraq much of its army's high technology used in the invasion of Kuwait and subsequent fight against the United States and its allies. And as other nations like Syria and Libya increasingly buy sophisticated Western technology, what kinds of threats to the West are these transfers likely to cause?

These questions also go the heart of theoretical debates among students of international political economy about the relationship between wealth, power, influence, and trade. Their answers have important implications for our definitions of security and for our broader theoretical understanding of how security and economics are linked in international relations. Indeed, scholarly discussions of trade vulnerability have been largely reserved for analyses of the less developed countries' (LDCs) economic relations with the Western world.[5] Poor countries are generally considered the vulnerable ones; they have weak states, little control over markets, and little to cushion them against shocks imposed by changes in the international economy that threaten their strength. Industrialized nations with their seemingly resilient political institutions, strong economies, and efficient bureaucracies, and control over markets and sources of raw materials supply possess the capabilities to withstand the international economic vacillations that render less developed countries vulnerable.

How does the concept of economic vulnerability apply to rich and powerful states? Barry Buzan has suggested a first cut at approaching this question with the distinction he makes between threats and vulnerabilities.[6] Although both have an important impact on national security, they are analytically distinct, and the policies through which each is reduced are quite different. The source of vulnerability can be found in a state's *capabilities* in relation to the capabilities of others; the source of threats can be found in a state's *intentions* toward other nations. In order to reduce threats, states attempt to affect the intentions of others; traditional means include the negotiation of treaties, like arms control or trade agreements. In order to reduce relative vulnerabilities, states must implement policies that expand their own industrial and military power, reduce the military and industrial power of others, and reduce their dependence on others.

Policies to reduce vulnerability in trade relations rub against the imperatives of the marketplace. Trade theoretically enhances the capabilities of all trading partners and facilitates a division of labor in which dependencies thrive and an assessment of vulnerability becomes difficult. Neorealist international relations theory tells us that in their economic relations with adversaries under international anarchy, even powerful states will focus on reducing potential vulnerabilities rather than on reducing threats.[7] From this perspective, the state must consolidate its control over markets in order to reduce vulnerabilities. State-directed and enforced export and import restrictions have been the chief mode of vulnerability reduction.

For over forty years in the United States, these state-directed export restrictions were driven by unexamined vulnerability assumptions. Vulnerability fears were focused on the Soviet Union: the assumption was that the centralized Soviet state and the centralized states of the Warsaw Pact were able to control markets to increase relative power. This meant that the Soviet threat would increase if the eastward flow of goods with possible military "significance" could not be blocked, if NATO imported too much of its vital energy resources from the USSR, and if East-West trade were subsidized through low-interest loans and official export credits. In part because, as noted above, the vulnerability assumption was untested and unexamined, export control policy clashed with other national policy goals. And because the U.S. attempted to coerce its allies into formulating their own policies on these untested assumptions, vulnerability claims gave rise to acrimonious debate within the NATO alliance.

Despite both the end of the Cold War and the Soviet Union, this debate continues unabated, focusing on an increasing number of countries that may pose security threats to the West. And in an ironic twist of history, the debate has come to refocus on the former Soviet bloc in a new way: the *weakening of central state control* means that the West has become vulnerable to the region's disintegration, turmoil, and potential economic collapse. Within the Cold War logic, the prospect of the fragmentation of a powerful Soviet Union was a welcome scenario. A fragmented Soviet Union was a less powerful adversary whose "threats" to Western security would be reduced. In 1991, as many states of the former USSR declared their independence, the threat was seen *not* as one of *intention*—of economic blackmail, leverage, and the use of economic relations for political and military ends—but rather as a threat of unintended *chaos* over which new and fragile governments would have little control. Many believed that if chaos did not overwhelm the region, many of the new states, particularly Russia, would eventually pose the threat of powerful trade competition and perhaps emerge as economically rejuvenated adversaries. In any case, Western vulnerability would be the result.

And whereas the South was previously considered a vulnerable economic region, many Third World countries came to be perceived as threats to the industrialized world; indeed the Bush administration warned that they may increasingly acquire the capability to beat imported Western plowshares into swords pointed at the West; these countries may engage in economic blackmail, leverage, and the use of economic relations for political and military ends.

Only once in the postwar period, in the early 1970s, the brief period of detente permitted Western trade with its most important adversary to flourish more than any other time during the Cold War. Western exports of machinery and transport equipment increased dramatically. The Soviet Union negotiated to greatly expand energy exports to Western Europe. And Western banks, awash in petrodollars, made lavish loans to Eastern Europe. In the 1980s, however, as U.S.-Soviet political relations deteriorated and as the Soviet Union engaged in a build-up of its nuclear forces, the Reagan administration claimed that these expanded East-West economic ties had damaged the West's security. It further claimed that the Eastern European debt had placed powerful constraints on the United States' political bargaining leverage with Warsaw Pact countries and that Western credits contributed to Soviet economic and military development. The argument for *more* trade restrictions was not only a response to increased political tensions, but was grounded in the assertion that trade enhanced Soviet economic and military capabilities and bargaining power and thus diminished the West's security. And capabilities, much more than intentions, govern the international security environment.

As a case study in the analysis of assumptions about economic vulnerability in international relations, this book will focus specifically on these vulnerability claims. Did expanded trade during the detente era provide the Soviet Union (and in some cases Eastern Europe) with power resources that it could have used to make the West vulnerable? As noted above, despite the reduction of old threats, the vulnerability question remains and has taken on new forms. An examination of the effects of trade on trading partners' capabilities in a previous era may offer guidelines to policymakers in the 1990s as they forge a new "post-Communist" trading order and as they formulate economic policies toward other potential adversaries and economic competitors. An examination of Western economic vulnerabilities in the postcommunist era can both contribute to a more nuanced view of the vulnerability concept and help provide a workable policy framework for strategic trade restrictions.

This book, then, will specify the arguments for trade vulnerability as it relates to advanced industrial nations and examine the available evidence from the detente and post-detente periods in East-West trade to test them. It will also offer a preliminary examination of new economic vulnerabilities in East-West trade as the postcommunist era begins. The historical evidence will certainly not resolve the vulnerability question; history does not usually repeat itself in the way one might expect. And, as noted above, policy debates involving symbolic gestures and diplomatic, political, and economic interests will not be resolved simply by making the vulnerability assumptions explicit or through a presentation of the "evidence." Often, as we shall see below, more is at stake in the debate than vulnerability. Nonetheless, a specification of the assumptions can help us distinguish between knowledge-based and politically motivated arguments and can provide a set of criteria by which to test future vulnerability claims in the policy debate.

In the remainder of this chapter, I briefly outline the historical evolution of the vulnerability debate in East-West trade to show how the unresolved vulnerability question exacerbated political tensions in U.S.-European relations. I then discuss how arguments over the extent of trade vulnerability have been modified by the Cold War's end, the disintegration and death of the Soviet Union, and declining U.S. industrial competitiveness. What emerges is a story of conflicting assumptions and efforts on the part of the U.S.—in the absence of agreement on vulnerability claims—to impose policies on its allies in order to reduce perceived vulnerabilities. The historical account tells us that not only did the vulnerability question remain unresolved, but that the United States attempted to reduce perceived vulnerabilities by trying to consolidate its political power over markets—in part by imposing controls on its allies. The coercive instruments of vulnerability reduction used by the United States clashed with the beliefs and policies of its allies; the clash was exacerbated by the international diffusion of control over high-technology markets, which made market control more difficult. This story sets the stage for the final section of this chapter, which outlines the plan of the book.

In short, this book will do three things: 1) examine the political debate over vulnerability and argue that political conflict resulted from unspecified vulnerability claims; 2) specify and test the central vulnerability arguments made in the policy debate; and 3) argue that, based on the specification of those claims and an examination of the evidence, vulnerability reduction—control over markets—is a function of more than state-imposed trade restrictions. The evidence suggests that, depending on the issue area under consideration, vulnerability reduction can be a function of private corporate strategies, multilateral agreement on vulnerability arguments, sacrifice on the part of vulnerable states, and the ability of those economic actors who can trigger vulnerability in the economies of their trading partners to stabilize property rights on the basis of market-rational behavior. State-imposed trade restrictions may be necessary but are not always the only or best way to reduce vulnerability.

Vulnerability Claims in the Policy Debate

Liberalism vs. Economic Nationalism

In debates over how to order trade relations with adversaries, two perspectives have vied for dominance: economic liberalism and economic nationalism. Whereas the liberal perspective is grounded in the philosophy of free trade, economic nationalists remind us that open markets actually increase the vulnerability of economic partners and often fail to provide for collective goods—like national security or even industrial competitiveness. In this section I simply paint the two arguments with broad strokes as "ideal types," that is, not all "liberals" would agree with every claim made for the liberal position and not all economic nationalists would agree with every claim made for economic nationalism. Nonetheless, it is important to distinguish the two positions analytically. In the following section I discuss the actors who, in general, make liberal and economic nationalist arguments; the historical account that follows is a description of how the two arguments were used by the participants in the political debate and how the terms of that debate were set in the early Cold War.

There is little question that, even from a liberal perspective, participation in the market increases the number of economic vulnerabilities a state faces. Indeed, all participants in the market face a fiercely competitive environment in which the prospect of losing always hovers. Markets impose harsh punishments on inefficient actors. Indeed, as Buzan rightly reminds us, because markets impose a condition of insecurity on all actors, they necessarily make states *economically* insecure as well, by increasing their risks of losing out to more efficient producers and reducing their certainty about economic prosperity in the future.[8] State actors often fear that even though all trading partners gain from the relationship, some will gain more than others, and therefore they must control markets.

Nonetheless, liberals believe that the absolute gains from economic interaction outweigh the costs. States that threaten the interdependent relationship by raising tariffs or implementing export controls are cutting off their noses to spite their faces; their partners may be hurt by protectionism, but they will also be hurt. Indeed, as we shall see below, liberals believe that the Soviet economic crisis of the 1990s can be partly attributed to its "protectionist" stance in the international economy throughout the postwar period.

Furthermore, the liberal believes that participation in international trade can reduce *political* and even military threats in a state's relations with others, because trade affects intentions. As we shall see in more detail, according to one strand of the liberal argument, trade can lead to more peaceful relations among adversaries by creating webs of interdependence that reduce the incentive for military conflict. Because this latter argument focuses on the impact of trade on trading partners' *intentions* rather than the impact on their *capabilities*, it does not address the vulnerability question directly. It assumes that if trade can lead to trading partners' more peaceful intentions toward one another, vulnerability becomes a decreasingly salient trade issue. Because liberal arguments do not address the vulnerability question directly, and because my interest centers on that question, I do not examine and test liberal assumptions here.

The economic nationalist *does* address the vulnerability question directly. From this vantage point, attention should be focused on trade's effect on relative national capabilities, rather than stated political intentions that are always subject to change. Free trade may be the engine of technological innovation and economic growth, adding to the capabilities of all trading partners, but it is the *distribution* of those capabilities—that is, whose capabilities are enhanced *more* in the relationship—that really counts. To the extent that trade enhances an adversary's economic and thus military capabilities, they claim, security is damaged. To the extent that one's trading partner gains in relative terms from the relationship, its relative power increases as well; within the relationship, one who gains less can become more dependent. To the extent that trade enhances the bargaining power of any trading partner by expanding its overall economic capabilities, increasing its number of bargaining "chips," vulnerability threatens.

For some economic nationalists, these considerations are as important with regard to allies as with regard to adversaries or potential adversaries. Of course they are much more pronounced in relation to adversaries, because enemies are more likely to translate vulnerabilities into political and military threats. But allies are never permanent, and even if they do not pose an immediate military threat, they can gain political influence if the distribution of the gains from economic activity are in their favor. Therefore, for example, as we shall see in the unfolding of the story below, economic nationalists in the United States argue that extensive economic interdependence with Japan is not in the national interest. Japanese firms, they argue, may be able to gain monopoly control over markets, leading to U.S. dependence on unreliable suppliers, a possible "hollowing out" of U.S. corporations, and the loss of an American capacity for innovation. As discussed in chapter 2 in some detail, this control over markets by one's economic partners—even if they are allies—can have important implications for national security, from the economic nationalist perspective.

Liberals, on the other hand, point out that economic competition can stimulate domestic innovation. In the U.S. auto industry, for example, the presence of Japanese transplants has stimulated domestic firms to upgrade product and production technology. Indeed, liberals argue that if the U.S. reduces its economic interdependence with Japan, the national interest might be compromised even more than with increasing interdependence. To reduce interdependence may mean running the risk of consigning the U.S. to absolute rather than simply comparative technological inferiority.

Many economic nationalists argue that trade with the postcommunist world is fraught with vulnerability as well, but the sources of vulnerability have changed. Indeed, for the moment, threats have decreased, but vulnerabilities remain: ethnic conflict, civil war and its prospect, and the possibility that leaner, meaner nuclear-armed adversaries can emerge from the postcommunist economic crisis. Liberals contend, however, that unless the West helps to ease the "transition process" in these countries with new trade and investment, future threats and vulnerabilities will loom larger than ever before.

The economic nationalist arguments with regard to trade vulnerability have only recently become part of the foreign-policy debate about alliance relations and relations with "friendly" nations. The same arguments, however, were clearly stated with regard to economic relations among adversaries, and in the United States particularly with regard to the Soviet Union. The vulnerability claims of economic nationalists were the foundation of U.S. policies in East-West trade, and liberals asserted throughout the postwar period that those policies decreased the odds of political stability and harmed Western commercial interests.

It is important to note here that in this book I systematically focus on the claims made by economic nationalists; I make no attempt to test liberal claims or examine other foreign-policy goals. This does *not* mean, however, that in those areas where I find vulnerability arguments weak that I automatically believe the liberal arguments to be stronger; liberal arguments about absolute gains and changing intentions should be similarly tested. To do so here, however, would be beyond the scope of this study. Nonetheless, the evidence presented here also suggests both support for liberal assumptions and a critique of them: the prospect of absolute gains from expanded trade with the West did have an impact on Soviet intentions under Gorbachev; but policies of Western trade restriction had a negative effect on Soviet capabilities and contributed to Soviet weakness. Because this is a study of Western vulnerability assumptions, these claims are not systematically explored here; I do, however, return to them in chapter 7.

The Actors

The central protagonists in this conflict between liberals and economic nationalists over multilateral trade restrictions have been the United States and Western Europe. Except for two brief periods—once in the 1960s and again in the 1970s—the United States has played the role of the economic nationalist and Europeans in general have taken the liberal position.

The conflict between the European liberal and the U.S. economic nationalist positions on East-West trade continued in part because vulnerability assumptions were never carefully examined, and unexamined assumptions reduced the policy choices down to coercive state trade restrictions. Underlying the conflict over beliefs and policies were differing interests served by liberal or vulnerability arguments to further specific goals. Unlike central decision makers in the United States who viewed foreign economic policy and national security policy as intimately related and therefore viewed trade with an eye to security concerns, Europeans saw these as two separate and distinct issues. This separation was reinforced by differences in institutional structure of export control administration between the U.S. and most of the countries of Western Europe. Defense ministries in Europe did not have the inclination, the influence, and the resources to take on international economic issues. Foreign-trade policy was made and implemented by the ministries of foreign trade and foreign affairs, and defense ministries deferred to them with regard to international economic issues.

In France, for example, the Ministry of Defense—which would have supported the economic nationalist position—was, until 1981, not involved in export licensing procedure at all. In the Federal Republic of

Germany (BRD), the Ministry of Defense has a veto on individual licensing decisions if vulnerability concerns are raised, but that veto has virtually never been used. And in Britain, the Ministry of Defense has only played an advisory role.[9] Therefore, in Europe, liberal assumptions dominated those institutions largely responsible for strategic trade restrictions, while in the United States, as we shall see below, economic nationalist assumptions were prominent if not dominant in the decision-making institutions.

Furthermore, unlike the United States, where business with its liberal views and commercial interests remained isolated from the policy process, European business was active in the formulation of East-West trade policy from the very beginning of the Cold War, and represented liberal views to government. Major trade-related groups in Europe and Japan joined government advisory councils that fed information into export control agencies, were consulted on the embargo list reviews, and lobbied for the relaxation of export controls. Influenced by exporters' interests, European and Japanese central decision makers became facilitators of trade with the Soviet bloc.

Particularly in West Germany, business had a strong influence on East-West trade policy and supported liberal views. In the early 1950s, the powerful industrial association, the Federation of German Industries (BDI), formed the Ostausschuss der Deutschen Wirtschaft, or the "Eastern Committee." This group was responsible for preparing documents for official trade negotiations between the BRD and the countries of Eastern Europe. Its task was to represent the interests of German business to the government on the issue of East-West trade. Between 1952 and 1955, when the BRD had severed diplomatic relations with the Soviet Union, the Ostausschuss conducted trade negotiations with the countries of Eastern Europe on its own. Thus it gained the status of a semi-official body. In the 1960s, the Ostausschuss prepared changes to export control regulations. These changes were accepted verbatim by the Ministry of Economics.[10] In Britain, too, the relationship between government and business in East-West trade policy formulation has been close, involving mutual consultation.[11]

As we shall see, within the United States, the Department of Defense has most consistently embraced the economic nationalist vulnerability arguments, and the Commerce and State Departments have most consistently taken the liberal position. The State Department and the National Security Council, however, have primarily seen trade with the Soviet bloc as an instrument of diplomacy—to extract concessions or induce cooperation on other issues like arms control or human rights; vulnerability arguments have suited these purposes at times, and at other times these agencies deemed liberal arguments more appropriate. Congress and the executive have often struggled for control of trade restriction policies and have used liberal and economic nationalist arguments in that struggle for dominance.[12]

Transnational coalitions have at times given support to liberal over vulnerability arguments. As we shall see, State Department officials allied with West European COCOM representatives to institutionalize the "exceptions procedure" in CoCom to permit higher levels of East-West trade than would have obtained under congressional restrictions grounded in vulnerability beliefs.[13] And in 1982 American firms and industry associations supported European governments in arguing that the Urengoi natural gas pipeline would not increase Western dependence on Soviet energy supplies.

I will also demonstrate that many actors used vulnerability arguments to further their own political purposes, and it is not surprising that vulnerability arguments were more powerful in both international and domestic debates when U.S.-Soviet tensions were high, whereas liberal arguments presided when tensions were relaxed. Throughout the Cold War, vulnerability discourse was highly politicized. The politics surrounding both the international and domestic Cold War struggles over trade restrictions has been extensively analyzed by scholars of East-West trade;[14] the vulnerability assumptions—which could have clarified the debates—have remained unspecified, however.

The Contested Vulnerability Assumption in the Cold War

From the beginning of the postwar period, the perspective of the economic nationalist dominated U.S. policy on East-West trade. That perspective was linked closely with American containment strategy. This strategy guided plans to defend the security of the Western alliance and rested on the unwavering belief that the Soviet Union was essentially an aggressive power and that unless contained, a confrontation was inevitable. "Economic containment"[15]—a national security approach to foreign economic policy—became a central component of this strategy. In 1944, George Kennan warned that the West should not continue to pursue an economic policy that would further the "military industrialization of the Soviet Union."[16] He cautioned, "The Soviet government views foreign trade in general as a political-economic weapon designed to increase the power of the USSR relative to other countries." He further warned that "it will view imports from our country only as a necessary means of hastening the achievement of complete military-economic autarky of the Soviet Union." The message was clear: exports to the adversary bolster his economic and military might and thus drain the relative power of the exporter, thereby increasing *his* military and economic vulnerability. He did not, however, state *how* Western exports to the USSR could pose the threat that he feared; nor did he offer evidence to back his warning.

The most important policy statement of this national security approach to foreign trade can be found in NSC 68, America's blueprint for waging the Cold War. NSC 68 began with the assumption that economic strength was a key foundation of Western security and that foreign economic policy was its essential building block. "Foreign economic policy is a major instrument in the conduct of the United States foreign relations . . . particularly appropriate to the Cold War."[17] International economic relations, then, must first and foremost be a weapon in America's national-security arsenal.

The weapon was two-pronged. First, relations with other industrial democracies were guided by liberal economic ideology and policies of economic "openness." Open markets in democratic societies would nurture economic growth, vitiate internal communist movements, and build a bulwark against Soviet expansion. In practice, however, although the U.S. government opened its own markets and pursued a policy of laissez faire with its allies, it permitted them to reindustrialize behind a wall of import restrictions against American goods.

The second prong of the economic weapon was an explicit denial of trade with the Soviet Union. Because the Soviet economy was geared to drive the Russian military machine, the argument ran, and because Western exports to the Soviets would simply satisfy their thirst for power, East-West trade would lead to the West's vulnerability—again, an unfounded claim. Policy, however, was formulated on the vulnerability assumption: economic liberalism, then, was harnessed to anticommunism to gain broad-based support for the building of international economic institutions that would create and maintain an international market economy from which socialist countries would be excluded (and from which they would attempt to exclude themselves).[18] Economic nationalism would necessarily drive U.S. economic relations with communist states.

Supported by these pillars of Cold War strategy in foreign economic policy—liberal policies toward other industrial democracies and economic nationalism toward Communist adversaries—congressional leaders and administration officials made sure that America's major trading partners would also be military allies, and, at the same time, they constructed a policy of economic warfare against the Soviet Union. The latter policy was embodied in the U.S. Export Control Act of 1949. This law stated that the "unrestricted export" of materials without regard to their "potential military significance" could "affect the national security" of the United States.[19]

Three lists of embargoed items were drawn up, the first containing items of direct military significance, the second containing industrial goods that the Soviets could potentially use to build economic and military power, and the third associated with atomic energy. On the second list were goods with no direct military significance but goods that could enhance Soviet economic performance, thus theoretically releasing resources that could add to military strength.

Although the United States had formulated a unilateral embargo rooted in the claims of the vulnerability thesis, it could not carry out the task of trade denial alone. Because the allies might sell the Soviets goods that the U.S. restricted, their compliance was needed in any export control effort. Thus, in 1949 the U.S. took the lead in creating COCOM, a multilateral "regime" to restrict Western exports to the Soviet bloc. From the perspective of the economic nationalists in the United States, the purpose of the unified embargo was to wage "economic warfare" against the Soviet Union and thereby protect Western security by creating a broad list of goods to be embargoed by all COCOM members. This embargo list would restrict both military and nonmilitary goods. The trick was to persuade the allies to accept these embargo norms based on vulnerability claims and to ensure compliance with the regime rules.

This would prove difficult, however, because even in the early Cold War period, Europeans based their East-West trade preferences on the assumptions of economic liberalism and cultural affinity with the East. Although there were variations and differences among them, they all advanced a similar argument: that all parties benefit from free trade, not just Eastern importers of industrial goods, but Western exporters as well.[20] It followed that the prewar structure of East-West trade had been beneficial to all trading partners, not simply the Eastern importers. For Western Europeans, this liberal perspective was convenient, because they needed the raw material imports the East could provide, and Eastern demand for Western manufactured goods could stimulate West European economic growth. Thus, ironically, while Western Europe restricted trade with the United States while paying lip service to liberal ideology, it used the same liberal arguments in debate with U.S. officials to restrict export controls, so that trade with rivals in the East could expand.

To many Europeans, Eastern Europe especially and even the Soviet Union were part of Europe in historical heritage and culture. The division between East and West, Europeans knew, was largely artificial, and at some indefinite point in the future, broken ties would again be resumed.[21] European elites questioned the "essentialist" view prevailing in Washington, which held that the Soviet Union was an aggressive power, bent on destroying the West. In contrast, they saw the USSR as a formidable adversary, but nonetheless one that they could bargain with, even live with.[22] Positive incentives like trade, the Europeans' counter-argument ran, could draw the Soviet Union into a web of interdependent relationships with the West, and the ties created could reduce the military threat in Europe.[23] Negative trade sanctions, however, would do nothing to reduce the Soviet menace, and would certainly not lead to a more conciliatory adversary. Indeed, as if to foreshadow Gorbachev's notion of a "Common European home," the belief prevailed among many Western European elites—even in the darkest days of the Cold War—that trade was an avenue of communication and conciliation that should not be closed.[24]

Nonetheless, there was general consensus among Europeans that some international restrictions on the export of goods with military significance were needed. They argued for a more limited embargo of military items and of those commercial goods that would have direct military significance. Indeed, by 1949 Britain had independently initiated export controls on military goods bound for the East. All recognized that a multilateral agreement on those controls was necessary to harmonize national policies in order to reduce discrimination among commercial competitors who might be handicapped by strict controls in one country and lax controls in another. It is important to note that, in general, the European incentive to join and maintain a multilateral export control organization was high, even though most did not agree with the broad scope of restrictions that the U.S. preferred. Because there was little consensual agreement on whether protecting security by the control of exports should be carried out through a broad or narrow embargo, political compromise rather than consensus characterized COCOM's decision rules, and became the basis of COCOM's authority.

The rules were straightforward; three sets of lists were created containing items all members agreed not to sell to the Soviet bloc: a munitions list, an atomic energy list, and an industrial-commercial list. Member states agreed to meet every three or four years to undertake "list reviews" in order to add, delete, and repair the lists of embargoed items. In preparing amendments to the lists, each member would propose changes four to five months before the beginning of the review; these proposals would be circulated among members for discussion. Counterproposals would then be submitted, circulated, and debated as well. In this four- to five-month period, members would negotiate tradeoffs from initial bargaining positions. Items to be embargoed would be debated on a case-by-case basis depending upon their export importance, and agreed upon by consensus. Within sixty days after the set of proposals had been agreed to by all member nations, the list would become effective.

The final embargo list then represented not an objective assessment of trade vulnerability but rather a political compromise. Members accepted the embargo of some items in exchange for free trade in other goods. On restricting items of direct military significance, consensus was easy to obtain. On items whose military use was indirect, however, Europeans tried to protect their exports by arguing that particular goods should not be embargoed.[25]

From the outset, U.S. leaders believed that Europeans should be pressured into compliance with a broad embargo. In fact, it had been difficult to push the European Recovery Program through Congress in 1947–48, partly because of the large volume of West European trade with the Soviet bloc.[26] Therefore, in December 1947, to gain congressional support for the Marshall Plan, the head of the National Security Council recommended the application of extraterritorial controls on all U.S. exports of strategic and scarce materials to Europe. In this way Washington could screen Western European trade with the Soviet bloc and stop the transshipment of prohibited U.S. goods from Western Europe to the East.[27]

This extraterritoriality measure, however, was not strong enough for

Congress. In 1951 it passed the Mutual Defense Assistance Control Act, generally called the "Battle Act." This law linked trade with communist nations to U.S. national security goals in its declaration that it was the policy of the United States to control the export of military and nonmilitary commodities to the Soviet bloc in order to "oppose and offset by nonmilitary action, acts that threaten the security of the United States and the peace of the world." It directed the president to curtail aid to any country that exported military or nonmilitary goods to the Soviet bloc, no matter whether these goods originated in the U.S. or in the target country. These threats of aid termination may well have been enough to dampen Europe's enthusiasm for trade with the East. On the other hand, despite numerous violations, the threats were never carried out. Why not?

The U.S. government was in fact split on the issue of vulnerability in Europe's East-West trade. In 1947 the central aim of U.S. export-control policy had been to limit strategic exports to the Soviets but to still ensure that Europeans could import goods and some strategic materials from the East, since such commerce was considered essential to Western European recovery. By 1949, however, Congress and the Commerce and Defense departments pushed for a Western policy of total trade denial.

The State Department agreed with the policy of economic warfare, but did not want the allies to be coerced into compliance. Specifically, State Department officials worried that a trade embargo would jeopardize upcoming negotiations over the creation of the new NATO alliance. Coercion would poison relations and dampen Europe's incentive to build up military strength against the Soviets. Secretary of State Dean Acheson's central fear was not a Soviet invasion of Europe but the "drift of Western Europe toward neutralism."[28] He knew that coercive export controls might actually irritate the Europeans so much that that "drift" would become a reality.[29] He therefore tried desperately to prevent passage of the Battle Act while still working toward policy coordination with the Europeans on economic warfare.[30]

Acheson's European strategy was three-pronged: first, he believed that European leaders could be reasoned with; they could be persuaded to accept an extensive embargo if they could also be persuaded to accept the embargo's underlying vulnerability arguments. At the same time, however, acrimony would have to be kept at bay by allaying European fears of coercion. Finally, if "reason" did not work to achieve

European consensus on an extensive embargo, Europe's trade with the East would have to be permitted in order to preserve the partnership.

State Department officials began this effort with an attempt to convince their counterparts in European foreign ministries that the menacing Soviet military machine threatened any minute to invade the West. That machine, they argued, depended for its vitality on Western capital goods. Therefore, U.S. officials reasoned, all industrial trade should be halted. At first it looked like these arguments would be persuasive. In 1949 the U.S. ambassador to the Soviet Union convinced the British ambassador there that "the whole [Russian] show would crack in five years" if trade could be stopped. His telegrams to the foreign office urged Foreign Minister Bevin to join the Americans in a total trade embargo.[31]

Bevin, however, did not buy the argument. The Foreign Office commented, "In view of the dollar crisis . . . the need for U.K. . . . trade with Eastern Europe is as strong as ever." Ministry of Defense experts denied the validity of the American claims, arguing that the Americans had their facts wrong and that even a 100 percent suspension of trade with the USSR would not slow down the Soviet economy.[32] Bevin himself believed that trade was an avenue of communication that could lead to conciliation, and it should not be closed. The overwhelming view that prevailed in the British Foreign Office was that economic sanctions would in fact harm the West more than they would harm the Soviet bloc.

In February 1949, Harold Wilson, then the president of the British Board of Trade, stated that Britain regarded the development of East-West trade as a healthy thing and that it should be divorced from politics.[33] British policy remained consistent. In 1950 Prime Minister Clement Attlee argued that it had never been a British policy to "raise an iron curtain in the commercial field between the countries of Eastern and Western Europe."[34] In France, official debate was less open, but in 1949, an article in *Le Monde* argued that economic relations between the two Europes were natural and that the U.S. should not impose extraterritorial restrictions on European nations.[35]

The Korean conflict provided Acheson with a second chance to persuade the Europeans to accept the vulnerability thesis by playing on fears of an imminent Soviet invasion. Even though he knew that intelligence reports interpreted the fighting in Korea as a "local affair," which would not necessarily foreshadow a communist attack in Europe, Acheson believed that it could be used to persuade the Europeans to quickly

tighten the military alliance with the United States, permit German rear-
mament, and voluntarily halt trade with the East. To get the British
and French to go along, he proposed more aid, U.S. troops in Europe,
and American leadership in NATO. To complement these moves in
COCOM, the State Department pressed Europeans to expand the list of
goods embargoed to the Soviet Union.

Nonetheless, Western Europeans stubbornly clung to liberal assumptions and the distinction between trade and security. They therefore
played on State Department fears of defection from NATO in order to
continue commerce with the East. Indeed, in September 1950, a few
months after the North Korean invasion, the British decided that normal levels of trade with the Soviet Union must continue in view of
Britain's need for Russian timber and raw materials, even though strategic exports to Eastern Europe and China, which might help the North
Koreans, would be restricted.[36]

Even during the height of the Korean War, the British complained
bitterly about American coercive tactics toward Europe with regard to
their East-West trade. The president of the British Board of Trade, Sir
Hartley Shawcross, in a 1951 speech, stated the British position and
offered a veiled threat of non-cooperation within the alliance:

> Our position was wholly different in East-West trade as in many
> other matters from that of the United States, because of the impor-
> tance of this trade to us. . . . This was not a matter which ought to
> be settled by the laying down of unilateral conditions or by the
> denial of supplies essential to our well-being. . . . The success of the
> Atlantic alliance must depend on understanding and confidence
> between our countries. . . . Harsh or unilateral action; the failure on
> either side . . . to understand the other's point of view, his special
> difficulties, and lack of confidence was something inimical to part-
> nership.[37]

Arguing that an expanded COCOM embargo could not be applied
effectively and that the East might retaliate and cut off their own trade
with the West, they balked at extensive COCOM lists of embargoed
goods.[38]

This early American effort to convince Europeans to accept vulnerability assumptions had clearly failed. Now the State Department had no
choice but to permit East-West trade to continue, while still appearing
tough to Congress. The only remaining alternative was to strike a bargain with Western European COCOM representatives. The COCOM list

would expand to encompass most of the items restricted by the U.S., but an "exceptions procedure" would be instituted, under which the committee could approve of individual exports to be excepted from the embargo.[39] With the exceptions procedure firmly in place, the COCOM list could expand in accord with vulnerability beliefs, but trade could legally continue in accord with liberal assumptions.

The bargain struck in COCOM clearly provided Europeans with the ability to continue trade, despite congressional threats of aid termination. The severest test of the strength of that ability was met by West Germany, a country highly dependent on its U.S. ties under the Eisenhower administration. Eisenhower was much more committed to coercive tactics than Truman had been. Recounting his visit with Secretary of State John Foster Dulles in April 1953, Konrad Adenauer wrote in his memoirs that in the course of their conversations, Dulles suggested that it was absolutely essential that West Germany cooperate with the United States to restrict exports to Eastern Europe, *even those exports not on the COCOM embargo list.* He remarked that Adenauer would have to reckon with the cancellation of all foreign aid if the Battle Act provisions were not taken seriously. For the West Germans, however, German reunification was a top foreign policy priority, and it would be endangered by a blanket policy of trade denial. Adenauer was able to steer an independent course under the protection of the COCOM compromise. He thus agreed only to restrict exports, "jointly with other trading nations."[40]

This episode points to Europe's steadfast disagreement with the United States over East-West trade, despite the Korean War fears raised by the U.S. Western European governments, in turn playing on State Department fears of creeping European "neutrality," struck a bargain within COCOM that would permit trade despite their agreement to longer lists of embargoed goods. To strike this bargain, they built a transnational coalition to tip the negotiating balance in their favor. Interviews conducted by Gunner Adler-Karlsson with 300 Western Europeans involved in the embargo sum up the success of that strategy. They revealed that "in view of the Congressional ties of foreign aid the West European governments had to *pretend* cooperation to get that aid, but a cooperation that was in reality not very strict."[41] Europeans tipped their hats to the U.S. by expanding the COCOM list, but the list itself was not fully legitimate in their eyes.

Although U.S. trade with the Soviet Union and Eastern Europe ground to a halt in the early 1950s, Western European exports to the

East as a whole actually increased steadily, albeit slowly.[42] Exports from COCOM members—which covered perhaps one-half of all internationally traded goods—decreased only slightly (11 percent) in one year, 1952; otherwise, they showed a modest increase. The large drop in trade between 1949 and 1950 occurred across the board, in non-COCOM as well as in COCOM nations. As I argue in chapter 3, this was due largely to Stalin's attempt at autarky and import substitution.

These early Cold War years therefore saw the airing of divergent positions on vulnerability in East-West trade between the United States and Europe and the forging of U.S. strategies of compliance and European strategies of independence in East-West trade policy with little consensual agreement between the two. The U.S. first attempted to use COCOM as the instrument of broad trade denial based on vulnerability claims, bolstering that attempt with unilateral threats of aid termination to Europe if European governments did not cooperate. Taking advantage of splits between the Truman administration and Congress, however, Europeans were able to preserve their liberal position on trade with the East by striking a bargain in COCOM that would provide for exceptions to a wide embargo and thus permit trade, albeit at lower levels. Their bargaining power was enhanced by veiled threats of noncooperation with the U.S. on NATO. Because NATO cooperation was a higher priority, State Department officials relented, and permitted the exceptions procedure that provided the appearance of a wide embargo without the substance of one. These strategies and counterstrategies had an important impact on the legitimacy of a broad-based embargo and would be repeated throughout the postwar period. There was little evidence of a broad political consensus on common definitions of vulnerability that could lead to common norms with regard to trade restriction. U.S. coercive efforts provided the glue that held the broad-based embargo together, but those same efforts prevented the evolution of a deeper legitimacy of COCOM's norms in the eyes of its members.

In sum, a clash of goals explains the tension between the United States and Europe on East-West trade issues. Underlying that clash are conflicting sets of beliefs on the role of East-West trade in foreign economic policy. In the United States, vulnerability arguments have dominated the thinking of those who constructed America's East-West trade policies, while in Europe, elite beliefs on trade with the USSR fell more in line with the philosophy of economic liberalism. These differing belief systems gave rise to quite different sets of institutional structures created to formulate and implement export control policies. Encased in persisting and differing institutions, the conflict in goals and beliefs and the struggle over compliance with U.S. preferences led to repeated disputes between the United States and Europe throughout the postwar period.

Nonetheless, throughout the Cold War, the United States continued in its effort to restrict East-West trade. Part of that effort was a proposal to limit East-West energy trade. In 1962, the U.S. Export Control Act was expanded to restrict trade in any goods that would make a significant contribution to the adversary's economic strength, regardless of the potential military significance. Among those items to be restricted were all petroleum and natural gas exploration, production, and refining equipment. U.S. officials, acting on CIA intelligence reports, believed that without Western energy technology, the Soviet Union could not improve its energy sector upon which its economic and military power depended. Those officials believed that expanded energy exports to the West would lead to Western dependence on an adversary's strategic commodity.[43]

East-West trade finance was also subjected to vulnerability claims. U.S. officials knew that the regulation of financial flows was the key to restricting the export of goods falling through the cracks of the COCOM embargo. Because their currencies were not convertible, and because their industrial goods were not competitive on the Western market, finance would be essential if Eastern Europe and the Soviet Union were to import from the West. When Western states regulate the flow of credits, they control Eastern demand for Western goods.

U.S. officials argued that if the West were to supply credits to Eastern Europe and the Soviet Union, it would be a virtual extension of financial aid, which could enable communist countries to divert more of their own resources to investment in military and other strategically significant areas.[44] European and Japanese lenders, however, ignored the logic of the vulnerability argument with regard to trade finance and throughout the late 1950s and 1960s, engaged in stiff competition with each other to provide low-interest loans to Warsaw Pact countries.[45]

Gradually, however, the "liberal" view justifying an expansion of trade between Western Europe and the Soviet Union and Eastern Europe began to influence U.S. policy. In 1965 President Johnson created the Special Committee on U.S. Trade Relations with Eastern Europe and the Soviet Union to explore the role of peaceful trade in "building bridges" between the United States and the Soviet bloc. The influence of the liberal perspective grew, and in 1969 a fundamental policy shift was reflected in the new Export Administration Act. The term *export administration* replaced the term *export control*, and the new law attempted to balance liberal views with efforts to avoid vulnerability.

Detente and Its Demise

By the 1970s, stimulation of trade had become a fundamental aspect of U.S. and Western European efforts to improve relations with communist countries. These efforts converged with the eagerness of the Soviet Union and the countries of Eastern Europe to enter into trade relations with the West that would give them access to Western technology, markets, and loans. As economic contacts expanded, a new kind of business venture was born: "one-shot-deals" in which the Soviet Union bought entire factories and prototypes of finished products gave way to "industrial cooperation"—the predecessor of Soviet joint ventures with the West—in which contracts were to extend over a number of years, resources were often pooled, and technology was transferred through cooperative production. East-West trade and industrial cooperation became a fundamental aspect of a detente strategy, which envisioned the entanglement of adversaries in webs of negotiated and cooperative interdependence, a fulfillment of the liberal's prescription. These webs of interdependence would then constrain competition and conflict on political and military-strategic fronts.[46]

Political efforts to stimulate trade had significant results. Between 1960 and 1975, trade between the Council for Mutual Economic Assistance (CMEA) and the Organization for Economic Cooperation and Development (OECD) countries showed a ninefold increase. The value of machinery imports from OECD to CMEA countries jumped from $1.0 billion in 1965 to $10.2 billion in 1977. During 1974, CMEA machinery imports from the West increased by 5 percent from 1973 levels, and in 1975 the increase was 55 percent.[47]

Nonetheless, as the 1970s drew to a close, the liberals and economic nationalists clashed on a number of East-West trade issues. Secretary of State Kissinger's detente goals of trade expansion, intended to give the Soviet Union a "stake in the network of relationships with the West,"[48] collapsed under the temptation to use trade as a diplomatic weapon to extract concessions on human rights and arms control. The uses of trade as an inducement to political cooperation and as a means to extract leverage were mixed with trade restrictions based on the vulnerability assumptions of economic nationalism. In the latter part of the decade, therefore, it was unclear, both within the U.S. government and to the Western European allies, which underlying assumptions guided U.S. policy.

Meanwhile, the Soviet Union was engaging in what some perceived to be a massive buildup of its strategic nuclear forces. In 1964 the USSR had only 389 strategic nuclear delivery vehicles, compared to the United States' 1,880. But by 1970 the USSR had surpassed the U.S. in number of land-based strategic missiles; by 1973 it had surpassed the U.S. in long-range bombers, and by 1975 it led the U.S. in number of sea-launched ballistic missiles.[49] This military buildup would later come to haunt the liberal proponents of East-West trade, and fuel the economic nationalists' vulnerability arguments. They assumed causality in the correlation between trade expansion and the Soviet military buildup.

The December 1979 Soviet invasion of Afghanistan put the final nail in detente's coffin; the invasion was interpreted by the U.S. as a renewed threat to world peace. And with regard to trade, economic nationalism again gained dominance in U.S. policy circles. The policy response was a unilateral embargo of all technology to the Soviet Union and a request issued to other OECD countries to cut in half all official and government-guaranteed credits needed to finance East-West trade. This time the allied response was overwhelmingly negative: France, West Germany, Italy, the Netherlands, Belgium, Denmark, Ireland, and Luxembourg independently denied the request. In open rebellion, Italy broadly publicized that it had won a major order to sell nuclear power plant equipment to the Soviet Union.

As the Soviet military buildup became apparent in the latter part of the 1970s, high-technology trade emerged as a central issue of heated debate over East-West trade in the Western alliance. Within COCOM, the United States had argued that the same high technologies that drive market competition also have a *dual-use*—both commercial/industrial and military applications. These include, for example, microchips used in advanced weapons systems that could also be found in toy stores; Apple II computers that could be used for weapons targeting; scientific systems that assess seismic data that could also be used as antisubmarine warfare devices; and robots and robotic mechanisms that were increasingly used in the production of both civilian and military equipment. U.S. economic nationalists staunchly claimed that if the West sold advanced technology to the Soviets, its technological superiority—the basis of its military power—would erode.

Europeans countered with the liberal argument that strict controls obstruct commercial diffusion of high-technology products and thus frustrate efforts to successfully compete for markets. High-technology trade with the Soviet Union and Eastern Europe again pitted European commercial interests against American security and foreign policy concerns. Perceiving a waning security dependence on the United States and a growing desire to broaden detente and expand trade with the Soviet bloc, European leaders were more harshly opposed than ever to the U.S. position on the restriction of East-West high-technology transfer.

The first Reagan administration took up economic nationalism and its vulnerability theme with renewed vigor, unambiguously returning the U.S. position to the earlier Cold War stance. It pledged to stem the eastward flow of U.S. technology and credits and the westward flow of Soviet energy supplies by more strictly enforcing curbs on technology exports to Eastern destinations (including the export of energy technology), expanding control over the flow of scientific communication, and by curtailing East-West trade finance.[50]

In his annual budget report to Congress in 1982, for example, Secretary of Defense Caspar Weinberger stated that "without the constant infusion of advanced technology from the West, the Soviet industrial base would experience a cumulative obsolescence, which would eventually also constrain the military industries."[51] Lawrence Brady, Assistant Secretary of Commerce for Trade Administration from 1981 to 1983, stated to a European audience, "We are pledged to limit the direct and indirect contribution made by our resources to the Soviet military buildup, and we are pledged to reduce substantially Soviet leverage over the economies of the noncommunist world."[52]

Were these claims correct? Did expanded trade and lax export controls contribute to the West's vulnerability during the 1970s? No convincing answer has yet emerged. What surfaced instead was policy confusion triggered by a conflict between untested liberal and economic nationalist beliefs about trade and trade vulnerability.

Despite the fact that conflicting claims were never tested, it is my contention, as will be discussed in chapter 4, that disagreement over the nature and extent of Western vulnerability in East-West trade actually appeared to weaken the norms of the COCOM regime. Strong common norms are crucial to COCOM's strength. Norms are "standards of behavior defined in terms of rights and obligations."[53] They exist in

COCOM when member states obligate themselves to place security above commercial gain in their international technology trade and are punished when they appear not to be acting accordingly.[54] When conflicting assumptions lead to differing standards for trade openness, common norms begin to decay. When regime norms weakened, corporations, competing with one another for market share, received conflicting policy signals from national governments and thus defied the rules. Continued violation of COCOM rules throughout the 1980s led one U.S. National Security Council official to state in late 1989: "The political climate is such that lots of companies in allied countries figure that even if they get caught breaking the law, they won't be severely punished."[55] Because the vulnerability assumption—the very foundation of COCOM's norms—was never clearly defined and tested, it became a bone of contention between the U.S. and its allies, clearly diminishing confidence in multilateral trade restriction policies.

The Postcommunist Era and Soviet Disintegration

The rapid introduction of Soviet foreign and domestic policy initiatives under General Secretary Gorbachev in the late 1980s raised the vulnerability question again. Although the USSR's military capabilities were as formidable as ever, Soviet intentions appeared to be changing. The INF Agreement of 1987 codified Soviet acceptance of the "zero option" proposal to remove Soviet and NATO intermediate-range nuclear weapons from Europe. In 1988 Gorbachev further promised to unilaterally withdraw troops and tanks from East Germany, Czechoslovakia, and Hungary.[56] By November 1989, it had become evident to most observers that the Soviet Union had reduced military spending as a percent of GNP.[57]

These initiatives, and the even more dramatic ones to follow, touched a fundamental political nerve throughout the West, among both elites and the public. Unilateral military reductions, as well as Soviet agreement to withdraw troops from Afghanistan (and later admit the "immorality" of the Afghanistan invasion), push for negotiated peace settlements in southern Africa and Cambodia, and relax—even relinquish—control over Eastern Europe triggered important changes in the Western public's perception of the Soviet "threat." For the first time in the postwar period, it was possible to see the end of the Cold War.

At the same time, Gorbachev began to take the measures necessary for radical internal economic reform. Because he partially blamed isolation from the discipline of the international market for inefficiency and waste in the Soviet economy, he took bold steps to expand trade with the West. In an attempt to gain access to hard currency reserves and Western markets, Soviet officials initiated informal contacts with the World Bank and the International Monetary Fund, applied for membership in the General Agreement on Tariffs and Trade (GATT), entered into trade negotiations with the European Community (EC), began to borrow on Western bond markets for the first time, and initiated sweeping changes in currency regulations. The boldest moves were the decentralization of the foreign trade bureaucracy and the legalization of joint ventures with Western firms and wholly owned subsidiaries on Soviet soil. For the first time, capitalist ownership of the means of production was permitted in the Soviet economy—and foreign ownership at that! Finally, as reform movements swept through Eastern Europe, the Soviet Union proposed that pricing within the Eastern trade regime, the CMEA, be based on world market prices. And the CMEA itself disintegrated as its newly "sovereign" members sought closer ties with the West.[58]

As the Soviet threat rapidly declined, liberal views of East-West trade gained new adherents, even in the United States. Liberals who believed that as part of the creation of a new European security order the West should "help" Gorbachev in his reform effort argued that trade barriers in U.S.-Soviet economic relations should be relaxed. Freer trade, they claimed, could lead to political stability among trading partners, and open economies would reduce xenophobia and fear. The West should not look at trade as a zero-sum game. It should not succumb to the temptation of trying to gain unilateral advantage by abusing Soviet restraint and domestic problems. They argued further that the Soviet economic opening would be primarily directed toward Europe, and Europeans would be responsive, especially if progress on arms control continued to reduce the European perception of a Soviet military threat. The United States should relax the technology blockade under these conditions, the argument ran; alliance conflict would be more harmful to Western security than expanded East-West trade.[59]

Skeptics, on the other hand, began to warn that despite these foreign policy initiatives and well-intentioned internal reforms, the Soviet threat persisted and its military power was more formidable than ever. They argued that Soviet defense spending did not diminish, and in fact, the 1980s saw a steady growth in Soviet military power with the aid of Western technology.[60] Despite Soviet retrenchment in Europe, the projection of Soviet power would still threaten U.S. interests. They reminded liberals that Secretary Gorbachev proclaimed in Vladivostock in 1986 and in Krasnoyarsk in 1988 that the Soviet Union was both a European and an Asian power. Although the threat of a direct Soviet attack on NATO had disappeared, the Soviet Union still intended to remain a military superpower, and its military capabilities still made it America's most dangerous adversary. In 1989, for example, a record tonnage of new ships was accepted by the Soviet navy, and the USSR continued to build nuclear missiles; and it not only expanded its naval base in Vietnam, it built another one in Syria.

Skeptics argued that because the Soviet threat persisted, U.S. national security policy must continue to stress the denial of Soviet hegemony at either end of the Eurasian land mass. And because the course of Soviet reform was uncertain—indeed Gorbachev's internal reforms placed the old system under considerable stress—the West must not change its policy or reduce its resource commitment to NATO. Finally, Gorbachev's intent was no different than that of his predecessors: to split the NATO alliance and expel the U.S. from Europe. Some argued that in the context of the Soviet Union's economic crisis, Gorbachev was using disarmament as a strategy to maintain the military advantage he could not afford to secure through military spending— Soviet troop reductions approximated the Soviet draft shortage. In addition, there had been no diminution of Soviet efforts to steal U.S. technology in order to enhance its military power. Therefore, the U.S. defense posture would have to be based on assessments of Soviet capabilities, not on guesses about Soviet intentions.[61]

Economic nationalists further warned that, whether successful or not in contributing to economic reform, expanded trade with the West would have a real impact on Soviet economic power. Joint production and joint ventures involve a qualitatively different level of technology transfer than outright sales of advanced products, and the expansion of those technology imports from the West could enhance Soviet military power. The very technologies that Gorbachev and his predecessors attempted to import from the West to modernize the Soviet economy would also benefit the military modernization effort.[62] The 1989 edition of *Soviet Military Power* stated authoritatively: "The long-standing Soviet program of legal and illegal acquisition of foreign technology has not diminished. That program, coupled with the pursuit of technology through joint ventures and exchanges, is vital to the Soviets' strategy of upgrading their competitiveness in military technology."[63] Soviet energy exports could lead to unacceptable levels of Western dependence, and the extension of credits to the East would only feed the Soviet military and exacerbates the vulnerability of the international financial system.

The final demise of the Soviet state decreased the Western perception of a *threat* from the region yet increased perceptions of *vulnerability*. However, as central authorities in the newly independent states lost control of their economies, as the delivery and supply systems began to break down and they reverted to barter trade, and as established trade relations with Western firms became even more uncertain, perceptions of the source of vulnerability in the West began to change. For example, the 1980s' view of financial vulnerability was one of *debtor leverage*; debtors could extract concessions from lenders who stood to lose significantly from defaults. The 1990s began, however, with a sharp rise in Soviet debt with a simultaneous collapse of central control over international payments. When independent enterprises and even banks began to borrow on international markets without central authorization, short-term debt skyrocketed, and by the end of 1991 the Soviet Union faced extreme liquidity pressures to which Western banks became vulnerable. In a similar fashion, the delivery of energy supplies became uncertain and Western investments in the post-Soviet industrial sector became insecure. Finally, the diffusion of military technology to the Third World, as desperate former Soviet scientists were forced to sell their knowledge to the highest bidder, became a real policy concern. In short, vulnerability fears based on assumptions about *too much* state control over markets were traded for vulnerability concerns about *too little* market control.

Of course, there were also those who warned of a continued threat to the West from Russia, arguing that Russian history could best predict the post-Soviet behavior of that state. They argued that eighteenth-century Russian modernization programs strengthened the state and the military, and that in the pre-World War I period Russia had geopolitical ambitions in the Balkans, Central Asia, and the Far East. Historically, Russian ambitions had always been difficult for her neighbors to deal with and had posed diplomatic problems for the West.[64]

Vulnerability and Declining American Industrial Competitiveness

Meanwhile, as these debates simmered and as new vulnerabilities emerged, the 1980s witnessed the rapid decline of many U.S. high-technology industries. This relative decline added two new complications to

East-West trade vulnerability arguments within the United States. First, foreign countries began to export high-technology goods. When high technology increasingly originates from abroad, economic nationalists argue, it can more easily find its way into the adversary's hands. To counter that threat, the U.S. engaged in a concerted effort to tighten export restrictions within COCOM. But as America's hegemonic position in high technology declined, its ability to provide leadership for COCOM diminished. On the eve of COCOM's fortieth anniversary in 1989, French officials told the Bush administration that they considered the Federal Republic of Germany to be the West's industrial leader, and despite U.S. military preeminence, the French government would follow West German policies on East-West trade.[65]

Furthermore, even the role of COCOM countries in the production of high-technology goods diminished in the 1980s, and the U.S. found it increasingly difficult to control non-COCOM countries' East-West trade. During 1989, for example, the United States pressed South Korea to restrict exports to the Soviet Union of 239 items, but failed to obtain the agreement of the South Korean government to do so. The Korean government argued instead that it would unilaterally "select" items for control from the COCOM list.[66]

Second, within the United States, the relative decay of American productive capability led to U.S. perceptions of vulnerability in relation to allies as well as adversaries.[67] For example, in the mid-1980s, the Defense Department expressed a growing concern that a general decline in the U.S. semiconductor industry could weaken the entire American electronics industry, which then would no longer be in a position to advance rapidly enough to offset any advantage the Soviet Union might have in numbers of troops or weapons.[68] The Pentagon's *Critical Technology Plan*, which compared the positions of the U.S., the Soviet Union, and America's allies in twenty technologies designated by the Secretary of Defense as "most critical to ensuring the long-term qualitative superiority of U.S. weapons systems," found that whereas the Soviet Union led in only one of those technologies, Japan led the U.S. in five.[69]

Relative decline in high-technology production and trade meant that the United States had become increasingly dependent on foreign technology for its military high-technology requirements. For example, the Pentagon worried that there would be no American suppliers for high-speed chips made from gallium arsenide, used in communications satellites, high-speed computers, and fiber-optic communications systems.[70]

This concern was deepened by noises from Japan that America's military strength was indeed dependent on Japanese technology. In a widely publicized book, *The Japan That Can Say "No,"* written with Sony president Akio Morita, Shintaro Ishihara wrote: "It has come to the point that no matter how much they [the United States] continue military expansion, if Japan stopped selling them the chips, there would be nothing more they could do. . . . If, for example, Japan sold chips to the Soviet Union and stopped selling them to the U.S., this would upset the entire military balance. . . . The more technology advances, the more the U.S. and the Soviet Union will become dependent upon the initiative of the Japanese people."[71] Even if such statements were exaggerated and intended for domestic Japanese political consumption, they confirmed the new trade vulnerability fears expressed by economic nationalists.

Some observers argued that to counter the dependence that may result from industrial decline, policies to enhance American competitiveness were required. These included granting industry the freedom to capture and maintain new markets, and an infusion of new (and sometimes foreign) capital into declining sectors. These policies, however, would compete directly with export controls. Ralph Thomson, former senior vice-president of the American Electronics Association, expressed the industry position succinctly when he stated that the relaxation of export controls would revitalize the competitiveness of American industry in the global marketplace: "In a situation where it's clear the principal confrontations now are economic rather than military, we certainly need to have the weapons released for use so we can fight the battle properly."[72]

Two industry-government conflicts in the 1980s illustrate the dilemma of clashing perceptions of vulnerability, and the resulting policy confusion. In 1987, General Motors and General Electric lobbied vigorously for export licenses that would permit their commercial communications satellites to be launched from the Soviet Union. The Soviets promised a "fast track to the stars" with their Proton rocket, at a cost of $30 million per launch, half the cost of similar launchings in the West. State Department officials, however, insisted that it would not be in the U.S. national interest to issue export licenses for these satellites, because using Soviet rockets would provide the adversary with access to strategic U.S. technology. The U.S. communications satellite industry, however, was in trouble. After the 1986 *Challenger* explosion, President

Reagan had ordered an end to commercial satellite launchings by U.S. space shuttles, and American rockets were booked with military orders through 1989. Without launching facilities, the industry recognized that it would be at a grave disadvantage vis-à-vis Europe and Japan, who were not only constructing their own rockets, but permitting the Soviet Union to launch their commercial communications satellites. Furthermore, to avoid U.S. extraterritorial export controls on their Soviet launchings, these competitors were designing out American components (that is, designing products in such a way that American components would not be needed and could be substituted), further harming the American industry. Congressional representatives, on the other hand, worried that if the U.S. communications satellite industry used Soviet launch facilities, the fledgling U.S. commercial rocket industry would be destroyed. NASA officials backed the communications satellite industry, urging the administration to drop restrictions in the interest of U.S. "competitiveness." At first, the government denied the export licenses to the Soviet Union, but permitted launches from China; later, however, it relented to allow some launches from the Soviet Union.[73]

A similar set of conflicts emerged when, in 1986, Japan's Fujitsu Ltd. announced plans to merge its semiconductor business with Schlumberger Ltd.'s Fairchild Semiconductor Corporation. Like many firms in the U.S. semiconductor industry, Fairchild was ailing. In exchange for 80 percent of Fairchild, Fujitsu would invest $400 million in the company over two years, making available all of its technology. Many observers estimated that the Japanese infusion of cash would make Fairchild a major player in the American market again, and Fairchild would leapfrog from thirteenth to tenth among world chipmakers. Again, the U.S. government was divided over its assessments of the sale's implications. Many argued that actions like the proposed merger were just what the U.S. semiconductor industry needed to become competitive again, while others countered that the merger would jeopardize U.S. security interests. Since Fairchild made defense products, worth $150 million a year, Fujitsu would conceivably have had access to contracts, catalogs, and Defense Department documents. And since Japan traded heavily with the Soviet Union, it was further argued, the sale might easily compromise U.S. interests. The controversy caused Fujitsu to withdraw the offer.[74]

These cases vividly illustrate the central policy problems generated by new perceptions of technological vulnerability: as international competition began to threaten the technological base of American industry, debates over export control exposed deep conflicts in U.S. policy circles over technology diffusion, the clash between public and private interests, and bureaucratic conflict within the U.S. government over whether U.S. competitiveness or technology security should guide policy decisions.

In an era of growing European and Japanese weight in the world economy, heightened struggle among the Western industrialized countries for technological dominance, and the lure of postcommunist markets, America's alliance partners and Western corporate officials increasingly argued for a redefinition of vulnerability. Vulnerability was no longer viewed simply as a Cold War threat from a military adversary but as a threat from military allies who were economic competitors in an increasingly "hot peace."

In response to these changes, the Bush administration began by espousing the vulnerability assumptions of Cold War economic nationalism in East-West trade. Secretary of State James Baker sided with the skeptics when he stated that "for all the talk of 'defensive defense,' Soviet military exercises still continue to show a marked inclination for taking the offensive."[75] The boldest official statement of this view and its economic nationalist implications came from Deputy Secretary of State Lawrence S. Eagleburger in September 1989 when he speculated that Gorbachev's relaxation of control in Eastern Europe and the Baltic republics could bring about damaging instability in Europe and lead many Western nations to provide economic assistance to Moscow without regard to their own national interests. He warned of "the danger that change in the East will prove too destabilizing to be sustained." Finally, expressing nostalgia for the relative stability of the Cold War period, Eagleburger warned that "Gorbachev is no anti-Communist and he intends to make the Soviet Union as strong as he possibly can."[76]

Furthermore, Bush administration officials began by also taking a hard line in COCOM against the liberal arguments of the allies. Europeans pressed the United States to offer a rationale for COCOM that would take into account the democratic revolutions in Eastern Europe. President Bush, however, at first refused to link those changes to export control policy and instead insisted in a letter to COCOM that trade controls could not be eased until Western European governments began to enforce existing restrictions. U.S. officials in COCOM warned that the Bush administration would be ready to impose sanctions on European companies who did not comply with U.S. export controls, even at the risk of trade frictions with Western Europe.[77] Europeans, however, were increasingly bold in their opposition to the U.S. position. In fact, to protect themselves from the extraterritorial application of U.S. export controls, they had begun to exclude American high-technology components from their products.[78]

The Bush administration, however, was thrust by events toward a more liberal policy position. Secretary of State Baker took a conciliatory tone when he stated that "we are prepared to provide technical assistance in certain areas of Soviet economic reform. . . . We want *perestroika* to succeed." He suggested that as part of that "assistance," the United States was willing to support "non-strategic trade with the Soviet Union."[79] By early 1990, Baker's views had set the tone for a significant turning point in America's long-standing opposition to relaxation in restrictions on East-West trade. The Defense Department relaxed U.S. controls on the export of computers to the Soviet Union, paving the way for new COCOM regulations. The United States proposed elevating the Eastern European countries in several stages to the same treatment that COCOM gave China, with the requirement that these countries provide safeguards that the technologies would not be adapted to military use.[80]

Economic nationalists within the Bush administration, however, were determined that these new terms should not apply to the Soviet Union.[81] The Bush administration's *Defense Planning Guidance*, issued in January 1990 to military commanders, argued that because the Soviet Union still represented a threat in the Third World, the United States should "preclude the transfer of militarily significant technology and resources to the Soviet Union."[82]

From Dual-Use to Triple-Use Technologies

In 1990 the United States was faced with yet another dilemma: in the (then still existing) Soviet Union and Eastern Europe, "dual-use" technologies suddenly became "triple-use" technologies. The technologies needed to enhance economic competitiveness not only had military applications, but they were also now the technologies needed to spread democracy. The most important facilitators of economic efficiency and growth—telecommunications equipment, computers, fax machines, copy machines, and other types of microelectronic equipment, as well as technical personnel trained abroad—could also help prevent despotic regimes from regaining political control. When civilians have access to high-technology information systems, opposition groups can grow and thrive, and it is more difficult for governments to exercise complete political control. Those economic nationalists who continued to desire restriction on the the eastward flow of technology were now faced with choosing between their fears of creating military and economic competitors and their hopes for the East's democracy and prosperity.

In June 1990, for example, economic nationalists in the Bush administration denied a license to U.S. West, Inc. to build a fiber-optic cable communications system across the Soviet Union. The proposed cable would have linked the former Soviet republics, Japan, and Europe for civilian phone service and business data communications. Opposition to the project was based on the fear that a transfer of fiber-optic telecommunication technology to the Soviet Union would threaten the security of the United States, because it would impair the ability of the United States to monitor military communications. Restrictions on projects like these, however, also impair rapid civilian communication; and U.S. Commerce Department liberals argued that the Soviet government maintained a separate telecommunications system for sensitive state communications anyway.

Despite continuing debates between liberals and economic nationalists in the United States, Western European business elites pushed their governments to tear down the Western-built economic walls embodied in COCOM's export restrictions in response to the collapse of the physical and political walls separating Europe. Of the 116 categories of restricted items remaining on the COCOM list, 30 were eliminated in June 1990.[83] These liberated items included certain categories of machine tools, computers, and telecommunications equipment—the same categories Europeans had pushed to decontrol in February. COCOM also accepted a British proposal that an entirely new list of controlled items be drawn up, in effect completely scrapping the old restrictions.

Even after the disintegration of the Soviet Union, the Bush administration argued against improving the military capabilities of the twelve former Soviet republics through the sale of advanced telecommunications equipment. They also argued that those states would be tempted to resell the equipment to potential American adversaries like Syria and Iraq. It was not until March 1992 that the U.S. government agreed to relax controls on the sale of fiber-optic cables to the former Soviet republics; that agreement was made over the heads of Defense Department officials who were still opposed because electronic eavesdropping would necessarily become more difficult.[84]

While controls on trade with former adversaries were being relaxed, new sources of potential economic vulnerability were discovered. In August 1990, Iraq invaded Kuwait, using military equipment and technology developed largely in both the industrialized East and West. The crisis sparked a new battle over the scope and direction of export restrictions to Iraq, as it was reported that between 1985 and 1990, the U.S. exported $1.5 billion worth of "dual-use" computers, chemicals, and communications equipment; indeed, in 1989, Iraq bought command and control equipment that U.S. planes targeted in the war just two years later.

Economic nationalists who supported strict restrictions argued that the Gulf crisis demonstrated the need to remain vigilant about dual-use technologies world-wide. Paul Freedenberg, a top export control official during most of the Reagan administration, stated in 1991 that the Bush administration was drawing back from the feeling that the Cold War was over: "It's all related to what happens in the Third World after Saddam Hussein." Administration officials began to prepare a set of far-reaching export controls on manufacturing, plant designs, and processing equipment that could be associated with the manufacture of chemical and biological weapons.[85] However, given the global diffusion of those technologies, only multilateral agreement and enforcement capability would halt the flow of dangerous technologies to potential adversaries.

Such an agreement was not easy to reach. The French deputy representative to COCOM argued that that organization's tasks should *not* be expanded to restrict technology to Third World countries—indeed such a task expansion could be interpreted as another form of North-South exploitation. The French position, even after Iraq's invasion of Kuwait, was that COCOM should not expand its country list to include states in the "South," that the threat from the Third World was very different from that of the Soviet Union and that their low levels of industrialization prohibit an easy diversion of commercial goods to military uses.[86]

This position, however, was overruled in the COCOM meetings of November 1992. At those meetings, members substantially redefined the mission of the organization in order to refocus controls on nations such as Iraq, North Korea, China, India, and Pakistan. Postcommunist countries would be removed from the export control list if they agreed to allow on-site inspections and guarantee that imported technologies would not be used for military purposes. They would also be required to establish export control systems of their own in order to prevent the proliferation of Western technologies to dangerous Third World countries. To help with the construction of these export controls in the post-communist world, COCOM members agreed to provide aid and technical assistance.

Nonetheless, in 1993 Western companies complained that COCOM was still fighting the Cold War in that it continued to deny technology to the former Soviet Union and Eastern Europe and that the structure of the organization itself—vigilant export control regulations and enforcement capabilities—prevented a redefined mission. COCOM, many argued, was a Cold War dinosaur that needed to be scrapped. COCOM officials stated, however, that strict controls were still required because of the weak states and political instability in the region.[87] So, despite a relaxation of controls on the former communist world, we can expect the struggle over strategic trade restrictions to continue for some time—given the "triple use" to which high technologies are put and new threats to Western security.

As Eastern Europe and the former Soviet Union open their economies to the West in the midst of deepening economic crisis, and as the U.S. experiences a relative decline in its high-technology industries, and as new potential security threats appear in other parts of the world, the central questions surrounding Western trade vulnerability are now more important than ever: At what level of technological sophistication should the export of machinery and equipment be forbidden? And to whom? To what extent should the kind of subsidized or guaranteed credit often found in international trade be extended to the liberalizing "East"? Should Western imports from these countries be expanded? Do Western and Eastern Europe rely too heavily on Russia for its energy supplies? How are we to assess new Western vulnerabilities in relation to the Third World?

Given the confusion, policy conflict, and potential harm suffered by American high-technology industries, what can Western nations learn from the experience of detente and its effects? Are there lessons from this period that can guide future policy? In the chapters to follow, I will address these questions.

At the heart of this inquiry is an examination of the claims advanced by the economic nationalists in their criticism of the economic strategy of detente in the 1970s. Those who fear a security threat in trade distinguish among three types of potential vulnerability: technology exodus, resource dependence, and debtor leverage. As these categories suggest, exporters, importers, and lenders each face different kinds of vulnerability in their relations with one another.

In chapter 2 I construct the arguments that form the assumptions behind each claim for vulnerability. I also examine the sources of vulnerability reduction and avoidance—that is, "the consolidation of control" over potential or actual sources of vulnerability. In all three issue areas vulnerability is assumed to be caused by an adversary's or competitor's control over resources or markets for resources. If vulnerabilities are indeed present, then their reduction requires either wresting that control away from the adversary or competitor or ensuring that he never gains control in the first place.

Throughout the Cold War policies to ensure low vulnerability implicitly assumed that control over markets must be in the hands of *the state*. Particularly in the United States, the thrust of policy has been toward the belief that states exercise coercive controls in order to prevent other states or private actors from endangering state security in their economic relations with adversaries and competitors. As the preceding historical account suggests, it is this "corollary" to the vulnerability argument that has often been the source of conflict over trade restrictions. Counterarguments have revolved around two questions: why coerce others to restrict trade when vulnerability is low, and why coerce at all when other means of vulnerability reduction are available?

After clarifying the economic nationalist vulnerability claims and vulnerability reduction arguments, chapter 2 moves beyond those claims and suggests four additional hypotheses about the "consolidation of control" for vulnerability reduction. First, even if adversary states regulate the import of commercial high technology, the reduction of associated vulnerabilities may actually rest with private *corporations* who sell technology; their strategies are often designed to withhold key technologies and entrap the technology importer in a relationship of dependence. In this way, their behavior supports the vulnerability reduction goals of exporting states.

Second, the vulnerabilities associated with the transfer of military technology or dependence on imports of the adversary's resources can be reduced through the coordination of the policies of potentially vulnerable states, rather than unilateral action or the coercive efforts of one state over others. This coordination is best achieved through a *normative* consensus: exporter agreement on which technologies at what level of sophistication or which imports in what volume should be restricted may be a powerful way to consolidate multilateral control over markets. Ironically, it is disagreement about vulnerability that weakens normative controls and triggers perceptions of the need for coercion. Coercion—and resistance to coercion—in turn causes political conflict among potentially vulnerable states, reducing the effectiveness of joint vulnerability reduction measures. Therefore, *agreement on vulnerability* is the key to multilateral coordination of vulnerability reduction.

Third, financial instability and debtor leverage can also be reduced through multilateral agreement among both private and public creditors, but because vulnerability in this issue area is mutual, its reduction may also require substantial debt forgiveness. Vulnerability reduction, then, may therefore be a function of *sacrifice* on the part of vulnerable nations. Finally, with regard to postcommunist nations, Western vulnerability is reduced when those states themselves gain enough strength to control markets. In order to reduce Western vulnerability fears, however, that control must be used to *establish stable property rights on the basis of market-rational behavior*, it cannot be used to establish the kind of coercive and total control attempted under communism.

These four vulnerability reduction measures fall outside of the economic nationalists' assumptions as they have been represented in the policy debate; yet they may provide guidelines for policymakers as they attempt to deal with the vulnerability question in the future. Therefore, chapter 2 does two things: it specifies and clarifies Cold War vulnerability claims so that they can be tested, and it "repairs" the vulnerability argument so that it can be a more effective foundation for future policy.

Using the vulnerability and vulnerability reduction propositions as a guide, chapters 3 through 6 assess the evidence from the 1970s and 1980s for each vulnerability claim. A note of clarification about the focus of the empirical analysis in these chapters is in order here. Chapters 3 and 4 submit vulnerability propositions about technology exodus to empirical analysis focused on the Soviet Union. The USSR was chosen because U.S. policymakers saw the Soviet Union as the most important source of Western vulnerability in this issue area. To the extent that a preliminary assessment of future vulnerabilities is presented, the focus on the former Soviet Union continues; the analytic focus of *future*

vulnerabilities is limited to Russia because of its size, resource endow-
ment, military capabilities, and potential for causing regional instability.

Chapters 5 and 6 on resource dependence and financial instabil-
ity/debtor leverage, however, bring Eastern Europe into the analysis.
Energy vulnerability concerns were focused primarily on Western
Europe during the Cold War; in the postcommunist era, as the East
joins "Europe," its energy vulnerabilities must also be considered. This
chapter still relies on the former Soviet Union as the chief source of
future vulnerability concern, because Russia still provides substantial
energy supplies to Western Europe. Moreover, Eastern Europe began
the postcommunist era almost wholly dependent on Russia for energy.
With regard to consideration of vulnerabilities associated with financing
trade with adversaries, Eastern European members of the Warsaw Pact
rather than the Soviet Union were the primary sources of future concern; therefore, Eastern European countries are the primary focus of
the analysis. With regard to the future, the former Soviet Union is again
brought into the analysis as a source of vulnerability.

Chapter 3 examines the warrants for the claim that technology exodus leads to the exporter's vulnerability in its contribution to the
importer's economic power. It analyzes the available evidence on the
role of Western technology in the Soviet economy between 1970 and
1990 and carries the analysis into the post-Soviet future. The evidence
suggests that the positive effects of technology transfer are only present
under certain specific conditions that did not obtain in the Soviet economy and are not likely to appear in the region in the near term, even if
economic reforms are effective. In their joint ventures with Russian
partners, Western corporations have pursued, and continue to pursue,
strategies designed to withhold key technologies from their customers.
The conditions under which Western firms control production technology may even slow the speed of future Russian industrial development.
Rather than exacerbate Western vulnerability, technology trade with
Russia—as was the case for technology trade with the Soviet Union—
may create a kind of dependence on the West that will inhibit Russia's
development of a competitive niche in the world economy. Western corporate strategy, then, contributes to the consolidation of the exporter's
market control and thus reduces vulnerability.

Chapter 4 assesses the role of Western technology in enhancing
Soviet military power and looks briefly to problems that may arise in the
post-Soviet future. The first section examines the direct contribution of
Western technology to Soviet military strength in the 1980s and con-

cludes that there is little evidence to support the claims that Western technology made a contribution to technological progress in the Soviet military sector. The second section looks at the role of the Western embargo in preventing Soviet acquisition of militarily significant technology. An examination of the struggles within COCOM over technology transfer suggests that disagreement over the scope of the COCOM embargo among its members weakened the embargo regime and opened the way for private firms to violate COCOM rules, increasing the number of illegal technology transfers. An examination of Toshiba Corporation's illegal sale of submarine-quieting technology to the Soviet Union provides an illustration of those violations and their vulnerability effects. The analysis shows that the vulnerability effects of the Toshiba sale were probably low and, in a broader sense, studies conducted by Reagan administration officials presented evidence that COCOM was largely effective in preventing the sale of militarily significant technology to the Soviet Union. This analysis therefore provides us with mixed results: while agreement on definitions of vulnerability leading to consensus on norms would have enhanced multilateral consolidation of control over technology exports—particularly control over illegal transfers—the multilateral embargo itself, with all of its flaws and weaknesses, was effective enough to control critical technologies that would have enhanced Soviet military power. The illegal sales may have included some critical items but probably not enough to have made a difference. Nonetheless, although the embargo generally proved effective, this lack of consensus signals problems for COCOM's "repair," focusing on new areas or the construction of new multilateral export control regimes.

Unlike the continuity suggested in chapter 3, events that took place in 1992 suggest that the economic vulnerability problem with regard to the export of military technology will be different for the West in the near future than it was in the past. Uncertainty over control of economic forces and the demise of the Soviet state began to force thousands of Soviet scientists trained in building nuclear and chemical weapons to sell their expertise to states like North Korea or Iraq; the United States has taken measures to reduce such vulnerabilities associated with a *lack* of state control in the region by providing financial support to many of these scientists.

Chapter 5 assesses the argument for resource dependence. It focuses primarily on Soviet natural gas exports to Western and Eastern Europe during the 1980s. This approach was chosen both because of the controversy over vulnerability in the Urengoi pipeline dispute of 1982, the increasing importance of natural gas in the energy mix of the USSR and of the OECD countries, and because of its increasing significance in Soviet-European trade. Based on the assessment of the circumstances under which Soviet natural gas is imported into Western Europe, and particularly into Germany, the evidence suggests that claims of Western European dependence on Soviet energy supplies were vastly overstated at the time of the pipeline dispute. Even though vulnerability was minimal—Western Europe had diversified its suppliers and contingency plans were in place—multilateral measures were taken to consolidate control over natural gas imports in the wake of the pipeline dispute that provided assurance against possible future vulnerabilities. The analysis concludes that the conditions under which Western Europe imported energy from the Soviet Union and now imports energy from Russia and other former Soviet states show clearly how the vulnerability faced by importers of strategic commodities can be reduced.

Eastern Europe, however, is vulnerable to supply interruptions and a deterioration in their terms of energy trade with Russia. Prices for Russian oil and natural gas have increased sharply for these countries, and Eastern Europe suffered additional energy shocks as a result of the Gulf crisis, which led to a higher price for world oil. Disruption in oil and natural gas deliveries will be difficult to swallow, until the countries of Eastern Europe diversify supplies and develop contingency plans to counter the effects of supply shortfalls.

Chapter 6 assesses the argument for debtor leverage under the condition of financial instability. It analyzes the events leading to the East-European debt crisis of 1982 and analyzes the potential for a debt crisis in the 1990s in the aftermath of communism's collapse. The evidence suggests that while claims of Western vulnerability were exaggerated in the other issue areas, *mutual* vulnerability was high in East-West trade finance and it will increase as the Central Eastern European countries integrate their economies more fully with the West. The new political status of Eastern Europe has changed perceptions of vulnerability; no longer is debtor leverage the central concern, but perceived vulnerability is similar to that of the financial community during the Latin American debt crisis. Much can be learned from that crisis in order to bring stability to the economies of Eastern Europe and, by extension, stability in the financial relations between Western lenders and Eastern borrowers. Mutual interdependencies created in international financial relations, however, constrain the implementation of other U.S. foreign policy goals, and thus financial vulnerabilities can inhibit important foreign policy aims.

In the concluding chapter I will reinterpret vulnerability arguments in light of the evidence presented and discuss the political effects of the vulnerability debate. Although the evidence in the four cases varies, in general, it does *not* support the vulnerability claims that fueled Cold War thinking during the Reagan years. This does not mean that the West was immune from vulnerability; it does, however, suggest both that vulnerability claims were questionable and that Western states, private corporations, and multilateral institutions were able to "consolidate control" over markets in ways that reduced vulnerability, despite the Reagan administration's dissatisfaction with the level and intensity of that control, and insistence on the unilateral consolidation of U.S. power over East-West markets. The evidence further suggests that Soviet disintegration resulted in part from the vulnerabilities the Soviet state faced in its international economic relations. Its inability to consolidate control over markets partially explains its collapse.

The book's arguments are then applied in a preliminary way to a discussion of new vulnerabilities in the former Soviet Union and Eastern Europe and to the issue of high-technology proliferation to "dangerous" Third World countries. This discussion of "new vulnerabilities in old places" suggests that because a loss of market control will be the source of Western vulnerability in economic relations with the former Soviet Union, policies to assist the new states to establish stable property rights and stabilize their economies on the basis of market-rational behavior are appropriate. Export controls must be based on the presumption of open trade rather than trade denial, and Western nations should provide a market for Soviet exports of high-technology goods. With regard to "old vulnerabilities in new places," new "hi-tech nonproliferation regimes" must be grounded in consensual assessments of vulnerability in order for them to be truly effective.

Debates over economic vulnerability in international relations have important implications for the policy environment; many of the vulnerability claims examined in this book have unnecessarily militarized international economic relations and national industrial policy, and they are certain to be made in future political debates over trade with adversaries and even trade competitors. This book raises questions and presents historical evidence that does *not* promise to resolve but does promise to clarify that future debate.

2

The Case for Economic Vulnerability
in International Relations

The economic nationalist's view of vulnerability in international relations can be best understood within Keohane and Nye's paradigm of "complex interdependence."[1] Although their argument is clearly framed within the liberal tradition, much of it can be used to support the economic nationalist position. Complex interdependence has its roots in the close contact among societies that arose in the wake of the postwar explosion of international trade and finance. Like a virus, trade spread the effects of domestic policies—such as inflation or deflation—to their trading partners' economies. States that trade with one another become sensitive to an increasing number of events in each other's societies.

This sensitivity confers upon states new levers of power over others. As a result of their ability to withhold or expand trade, states can exercise influence over the policies of their trading partners and can actually enhance or reduce their economic power. For example, states can prey on their trading partners' dependence on imports and exports to extract concessions in other areas of concern; they can tactically link trade issues to other unrelated issues in international negotiations to achieve their wider goals.

States become vulnerable in a trading relationship when interdependence is asymmetrical in their trading partners' favor. That is, a state is vulnerable when the relationship confers more power on the partner than it can maintain within the relationship. A state is also vulnerable when it loses control over markets or when the partner controls markets upon which the vulnerable state depends for strength and autonomy. From the perspective of economic nationalism, trade between adversaries makes them particularly sensitive to the source of market control that can arise within the trading relationship. For example, the United States would be vulnerable if it sold technology to an adversary that changed the balance of military power between the two countries in the adversary's favor. Western Europe would be vulnerable if it became dependent upon an adversary's energy imports, and if that dependence gave the adversary the power to extract concessions in other areas by threatening to cut off energy supplies.

Vulnerability also lurks in a relationship of symmetrical interdependence. Although the fates of both partners may be linked, one partner can play "chicken," exploiting the other's fears of the high cost of breaking the relationship and thus extracting concessions. As I suggest in more detail later, lenders risk this kind of vulnerability.[2] For example, the growth of Eurocurrency market finance of Eastern European imports in the 1970s led to dangerous levels of Eastern debt in the 1980s, leaving the Western financial system vulnerable to collapse or to debtors' bargaining demands.

States can reduce their trade vulnerability by changing their own policies to diminish the power their partner gains within the relationship. They can also minimize their vulnerability by building international "regimes" that establish norms of reciprocity and rules and procedures to determine who controls markets and to limit the power trading partners can exercise over one another. For example, as we saw in chapter 1, the United States established an export control policy to limit those exports to the Soviet Union that could tip the balance of military power in the Soviets' favor. It also took the lead in establishing COCOM, an international regime of Western states whose purpose was to jointly restrict those exports that might endanger Western security. Western nations can also establish policies to diversify their energy suppliers, so that one exporter does not control the markets and thereby have the power to extract concessions with threats of a supply cutoff. Finally, they can formulate and implement policies that limit or place conditions on lending in order to reduce the power borrowers may have when they threaten default. These are simply examples; we will examine additional vulnerability reduction measures below.

Because exporters face different vulnerability problems than importers, and because asymmetrical trade relations create different problems than symmetrical trade relations, it is useful to distinguish among three types of vulnerability that powerful industrialized nations may encounter in international economic relations. Exporters face problems associated with technology exodus; importers risk dependence on a particular resource supplier; and lenders risk not only potential default on the part of borrowers but also a weak bargaining position with debtors who can *threaten* default or simply stop interest payments to obtain concessions. Although these are not the only vulnerabilities industrialized nations face in their international economic relations, they were the key vulnerabilities that U.S. central decision makers argued the West faced in East-West trade during the Cold War.

Technology Exodus

At the heart of exporter vulnerability is the hypothesis that exports of commercial high technology give a disproportionate increase to the power of the recipient.[3] Instead of simply purchasing pieces of equipment and technology, importing states seek to build up an indigenous military-industrial base that will be safe from the vicissitudes of international trade. If indigenous innovation is inadequate to this task, these states seek to acquire from abroad the advanced technology necessary for increased production efficiency. As these high-technology imports increase, the exporter's vulnerability in the face of the recipient's increased power increases as well. As the exporter's vulnerability increases, security declines. It follows that if the recipient of those exports is an adversary, the export of that technology should be restricted. For example, both before and in the wake of Iraq's invasion of Kuwait, a rash of reports appeared throughout Europe and the U.S. accusing Western firms of selling to Iraq the very technology that now jeopardized Western security in the Persian Gulf. Most of those purchases were legal and were authorized by Western governments.[4] Even if the recipient is an ally, the technology exporter may become vulnerable to the importer's enhanced competitive position in international trade; reduced economic competitiveness translates into reduced political power and influence.[5]

This claim for exporter vulnerability is based on three related arguments. First, cutting-edge commercial production technology and other commercial high technology have increasing military significance; thus, those who have a competitive edge in the development of commercial high technology possess a military advantage as well. It follows that because technology is important to military power, those nations who are trailing in high-technology development will attempt to acquire it abroad in order to close the technology "gap" between themselves and those more powerful. Finally, the increasing ease of international technology transfer through the internationalization of production permits trailing states to successfully acquire foreign technology, and thus weakens the restrictive effects of existing technology export controls. I now turn to a discussion of each of these arguments.

Technological Excellence and Military Power

Technological excellence is a crucial component of military power. Its contribution is both *direct*, through improvement in weapons systems, and *indirect*, because it enhances a nation's ability to acquire and maintain an internationally competitive industrial position.

In the most elementary sense, the adoption of a new military technique can give a state a distinct military advantage over its adversaries. This is because new techniques can diminish or even invalidate much of the adversary's military capability. Technologies that improve accuracy, speed, target coverage, and destructive capability of new or existing weaponry can be decisive to military victory. Technologies that enhance real or perceived defensive capabilities or the hazards of combat by improving flexibility, maneuverability, invisibility, and undetectability are also considered crucial to military advantage.

For example, the invention of the stirrup permitted soldiers to use horses for enhanced target coverage. The invention of gunpowder and artillery gave the military the advantage of high speed and broad target coverage to the societies that introduced them. In the 1930s, mechanization and aviation technology provided a decisive edge in both speed and target coverage; the recent development of "stealth" technology makes cruise missiles invisible to Soviet radar, and thus negates the capabilities of the USSR's air defense system.[6] Needless to say, nuclear technology in the postwar period has led to a dramatic break with the past in weapons' destructive capability. Microelectronics to improve accuracy and target coverage and directed energy to improve speed are examples of current innovations that promise to grant their developers a decisive strategic edge even, some say, in the event of a nuclear war.

States have not always recognized the importance of technological innovation to military strength. Before World War II, the pace of military innovation was glacial; the introduction of new techniques consisted of isolated inventions of single, scattered entrepreneurs. Innovation was sometimes even resisted by military bureaucracies.[7] The invention of the atomic bomb, however, represented a decisive break with the past, making technological superiority the key to military power. As a result, the link between technological prowess and military might has led to significant change in the organization and objectives of the scientific and technological community.

The United States in particular relied on its technological superiority in weaponry in the postwar period to offset the Soviet Union's alleged quantitative advantage. This reliance is reflected in U.S. federal spending for research and development. Between World Wars I and II, the government provided only about 15 percent of all R-and-D funds; by 1984 it funded over 60 percent of all R and D, and 75 percent of those funds were earmarked for military research and development.[8] In the industrialized world as a whole, military research and development is now highly organized and well funded; by 1977, one-third of the world's R-and-D expenditures went for weapons innovation.[9]

A more complex and indirect relationship exists between the technological level of a nation's *economy* and its military power. First, an advance in manufacturing technique is an important source of labor productivity.[10] Advanced machine tools, numerical control, statistical process control, computer-aided design and manufacturing, and advanced management techniques are all examples of innovations that have resulted in dramatic bursts of productivity and higher-quality products.[11] The more productive a country's labor force, the stronger its industrial base will be. In the long run, the strength of a nation's military is a distillate of its industrial power; a superior economy can be converted into a stronger war machine. No modern state has been able to maintain a first-rate military capability with a declining industrial base.[12] Furthermore, a highly productive labor force releases resources for military production by allowing for changes in domestic investment allocation. With increasingly efficient industrial production, economies grow and expenditures can more easily be diverted to the military sector of the economy, despite the costs relative to other national choices.

Second, technological advance increases military strength by virtue of the fact that both military and industrial innovations can enhance one another's production capabilities. This capability for mutual enhancement, although as old as the industrial revolution itself, has given rise to the modern notion of "dual-use" technologies—technologies that can enhance both civilian and military capabilities.

Sometimes technologies developed in the military sector are later employed to drive overall economic development. On the eve of the industrial revolution, military innovations were often adapted to industrial use. Indeed, the search for weapons improvements actually contributed to the rise of industrial civilization. For example, boring machines were invented to produce smooth barrels in cannons, but they were later adapted to produce parts of steam engines. The development of mathematics, particularly descriptive geometry, at the time of the Napoleonic Wars, was part of a deliberate attempt to increase the accuracy of artillery fire.[13] In the aftermath of World War II, military innovations proved to be a tremendous spur to growth in civilian industry. The development of the electronics and aerospace technologies in the United States was the result of military research-and-development efforts in the space program and the development of strategic nuclear weapons.[14]

Civilian technologies, of course, often can have important military applications, and many observers argue that this importance will increase throughout the 1990s. First, a technologically advanced industrial base can provide the foundation for broad-scale industrial mobilization crucial to warfare. For example, at the end of the nineteenth century, Germany began to develop an internationally competitive chemical industry. It was nurtured in part because Germany was limited in natural resources and synthetic substitutes were required for the development of a modern industrial infrastructure. During World War I the chemical industry contributed decisively to Germany's military power. When Britain curtailed the export of essential nitrates to Germany, the German chemical industry provided gunpowder and explosives through synthetic production. Again, during World War II, when petroleum supplies were embargoed, virtually all of the German aviation fuel was synthetically produced.[15]

Second, civilian technology is immediately applicable, often without adaptation, to military use. For the present, the contribution of commercial technology to military applications may be far more significant than military technology "spinoffs" to commercial industry. John Zysman has argued that the requirements for technological sophistication in industries that produce and use high-technology goods are now similar to those in the military sector. For example, in sophisticated automobile models, semiconductor chips have been developed that operate in real time to control the mechanical systems of automobiles in environments that are often as hostile as the battlefield.[16]

Similarly, the development of commercial high-definition television (HDTV) will have immediate military applications. HDTV promises to deliver cinema-quality pictures to consumers' living rooms because the picture can carry four times as much information as conventional television, making possible high resolution and vivid color even on large screens. Based on a new generation of semiconductors, HDTV is expected to have many applications in other fields, including personal computers, telecommunications, and manufacturing equipment. The U.S. Department of Defense has allocated $30 million for HDTV research that will be applied to manufacture high-resolution computer screens for improved accuracy and coverage in target weapons.[17]

In another example, West German firms legally sold Iraq machinery for making gas centrifuges—which can separate inert uranium 238 from radioactive uranium 235, an essential step in creating weapons-grade nuclear material. The firm, however, claimed to have sold the equipment for commercial purposes and insisted that the machinery was not precise enough for weapons applications. Indeed, many German exporters to Iraq claimed that they did not know that their machinery would be used to manufacture weapons.[18]

Two causes contribute to this growing importance of commercial technology to military power. First, since World War II, weapons have been increasingly developed as integrated systems. They include delivery mechanisms, logistics support, training facilities, and deployment tactics. For example, a ballistic missile defense "system" consists of tracking, engagement, and interceptor technology, sensor technology and signal processing for improving launch detection, and fixed radars for early warning, all developed in the commercial semiconductor, computer, and telecommunications industries.[19]

Second, since World War II, weapons systems have been developed for environments that were not previously considered part of warfare.[20] This expansion of military environments led to overlaps in the application of civilian and military technologies. Devices developed for oil and gas exploration are implanted on the ocean floor to enable submarine detection; satellites provide global surveillance and communication that can enhance both welfare and warfare. Chemical herbicides can also destroy vegetation in warfare as a battlefield tactic, and weather modification techniques developed for agriculture are being tested for use in battle.[21]

The development of integrated weapons systems and the expansion of military environments greatly increase the possibility that advanced commercial technology will increasingly have military applications. Microchips used in advanced weapons systems can be found in toy stores; Apple II computers can be used for weapons targeting. Scientific systems that assess seismic data are significant as antisubmarine warfare devices. Robots and robotic mechanisms are increasingly used in the production of both civilian and military equipment. Infrared sensors are equipped with the same silicon chips for data processing that are used in pocket calculators and digital watches. Telecommunications equipment, developed commercially, can be adapted to withstand hostile electronic warfare environments with laser optics. Thus equipped, they can significantly improve military command, control, and communications systems. Personal "compact" computers, developed for business and home use, have been adapted to military operations on the battlefield. Their usefulness lies in their small size, low weight, high power, and rugged packaging. Krypton switches which are used in office copy machines, can also be used to trigger nuclear weapons and separate stages in missiles.[22]

The Impact of Exports on the Technology "Gap"[23]

Because technological excellence contributes to military strength both directly and indirectly, states feel compelled to protect any technological advantage they may have over their adversaries. At the same time they must move to erase any advantage that their adversary may enjoy. Thus, trailing states attempt to "catch up" with those who are ahead. The second claim in the exporter vulnerability thesis, then, is that depending on whether they see themselves as leading or trailing in levels of technological competence, states attempt to either widen or narrow the so-called technology gap between themselves and their adversaries and economic competitors.

The size of the gap is usually measured by comparing the years in which certain key technologies are employed in the economies and defense industries of both leading and trailing states. In other words, the gap between two nations is assessed by how far one nation is ahead of the other in its ability to quickly deploy a new technology in production or weapons systems or bring it to market in the form of new products. The export of technology from leading to trailing states is believed to reduce that gap. Economic nationalists in leading states *fear* for the closing of the gap, and economic nationalists in trailing states *hope* that the technological lead between themselves and their competitors can be narrowed.

Albert O. Hirschman got to the heart of this issue when he wrote that "an increase of wealth of any country, if brought about by foreign trade, is necessarily a loss of wealth for other countries."[24] It follows that if a state imports the technology that is the very foundation of another country's wealth, it increases its own power and military might relative to the exporting country. Certainly in the nineteenth century, Russia and Germany experienced rapid economic growth, which was translated into military power in the twentieth century. They did this largely by adopting technology developed by their economic and military competitors, reducing technology gaps and thus reducing the power gaps between themselves and their adversaries.[25] In the postwar period, Japan improved its competitive position by borrowing technology from abroad to improve production and capture new markets.[26] When those states that import another's technology are able to narrow the "gap," the technology exporters must spend even more to stay ahead.

In order for the gap to be significantly reduced, however, imported technology must be efficiently employed in the targeted economic sector or throughout the economy as a whole. This involves the *internal* diffusion of technology. For diffusion effects to be realized, economic linkages between raw materials suppliers, manufacturers of equipment, makers of components, providers of skilled services, and makers of finished products must be strong throughout the economy. When linkages are strong, technological improvements in manufacturing can spur advances in related sectors and can thus lead to improved price/performance in downstream products and generate new markets.[27] Although, as we shall see in chapter 3, economic studies attempted to assess the diffusion effects of Western technology on the Soviet economy, the policy debate did not address the diffusion issue.

The Increasing Ease of International Technology Transfer

The fear on the part of economic nationalists in the West that trade narrows the gap has been heightened by the fact that since the 1960s international diffusion of technology has become increasingly easy. This fear can, in part, be blamed on the rise in multinational corporate activity. Rapid technological advances in communication and transportation reduced the costs of overseas investment, and corporations responded to incentives to locate production facilities abroad.[28] The overseas production facilities they constructed now provide the vehicle by which technology is diffused internationally.

Many observers have argued that this rapid international technology diffusion threatens to close gaps between advanced and trailing states more quickly than ever before.[29] States who are able to close the technology gap by importing technology can eventually compete with their exporting states for export markets, and as they increase market share, they can contribute to the technology exporter's economic decline. As technology is diffused internationally through the multinational corporation's policies of direct foreign investment and licensing, those nations that allow their firms to export technology will lose not only their technological lead, but their domestic market share of the goods they produce. This is because states that import technology can begin to export products back to the exporting state, disrupting their firms' domestic markets. The exporting state then becomes vulnerable to the importer's increased economic strength.

Furthermore, changes in *how* multinational corporations transfer technology have even further reduced the technology gap by shortening the time that it takes the importer to acquire the exporter's technology. This was a conclusion of the controversial but influential "Bucy Report" (named after J. Fred Bucy who presided over the writing of the document), which set the guidelines for Defense Department policy on East-West technology transfer throughout the 1980s.[30]

The "Bucy Report" argued that the traditional transfer modes of direct foreign investment and licensing, dominant in the 1960s, released to the importer only standardized production techniques and "mature" technologies on the verge of obsolescence. In the 1970s, however, industrial cooperation, a new technology transfer mode favored by the Soviet Union and Eastern Europe, seemed likely to narrow the technology gap. These arrangements created sustained contact between exporting firms and importing enterprises. This sustained contact permitted the importer to acquire state-of-the-art production technology rather than simply standardized production techniques, since the transferring firm had a keen interest in capturing markets from competitors. The "Bucy Report" thus termed joint ventures and coproduction the most "effective" forms of technology transfer, i.e., the forms that ensure the highest degree of technological advance in the importing country.

Often called "strategic alliances" in the West, these agreements take the form of joint ventures, coproduction agreements, subcontracting, distribution agreements, joint marketing and development agreements, or the sale of entire production facilities, among others.[31] The contract usually involves long-term training and service, one of the most important factors in effective technology transfers.[32] Often payment for these plants is in the products they produce, called a "buy-back" agreement. In high-technology industries especially, with R-and-D costs prohibitive, where customized production requires direct contacts with end-users, where protectionism threatens exports, and where converging technologies require firms to integrate a full line of products rather than sell a single piece of equipment, cooperative efforts begin to spring up.

In the Soviet Union and Eastern Europe, two kinds of cooperation agreements dominated in the 1970s and 1980s: joint ventures (not introduced in the Soviet Union until January 1987) and coproduction (a form of subcontracting used during most of the Cold War in which the Eastern firm manufactured certain parts of a product). The technology transferred through these more efficient modes was claimed to increase the importer's economic and military power because they permit the transfer of state-of-the-art dual-use technologies. Furthermore, because the imported production technology would be advanced, allowing the importer to leapfrog over older technologies painstakingly developed in the exporter's economy, and because the number of buy-back agreements grew throughout the 1980s, industrial cooperation would also result in exports that could potentially disrupt Western markets.[33] And because dual-use technologies were increasing, the danger of exporting technologies with military significance rose as well. Secretary of Defense Caspar Weinberger claimed in his 1984 Defense Department budget request to Congress that "the most successful overt [Soviet means of acquiring Western technology] include purchase of equipment, purchase of whole manufacturing lines including turnkey factories, and training of students and others in Western nations."[34]

Indeed, in the rush to negotiate joint production agreements in postcommunist economies, Western high-technology firms are finding that their deals will have the "advantages" of these countries' technological "backwardness." For example, in early 1990, Motorola, Inc. negotiated to sell cellular telephone networks in Poland and Bulgaria. Because fixed phone networks are scarce and operate on obsolete telecommunications equipment—in Eastern Europe there is one telephone line for every twenty people, compared with one for every two people in the West—mobile systems can make easy inroads in the East. These countries have the potential to leapfrog over older technologies that are widespread in the West. Thus their own technological development will be speeded up, the gap can be more rapidly narrowed, and they can begin to produce for export more quickly.

In the 1980s, a new form of "efficient" technology transfer was added to the old: foreign firms began to acquire a stake in other nations' high-technology firms and could thus gain access to technology on a long-term basis. Indeed, this was the reason for the U.S. government's opposition to Fujitsu's attempt to acquire Fairchild Semiconductor Corporation, discussed in the previous chapter. Opponents of the acquisition argued that it would have given Japan access to sensitive American defense technology. In reports of Western firms' role in the development of Iraq's defense industries, it was revealed that a London-based firm controlled by Iraq acquired a 50 percent interest in a small German firm that manufactured high-quality steel components used in Iraq's missile program. It was further revealed that the same Iraqi firm spent billions of dollars acquiring many Western companies that made industrial equipment with weapons applications.[35]

The underlying assumption, then, is that these new modes of technology transfer have made available to adversaries or potential adversaries advanced Western industrial technologies. These technologies not only have military applications, and release resources for military use, but can enhance the overall industrial base of military power and increase the competitiveness of an adversary's industry. Furthermore, these new transfer modes are difficult to control through traditional embargoes on goods and technical data because they involve sustained personal contact among engineers and technicians from both importing and exporting states.

In sum, because of the key role that technological superiority plays in the creation and maintenance of military strength, the case that security threats to exporters increase with the exodus of this technology rests on two arguments: that commercial technology transfer is increasingly damaging to the security of the exporting state, and that the transfer of advanced technology is growing easier, erasing the effects of earlier restrictions. Because a technologically advanced manufacturing base is crucial to a state's international power position, and because most important product and process innovations have both military and civilian applications, the adversary's acquisition of a state's advanced technologies through joint ventures and other forms of industrial cooperation with multinational corporations (MNCs), is believed to increase the exporter's vulnerability. Both arguments point to the increasing ineffectiveness of traditional embargoes and the need for expanded state control over the movement of ideas and people as well as tighter regulations on trade, finance, and capital flows.

The two postwar trends—the development of weapons as integrated systems and the expansion of military environments to include new "battlefields"—along with the belief that trade and technology transfer closes the power gap between nations, were central reasons for the establishment of peacetime export controls in the postwar Western world. Ironically, however, these two trends gave increasing importance to dual-use technologies: it is, in fact, the emergence and proliferation of dual-use technologies in the postwar era that gave rise to the paradoxical relationship between technological innovation and military security in the industrialized world, discussed in the previous chapter.

Reducing Technology Exodus

In order to minimize the negative effects of technology exodus in trade relations with adversaries, leading states may attempt to maintain or widen the technology gap by placing export restrictions on those goods and technologies they believe would enhance their adversaries' military power. Trailing states, however, will try to close the gap through imports of those same technologies. If leading states are able to maintain an effective embargo as well as an advantage in innovative capability, they reduce the odds of increasing their own vulnerability through exports.

Two factors have both increased the importance of an embargo on technology exports and made export restrictions more difficult. The first is the dramatic rise in "dual-use" technologies and the resulting blurring of distinctions between trade in military and civilian goods discussed above. Private corporations are the developers of high technologies, and innovation carries with it proprietary rights. Even when firms develop new products and processes under defense contracts, they produce goods with an eye to commercial markets. Strict government technology controls obstruct diffusion of high-technology techniques and products and thus frustrate corporate efforts to successfully compete for markets. The logic of political judgments with regard to export control often contradicts the steady dynamic of market expansion on which the competitiveness of high-technology firms depend. Because private firms are the developers and traders of commercial high technology, business increasingly has a stake in influencing policy. Furthermore, as I have argued above, within the policy process, the ideology of liberalism, which bolsters free-trade policies, competes with the ideology of economic nationalism, which underlies policies of technology export denial.

Thus the emergence of dual-use technologies has given rise to a clash between public and private interests and bureaucratic conflict over export controls. Because export control conflicts with other policy goals on the domestic agenda and will sometimes be sacrificed to other goals, consistent and unitary export control policy cannot easily be pursued. Clashing policies reduce consensus among diplomats over what should or should not be embargoed and can lead to ineffective controls or a "leaky" embargo. U.S. policy, as we saw in the previous historical account, has been almost entirely focused on expanding the powers of the state to either cast the embargo net wider or make enforcement more effective. This has often meant the exercise of coercive policies vis-à-vis allies in order to pressure them to expand their own state control. The characteristics of the technology exodus problem as described here suggest two additional vulnerability reduction options.

First, contrary to the arguments of the "Bucy Report," the strategies of multinational corporations can actually *inhibit* the transfer of those commercial high technologies that could have indirect effects on the importer's military power. Four kinds of strategies have an effect on the level of technology entering the host country's economy. First, if corporate investment is targeted toward production for the domestic market, rather than for exports, then what is produced is generally sheltered from international competition, and therefore state-of-the-art technologies are not imported.[36] Second, even if foreign technology is used for the production of exports, unless those exports are manufactured goods rather than primary products, only standardized and not state-of-the-art technology will be exported. Third, the form of business organization chosen for the joint venture determines whether and what kind of technology is transferred. If, for example, the form chosen is a complex business organization, the kind of technology transferred will usually be at the highest level available, approximating the level developed in the home market. But if the joint venture is simply an assembly plant, it will require relatively low levels of technology. Finally, corporate officials negotiating joint venture agreements or strategic corporate alliances can ensure through contractual provisions that the most advanced technologies are withheld from the host country. Indeed, their primary goal is to sell *products* not technology, and therefore they attempt to limit the sale of technology in the contract. I discuss these means of vulnerability reduction in commercial technology exports more extensively in chapter 3.

Second, multilateral agreement on norms may be the key to compliance with embargo injunctions on the control of militarily significant and other dual-use technologies. Common norms form the core of international regimes; the stronger the consensus over the norms, the stronger the regime. The key indicator of regime strength is the degree to which member states comply with regime injunctions. A strong multilateral embargo depends on a common agreement on the necessity of restricting trade with adversaries and agreements on what should be restricted. Without agreement on these norms, the embargo regime will be weak, and weak, unstable embargo regimes are by definition ineffective.

The key indicator of regime strength is the degree to which member states comply with regime injunctions. In the COCOM case, compliance was difficult for member states because private corporations were the "agents" of international technology transfer. Members may have been unwilling to violate COCOM rules, but they were increasingly unable to control those firms that did. This is what Robert Putnam has called "involuntary defection" from international regimes.[37] Stephen Haggard and Beth Simmons argue that this involuntary defection "is not the result of calculating unified actors, but the outcome of domestic political conflicts which no single actor can control."[38]

Both blatant noncompliance and involuntary defection from international regimes can be muted in two ways: first, a dominant power within the international regime can offer rewards to member states for compliance and punishment for noncompliance. Second, compliance can be achieved through a broad political and social consensus on common norms. Whereas compliance without consensus can be achieved if a dominant power is willing and able to offer rewards and enforce threats of punishment, such forced behaviors do not enhance the regime's legitimacy. Consensus on a common set of norms, however, can bolster the legitimacy of an international regime since compliance based on consensus is voluntary.

If established norms have not been reached by consensus, enforcement problems arise. A multilateral embargo that loses its legitimacy by restricting trade in goods that have little direct military significance, or that restricts its members' sale of goods widely available outside the regime, will trigger hostility and resentment, lead to the decay of established norms, and will be increasingly difficult to enforce. It will thus be less effective than a more legitimate regime whose norms are established consensually.

One way to establish consensus on the basis of common norms would be to specify and test vulnerability claims upon which the joint embargo is based. Joint attempts to define vulnerability can lead to shared definitions of the problem and the collective search for information to resolve uncertainty about the consequences of relaxed or tightened export controls. Technical information can be useful as a basis for shared meanings of the terms of agreement on what items should be embargoed and what items should be sold. For example, as we shall see below, political disputes can arise if key terms in the vulnerability argument are not specified. The term *strategic*, for example, had different meanings for different COCOM members, and differences in meaning led to disagreement over which items should be restricted for "strategic" reasons. Even the terms *technology* and *technology transfer* held different meanings for different actors, and throughout the 1970s, negotiations tried to arrive at common definitions.[39]

Resource Dependence

A second source of trade vulnerability is the importer's dependence on foreign sources of necessary goods. Because the world's resources are distributed unevenly, and because international trade leads to industrial specialization, states come to depend on one another for goods that are vital to their strength. From the perspective of the economic nationalist, importer dependence translates into political and military vulnerability and a threat to national security. The dependent relationship creates the conditions for the exporter to exercise political control over the importer. It provides a channel through which it can influence the importer's foreign and domestic policies. In the event that the importer balks at these influence attempts, the exporter can cut off supplies of needed material, thus weakening the importing state.

The key to importer vulnerability is its *dependence* on the exporter. That dependence is fostered by two interrelated factors: a high level of importer demand and clear exporter control over supply.[40] First, to become dependent, the importer must have an intense need for goods provided from abroad. For example, Western Europe and Japan lack sufficient indigenous energy supplies, and sufficient energy is a crucial requirement for the viability of their industrial economies. Fifty-six percent of the world's proven oil reserves are in the Middle East, mostly in areas where there is significant risk of political disruption; 20 percent of the world's oil reserves are in Iraq and Kuwait. Thirty-eight percent of the world's proven natural gas reserves are in the former Soviet Union and three-fourths of all Soviet natural gas deposits are in the Russian Federation. A further 25 percent are in the Middle East; 16 percent of Middle Eastern natural gas reserves are in Iran. While OECD countries account for 58 percent of world natural gas consumption, they have only 17 percent of reserves. Western Europe and Japan's intense need for imported energy thus creates dependence on external energy sources.[41]

An intense need for goods from abroad is not a security threat per se. One exporter or group of exporting states must have a near-monopoly control over the needed supplies or be able to supply the good under terms that make it difficult or impossible for the importer to switch suppliers. Western Europe and Japan were vulnerable to the cutoff of Arab oil in 1973 because OPEC had gained near-monopoly control over oil supplies. But, as Stephen Krasner has argued, oil is the exception.[42] In other commodity markets, exporting states acting alone can rarely create importer vulnerability since they have not been able to control a market; nor have they been able to reach the agreement needed to act in concert.[43] For example, although the Soviet Union had an intense need for foreign food supplies in 1980, it was not vulnerable in the face of the U.S. grain embargo because the U.S. could not muster support for collective sanctions among grain exporters and the Soviet Union quickly found alternative suppliers.[44]

Yet despite the fact that exporters rarely have a monopoly on supply, conditions can be created under which it is difficult for importers to switch suppliers. Of the Western European-Soviet energy connection, Richard Perle stated that "practical men will find alternatives to angering their suppliers more easily than they will find new suppliers."[45] Four examples of the effects of both monopoly and nonmonopoly supplier pressure illustrate this point.

In 1965 the United States suspended PL 480 food aid to India in order to force the Indian government to increase its own food production. The United States promised that if the Indian government stimulated domestic production, the U.S. would resume aid. This policy was successful because over 56 percent of all of India's food aid came from the United States, and other sources of cheap food were not available. India was also facing the prospect of famine. The Indian government did not want to publicly ask for aid from other countries because the admission of need would cause domestic panic, hoarding of stocks, and pressure on food prices, thus increasing the likelihood of widespread starvation, not to mention widespread riots and demonstrations. Under pressure, the Indian government complied with U.S. demands. Thus, while the United States was not a monopoly supplier, the opportunity costs of finding alternative suppliers were unacceptable to India.[46]

Cuba's dependence on the Soviet Union was also instructive in this regard. Ironically, in the early 1960s the Cuban government proposed to diversify Cuban industry and agriculture to avoid dependence on the Soviet Union for vital industrial imports. The Soviets, however, wanted Cuba to concentrate on sugar production instead of industrial development and exchange sugar for Soviet manufactured goods. In response to Castro's pursuit of economic diversification in 1968, the Soviet Union reduced shipments of subsidized oil to Cuba. Because he could not find alternative supplies of oil at an acceptable price, and was therefore faced with the choice of economic collapse or conformity with Soviet demands, Castro complied.[47] In the the late 1980s the Cuban government made no secret of its hostility to Gorbachev's reforms. By February 1990, the Soviet Union had fallen seriously behind in its grain shipments to Cuba, forcing the Cuban government to cut the bread ration outside Havana and raise prices in the capital city,giving rise to speculation that the Soviet Union was pressuring Cuba to soften its Stalinist line.[48] The Soviet Union had created an enduring trading relationship with Cuba throughout the postwar period that had made it difficult for Cuba to switch suppliers.

Third, 1990 proposals to put CMEA trade on a hard currency basis exposed Central Eastern Europe's dependence on Soviet energy supplies. Throughout the postwar period, the Soviets supplied energy to Eastern European economies at preferential prices; by 1990, the CMEA oil price was based on an average of the previous five years. Between 1976 and 1985 the CMEA oil price did not rise as fast as the world market price. Between 1985 and 1990, however, because world prices dropped sharply, CMEA prices were higher than prices in the West. Eastern Europe, however, was dependent on Soviet energy supplies at any price because its trade with the USSR was based on the "transferable ruble"—simply a unit of account. This meant that Soviet buyers would pay transferable rubles for the merchandise they acquired from Eastern Europe, and the Eastern Europeans would then use these same units to buy energy supplies and other raw materials from the Soviet Union. In this way, the Soviet Union provided an assured market for Eastern European manufactures and an assured supply of energy to Eastern Europe. Because imports and exports were so tightly linked, making a switch in energy suppliers difficult, Eastern European dependence on Soviet energy supplies was high.

Finally, in February 1990 Lithuania held parliamentary elections in the first multiparty vote in the Soviet Union since shortly after the Bolshevik Revolution. The electorate rejected the Communist party and provided a parliament with a firm mandate for independence. When the Lithuanian parliament subsequently voted to secede from the Soviet Union, President Gorbachev not only sent troops to Lithuania in a show of force, but imposed sanctions: all shipments of oil and most shipments of natural gas and other raw materials were curtailed. By June 1990, the Lithuanian parliament had agreed on a moratorium for its declaration of independence in return for an end to the economic embargo.[49] But the Lithuanian independence movement continued and was ultimately successful in the aftermath of the failed Soviet coup of August 1991.

The promises and threats illustrated in these episodes are a form of blackmail exercised by the exporters over the importers within the relationship.[50] Furthermore, these examples illustrate the dependence of weaker countries on dominant states and their vulnerability to supply cutoffs or changes in the terms of supply. But dominant states may also be dependent upon those less powerful—the economic nationalist's fear of importer vulnerability. Certainly the 1973 oil embargo illustrates the vulnerability of "stronger" nations at the hands of a coalition of "weaker" ones. If the perceived costs of doing without the good, switching suppliers, or jeopardizing the relationship are higher than the costs of compliance with the exporter's demands, we can say that the need is intense, the exporter controls supply, and the importer is highly vulnerable, no matter what the overall power relationship might be.

The dependent importer is vulnerable to the exporter's attempts either to influence the importer's intentions or weaken its capabilities. The distinction is important. Attempts to influence intentions are exercised *through* the dependent relationship. Often the dependent relationship alone is enough to influence the importer's intentions without any overt attempts on the part of the exporter.[51] Attempts to weaken capabilities are exercised *by curtailing* the relationship. Exporter attempts to influence intentions are usually short-term, if they are successful. Unsuccessful attempts to influence intentions can result in a stepped-up effort to weaken capabilities through a long-term curtailment of supplies. So, although implementation of an influence attempt may lead to an effort to weaken the importer's capabilities in the face of noncompliance,[52] these objectives can be treated separately since each leads to a different kind of vulnerability.

Exporters attempt to influence importers' intentions within the dependent relationship through the exercise of both positive and negative sanctions.[53] Positive sanctions are actual or promised rewards for compliance with exporter's demands; negative sanctions are actual or threatened punishments for noncompliance. These concepts shade into one another because withholding a reward can also be regarded as a punishment. Each day of Soviet oil deliveries to Cuba was a promise that there will be deliveries the next day if Cuba complied with Soviet policy. Implied in that promise, however, is the threat that the Soviet Union would cut off Cuba's lifeline if the Cuban government deviated from Soviet demands.

Alternatively, the exporter can curtail the relationship in order to weaken the importer's economic and military capabilities. Historically, importers face this kind of vulnerability in wartime or in times of political tension, when exporters and importers find themselves in an adversarial relationship. Recall that during World War I, the United Kingdom cut off all supplies of industrial goods to Germany, and again during World War II, the Allies cut off all petroleum supplies to Germany. In both cases, the German economy suffered but indigenous German industry was able to produce substitutes for the war effort. The Arab cutoff of supplies to Israel since 1948 was a deliberate attempt to weaken the military and economic capabilities of the state of Israel. The multilateral embargo against Iraq that began in August 1990 was intended to weaken Iraq's capabilities and to force Iraq to withdraw from Kuwait, and was further intended to be a substitute for military pressure. For reasons described above, which focused on Soviet capabilities, the United States throughout the postwar period refused to provide certain industrial goods to the Soviet Union.[54]

Economic nationalists have argued that Western Europe faced importer vulnerability when it relied too heavily on Soviet energy supplies. They claimed that Europe was not only vulnerable to influence attempts, but to supply cutoffs as well. Indeed, in 1984 the Soviet Union briefly reduced its supply of oil to Britain in support of a miner's strike there.[55]

It is important to remember that dependent importers are not only vulnerable to influence, bargaining leverage, and outright coercion exercised by exporters, but also to supply disruptions, reductions, and cutoffs triggered by economic changes, technical failures in supply and transport, and increases in demand. Dependence on supplies from abroad can lead to importer vulnerability even if the exporter does not intend to manipulate supplies in ways that weaken the importer's economic and military capabilities, and even when importer and exporter are closely allied.

For example, charges were made in the U.S. media against Japanese firms about their tardiness in delivering important electronics parts for weaponry during the Gulf War. Japanese electronics firms maintained that they could not curtail existing commercial contracts to meet the needs of U.S. forces in the Gulf. Some observers maintained that the Japanese government feared the domestic political opposition that might arise if it pushed its firms to favor military over commercial customers. Indeed, in 1989 the Center for Strategic and International Studies stated that the U.S. military's dependence on foreign suppliers was so acute that the United States could not support the use of force on the scale of the Vietnam War without rebuilding domestic production capability.[56] No matter what the source of vulnerability, however, it is crucial that the importer find ways to limit dependence, in order to bring about a set of stable expectations and policy autonomy.

Reducing Importer Dependence

Importer vulnerability is reduced when one or both of two conditions hold. First, importers are less vulnerable when dependence is mutual. Put another way, vulnerability is reduced when trading partners are interdependent and when that interdependence is roughly symmetrical.[57] This is because the exporter's threats to reduce or curtail supplies are less credible when its own costs of ending the relationship are high. Simply put, when an exporter is also dependent on an importer, it is less willing to cut off its nose if it spites its own face.

The first condition for reducing importer vulnerability, then, is a degree of *exporter dependence*. The classic analysis of this situation is Hirschman's study of Bulgaria's dependence on Nazi Germany as a market for its exports in the 1930s.[58] Germany bought Bulgarian grain at higher than world market prices, raising Bulgaria's dependence on grain exports to Germany. At the same time, Germany also tied Bulgaria to its imports by paying for grain with nonconvertible currency. Thus Bulgaria's incentive to curtail exports to Germany was sharply reduced by its dependence on those exports.

In the present day, the same situation is true for some oil-exporting states. Indonesia, Nigeria, Gabon, Ecuador, Venezuela, and Mexico, for example, are all dependent upon oil exports for the health and vitality of their economies. They cannot easily cut supplies because their economic development plans would be jeopardized, and their governments would, in some cases, be destabilized. For these countries, the costs of pursuing policies that would make importers vulnerable would be immediately very high.[59] Thus, they are dependent upon exports, at least in the short term. As the U.S. government discovered in 1980, American farmers were more dependent upon their grain exports to the Soviet Union than the Soviet Union was dependent upon American grain imports. As a result of the embargo, farm prices fell below acceptable levels, and the Reagan administration was forced to lift the sanctions as a result of domestic pressure.[60]

These are cases in which exporter dependence is higher than importer dependence, and exporters are more vulnerable to the importers' ease of switching suppliers. This asymmetrical exporter dependence substantially reduces exporters' incentives for curtailing supplies, and importers are less vulnerable.

It is less clear, however, who is more vulnerable when dependence is mutual, that is, when the costly effects of curtailing supplies would be reciprocal. These costs can be political and strategic as well as economic. For example, if the United States cut all trade with Western Europe and Japan, it would be much *less* vulnerable than its trading partners if vulnerability is measured in economic terms. The damaged alliance relationships that would result, however, might substantially diminish the security of the United States. In this case, interdependence and vulnerability are mutual, and the incentive to maintain orderly trading relationships is high for all parties. Although there is certainly much leeway for threats to reduce trade and promises to expand it, the possibility that one trading partner or the other would curtail trade is low because the costs of such an action would be unacceptable to both.

In the post-Soviet environment, mutual economic dependence was evident in Eastern European economic relations with the former Soviet Union. Although the Central Eastern European nations depended on its energy supplies, the former Soviet Union also depended on Eastern Europe as a key source of badly needed consumer goods. In 1990, on the eve of the Soviet collapse, the USSR had an assured supply of these goods without the expenditure of precious hard currency. As the nations of Eastern Europe increasingly turned to Western markets, however, the Soviets suffered shortages, indicating a high dependence on imports of Eastern Europe as a source of supply of manufactured goods, constraining the Soviets' ability to use energy exports to Eastern Europe as a source of leverage.

A second way to reduce importer vulnerability is simply to change policies in order to reduce dependence. Keohane and Nye argue that "the key question for determining vulnerability is how effectively altered policies could bring into being sufficient quantities of . . . a comparable raw material, and at what cost. The fact that the United States imports approximately 85 percent of its bauxite supply does not indicate American vulnerability to actions by bauxite exporters, until we know what it would cost (in time as well as money) to obtain substitutes."[61] Of course, as we saw above, switching suppliers is not only a matter of time and money, but an entanglement in domestic politics and foreign policy, making this form of dependence reduction more difficult.

Nonetheless, two kinds of policies can reduce importer dependence and thus vulnerability: the first are policies that reduce dependence *within the trading relationship* by diversifying suppliers at the outset. This reduces the exporter's *incentive* to curtail supplies since supply cutoffs would not yield the desired result.

The second set of policies to reduce vulnerability are those that can go into effect *after* a supply cutoff. These include stockpiles of vital materials, the potential for substituting materials that are plentiful, and the preparation of citizens for sacrifice of imported goods. These policies impinge upon the exporter's *capability* to weaken the importer by curtailing supplies. If the importer communicates these policies to the exporter, its incentive to curtail supplies will also be reduced. Exporters that wish to exert economic pressure on importers to achieve foreign policy goals must believe that importers will be vulnerable to that pressure. These two kinds of countermeasures will change that belief. Both of these policies are easier to pursue when supply of the vital material is spread out among a number of exporters and when they are unable to coordinate their export policies.

In sum, the case for importer vulnerability rests on the extent of the importer's dependence on an unreliable exporter. Dependence can be measured by the intensity of the importer's need and the tightness of the exporter's grip on supply. If the importer has diversified its supply of the needed good and created stockpiles, planned for substitutes, arranged for potential alternative suppliers, and prepared its citizenry for a possible supply cutoff, dependence can therefore be reduced. Importer dependence is also reduced if exporters have the incentive to be reliable. That incentive is created by the exporter's dependence on markets abroad. To the extent that the relationship and its future is important to both importer and exporter, reliability of supply is increased and dependence and vulnerability are reduced.

Debtor Bargaining Leverage and Financial Instability

A third source of vulnerability to be discussed here is that which creditor nations face in international lending. They generally employ two kinds of arguments to support their case for vulnerability. The first maintains that because money is fungible, and because increased industrial efficiency results in savings that can contribute to a state's military capability, any infusion of foreign capital into an adversary's economy can be redirected to the military. Debtors, then, can increase their military capability and exercise the same kind of power and foreign policy leverage that economic nationalists who fear technology exodus predict. As

Judy Shelton argued, "the West to East flow of financial capital constitutes the "transfer of a strategic resource" and must be curtailed.[62]

Second, creditor nations are vulnerable when debtors threaten insolvency. In this case, creditors may face the prospects of default and debt restructuring that offers more favorable terms for the borrower than the lender, which in turn can provide incentives for threats of a moratorium on interest payments. In this way, creditors are vulnerable to both a breakdown of the financial system and the leverage debtors can exercise by manipulating creditors' fears of that breakdown. Furthermore, the "interdependence" between debtor and creditor and between creditor nations constrains the foreign policy options of creditor governments.[63] Negative economic sanctions will be an ineffective foreign policy instrument if trade and capital flows must be maintained in order to ease financial instability.

Vulnerabilities associated with threats of insolvency were probably most pronounced when the Mexican government approached the international banking community in 1982 with empty pockets. In August of that year, Jesus-Silva Herzog, the Mexican minister of finance, announced to the world that Mexico could not continue to service its debt. The danger lurking behind the announcement was the "domino effect"—that other debt-burdened countries would follow in Mexico's footsteps. For example, by 1984 the nine largest banks in the United States had lent more than 250 percent of their capital reserves to risky countries. In the worst case, if they all would have been unable to recover even less than one half of the sums, they would have been left without any capital at all. And even if a much smaller percentage were lost, the impact would have endangered their stability and ultimately the stability of the entire banking system.[64] The vulnerability fear was evoked by statements such as that made by Mexico's director of public credit:

> We didn't crawl to the international financial community as debtors seeking relief through some minor adjustment that could be made backstage. We walked through the front door. We said we had a major problem with a capital P. We didn't say the problem was a particular debt. We said it was the whole international financial structure. We said it was everybody's problem.[65]

When debt is "everybody's problem," debtors have fertile ground to exert leverage over lenders in their attempts to extract bargaining concessions from them. Needless to say, the threat of debtor leverage is heightened when nations enter into financial relationships with their adversaries or competitors. In the late nineteenth century, for example, France instituted an official ban on the purchase of German bonds, as French-German enmity escalated, because France chose not to risk having the force of loaned capital turned upon itself.[66]

Even when states lend money to their allies, they are vulnerable to the negotiating leverage borrowers can exercise. Before the dissolution of the Warsaw Pact, Poland proposed to the Soviet Union that it would put its trade with the Soviet Union on a hard currency basis if the Soviets would simply erase Poland's $8 billion Soviet debt. Polish negotiators believed that Poland's debt gave them bargaining leverage.[67]

Creditor vulnerability to debtor bargaining leverage has its roots in the structure of the international financial system, which provides debtors with a source of power in the relationship. Five related causes contribute to a structure fostering financial instability, that is, a structure that increases the risk of debtor insolvency: rapid debt expansion that outstrips the ability of borrowers to service the debt; rapid growth of unregulated commercial lending; the worldwide overcommitment of an interlocking banking system; the inadequacy of debtor government guarantees; and the practice of debt restructuring that overburdens the debtor's economy and restricts its export possibilities.

The first source of financial instability is a debt expansion that outstrips the borrower's ability to service the debt. When a debtor's imports outpace its exports, it becomes increasingly incapable of repaying the debt in convertible currency. Whether or not a country can service the debt depends on the maturity and interest rate structure of the existing debt, the possibility for increased exports, and the nation's ability to reduce imports. A sudden drop in exports would make it difficult for a country to continue essential imports and at the same time service the debt. Many developing countries that depend on the export of commodities whose prices are volatile face this possibility. This situation would not be politically feasible on a sustained basis, because it would require debtor governments to enforce austerity measures just to pay back the interest, and such measures can lead to dangerous political instability, tempting the borrower to default on its loans rather than allow its government to fall. One factor leading to the debt crisis of the early 1980s was the banks' inadequate assessment of borrowers' long-term export capabilities and abilities to cut imports in order to service loans; terms of repayment were generally fixed by loan contracts and are not related to the borrower's economic performance.

A second force for financial instability in international lending is the trend toward commercial over official (e.g., intergovernmental) financing. This trend leads to increasing instability because commercial lending is largely unregulated and strong creditor government guarantees are usually not forthcoming. Without guarantees, banks must face the full brunt of a default alone, and without regulation and supervision, loans can finance projects that are mismanaged and do not sustain growth to the extent needed to service the debt.

This recent trend in unregulated and unguaranteed lending is a direct result of the growth of the Eurocurrency market. Until the early 1970s, government and commercial financing were sought by borrowers for different purposes, and two patterns of external financing predominated in international markets. The first was long-term financing by multilateral institutions and export credit agencies. For borrowers, credits from these sources had the disadvantage of being tied to exports from the country that extended them; loans and credits had to be used to finance imports from the creditor country. The advantage was that they were guaranteed and usually carried lower interest rates and longer repayment periods than short-term commercial loans. Because private banks were reluctant to make long-term loans at fixed rates of interest, and because the risk was higher that the interest rate would change or that the borrower would default, government credit agencies usually took the risk of providing long-term credits to foreign countries.

The second mode of finance was short-term lending by commercial banks. Commercial loans were usually more readily available, for larger amounts, and carried fewer restrictions on their use than the government-financed long-term loans.[68] The less risky commercial loans were provided by banks with credit guarantees and interest rate support from their governments.

The growth of the Eurodollar market dramatically changed this pattern by allowing commercial banks to become involved in a major expansion of long-term lending by transforming short-term deposits into long-term loans. To meet demands for longer-term loans, commercial banks began to roll over short-term deposits. That is, they offered the borrower a series of short-term advances automatically renewable at intervals, typically every six months. The interest rate on the loan was floated at each interval. This variable interest rate is a fixed spread or markup over a base rate, usually the London Interbank Offered Rate (LIBOR), the rate at which banks in London are prepared to lend to preferred banks. The spread reflects the lender's appraisal of the default risk involved, the cost of servicing the loan, and the commitment period of the loan.[69]

Because these commercial loans were largely unregulated and unguaranteed, there was little creditor-government involvement to determine the size and conditions of lending and to prevent the misdirection of funds. Furthermore, there was little incentive on the part of debtor or creditor to scrutinize the viability of projects constructed with borrowed funds.

Two examples from Mexico and Argentina illustrate this problem. Lavish commercial loans to Mexico in the 1970s were based on prospects of vastly expanded oil revenues, which would then be used as a base to build a strong industrial economy with new export revenues from the sale of manufactured goods. Oil revenues, however, could not cover both rising import costs and interest payments on the debt. The export sector could not grow, because the peso was overvalued, and by 1982 the Mexican government had run out of money to repay the debt.[70] Similarly, Argentina invested its borrowed funds in weapons and on mismanaged state-run projects, like the nuclear power industry—a seemingly unnecessary investment in a country self-sufficient in hydrocarbons.[71]

Third, compounding the dangers of unregulated commercial lending is the interlocking nature of the global financial system. As a consequence of the sheer volume of the unregulated global debt, commercial financial institutions face increasing risk and thus join together to protect themselves against default, in what is called "cross-default agreements." These agreements are intended to deter the legal declaration of default and operate in the following way: a country is de facto in default when it fails to make either interest or principal payments on time. The creditor, however, must *formally* declare this failure for the debtor to be *legally* in default. Thus, a country may be de facto in default without suffering legal consequences until any one of its creditors declares the default. If a bank declares a country in default, it immediately seeks a court order to attach that country's assets. Those assets, however, are generally inadequate to cover the claims of all of that country's creditors. Therefore, there is a high incentive to be the *first* to declare default when a borrower refuses to meet its obligations. Large banks, which have the most to lose in this situation, have made efforts to prevent smaller banks from declaring a country in default prematurely. In some cases they have even bought out the portfolios of smaller banks in an effort to maintain stability, but in general, they have insisted on cross-default agreements in their syndicated loans. These agreements specify that if one bank declares a country in default and seeks a court order to attach that country's assets, other banks that are parties to the agreement must do the same. They stipulate that the entire loan obligation, both principal and interest, become payable immediately upon declaration of default.[72] In that event, the courts would be flooded with requests to attach a delinquent debtor's assets, and no creditor would be able to cover its losses. Because cross-default agreements raise the cost to creditors of declaring a debtor in default, every creditor will think twice before doing so.

Although these cross-default agreements are intended to provide only a safety net to prevent premature default declarations, they point to the deeper instability of the system as a whole. A default on one loan will not be isolated but will send a ripple effect throughout the entire banking system. Even when cross-default agreements are not in effect, banks will be reluctant to declare default in many cases,often because debtor government guarantees are inadequate, the fourth cause of financial instability.

Generally, a certain percentage of these commercial loans are guaranteed by creditor governments and declaration of default would force them to live up to their commitments. Then banks would only have to write off the nonguaranteed portion of these loans. But when banks are overexposed, any writeoffs would mean that assets would be significantly reduced and profits curtailed. Banks would have to sustain significant losses if they were to accept the government's offer to make good on its guarantee, and thus they are often reluctant to do so.

For members of the banking community, then, the overriding consideration is the desire to prevent nations that face an external debt crisis from dropping out of the international financial system altogether. Because they wish to protect their original investments, they are willing to restructure loans. The conditions under which restructuring takes place provide the fifth force for financial instability. Restructuring means that the repayment of the principal will be spread out over a longer period, usually after a grace period in which no payments are made. Creditors insist that interest payments continue to be made, however, usually at a higher rate.

Loan restructuring or rescheduling is also a route to business expansion in the face of ruthless competition among lenders. The pressure on commercial banks to restructure the debt on terms favorable to borrowers is high, both because of an overriding concern with the system's stability and because of internal business incentives. As we will see, these factors work to the negotiating advantage of the debtors.

Finally, this practice of rescheduling can cause further problems that increase the vulnerability of borrower and lender alike. Loans are generally denominated in convertible currencies, such as francs, marks, sterling, dollars, or yen. Both principal and interest must be repaid in these same currencies. In order to repay their debts in hard currencies, borrowers must achieve a trade surplus with hard-currency countries. But rescheduling of interest payments simply adds to the sums that they must pay and diverts resources away from economic growth. It is indicative of the uncertainty surrounding the international financial system that neither governments nor banks have attempted to estimate when it would be reasonable to expect debtors to achieve the export surpluses necessary to reduce their borrowing. Even in the absence of a debt whose repayment draws away scarce resources, healthy trade balances are difficult to achieve for many debtors. Even if debtors could drastically reduce their imports and vastly increase their manufacturing exports, protectionist pressures in the capital-exporting countries may let borrowers' exports go begging.

Given the high uncertainty and potential instability resulting from these five conditions, lenders generally face two interrelated problems when they extend large loans to risky borrowers: the first is the vulnerability to pressure that borrowers can bring to extract lower interest rates, longer repayment periods, or other concessions from lenders. Borrowers can bring this pressure when lenders are overexposed and would be faced with financial insolvency if debtors fail to repay the loans. If debtors do default, however, lenders are vulnerable to the very instability that defaults can bring to the international financial system. Borrowers who default are vulnerable as well, because their foreign assets will be frozen and their creditworthiness will therefore be jeopardized.

Both kinds of vulnerability place borrowers and lenders in a situation analogous to the dilemma of nuclear deterrence. Three aspects of the two situations are strikingly similar. First, vulnerability is mutual, creating a common interest in systemic stability. Second, cooperation is not assured, because one party can play "chicken," exploiting the other's fears of total system breakdown. And third, threats must be credible, but credible threats increase vulnerability.

With nuclear deterrence, if neither side has a first-strike capability and both sides have a second-strike capability, neither side can inflict damage on the other without incurring unacceptable costs. This situation actually creates an unprecedented common interest among adversaries. As Robert Jervis has written, "their fates are linked together—or the fate of each is in the other's hands—in a way that was never true in the past."[73] The fates of borrowers and lenders may be similarly linked together if the lender is dependent on repayment and the borrowers are equally dependent on future loans and free access to their own assets abroad. A default may then be equally damaging to both. Under these conditions, interdependence is mutual. Vulnerability is also mutual when the international financial system is unstable and uncertainty is high.

For example, in 1976 North Korea failed to meet interest and principal payments on a $1.6 billion hard-currency debt accumulated in the early 1970s. Principal creditors (Japan, BRD, U.K., and France) did not want to declare North Korea in default, because that country's assets in the West were so meager. But North Korea's access to international credit was dramatically affected, and its credit rating dropped to ninety-ninth among one hundred countries listed in the *International Investor* and future loans were simply not forthcoming. In this case, then, vulnerability was mutual.[74]

Unfortunately, however, this mutual vulnerability in both the nuclear and financial arenas does not necessarily lead to cooperation and stability. Under conditions of mutual nuclear second-strike capability, "the shared common interest of avoiding all-out war can be competitively exploited, because achieving this goal requires that only one side, not both, makes concessions. Indeed, the very strength of the shared incentives not to let a conflict lead to war permits the side with greater resolve—or foolhardiness—to shift to the adversary the burden of avoiding mutual destruction."[75] In the same way, lenders may be vulnerable to borrowers' exploitation of mutual dependence. If default is the only alternative to loan restructuring, debtors may be able to extract concessions from lenders in negotiations on more favorable terms that lenders would prefer, since lenders wish to avoid default. In essence, they may decide to play the game of "chicken," as Vinod Aggarwal has persuasively argued, using as leverage the other side's need to avoid instability in the international financial system.[76] Because default is "unthinkable," lenders might be willing to make concessions on other, less important issues that would appear less costly.

For example, in September 1989 Brazil suspended interest payments on all of its $65 billion medium- and long-term commercial debt. In March 1990 payments had not resumed, and Brazil's economics minister, Zella Cardoso do Mello stated that Brazil would resume interest payments on its debt *only* after renegotiation. Clearly the banks were reluctant to declare Brazil in default and would be obliged to renegotiate the debt on terms favorable to Brazil.

In order for borrowers to extract concessions, however, the threats must be credible; that is, the borrower must convince the lender that it would carry through with the threat.[77] The ability to make credible threats, however, is a double-edged sword. If threats are indeed credible, the odds are high that the vulnerable lender will retreat. At the same time, if the threat is to be credible, the borrower is locked into its decision to carry through if the lender does not make concessions. This increases the instability of the situation, and threatens the breakdown of the financial system, again increasing the vulnerability of the lender. If the threat is credible and the lender does indeed make concessions, the borrower experiences less vulnerability than the lender. If, however, the lender does not respond to the threat, the borrower will be just as vulnerable as the lender to systemic instability.[78]

The sheer volume of debt, the mutual vulnerabilities it entails, and the complex linkages among bankers, and bankers and lenders, means that creditors' foreign policy choices may be constrained. Benjamin Cohen makes the clearest statement of this kind of vulnerability.

The government may find it more difficult to support or reward its friends or to thwart or punish its enemies. Generous debt assistance to countries with poor records on human rights, for instance, or to regimes that support international terrorism may easily undermine efforts by Washington to exercise influence through the withholding of public moneys; states deemed vital to U.S. security interests may be seriously destabilized if they are suddenly "red-lined" by the financial community.[79]

Reducing Financial Instability and Debtor Leverage

To reduce financial vulnerability in the short term, lenders have a number of means at their disposal. First, they can pressure debtors to seek new money in the form of equity rather than loans.[80] With market reforms rapidly advancing in Eastern Europe, and postcommunist governments seeking foreign investment, this option appears increasingly attractive; indeed, foreign investment in Eastern Europe is targeted for the export sector. This strategy could simultaneously reduce the debt and increase output and hard-currency exports.

Second, banks can convert existing loans into equity through debt-equity swaps. In this arrangement, a debtor buys existing debt using local currency that must then be invested in the debtor country. These debt-equity swaps are not unproblematic. In the first place, the repurchase will mean an increase in the money supply of the debtor nation and can thus trigger inflation. To offset inflationary pressures, debtor governments may sell a bond in the domestic financial market. An external debt is thus traded for an internal debt; interest rates are usually higher in the domestic market, and thus overall debt payments tend to rise.[81]

Third, creditors can appeal to the IMF and the World Bank to guarantee loans and to monitor the economic performance of debtors. Indeed, between 1982 and 1988, the role of the IMF in Latin American debtor countries became increasingly visible. What this meant, of course, was that when the IMF provided bridge loans and arranged refinancing agreements, it also wrote stabilization programs and devised deflationary economic policies to reduce balance-of-payments crises. These policies, however, actually exacerbated debtor countries' problems, squeezing their economies so that they could service existing debt. In order to reduce budget deficits, for example, many Latin American countries were forced to curtail social programs, which in turn affected consumption standards as well as programs that supported productive capacity, such as energy, transportation, and communication,[82] thereby wiping out earlier development gains, and triggering political unrest.[83] In fact, noncompliance with IMF programs grew in the second half of the 1980s because the programs imposed austerity measures that would enable debtors to make interest payments but at politically unacceptable costs.

Fourth, in order to directly counter the threat of debtor bargaining leverage in negotiations, creditors can negotiate cooperative agreements among themselves in order to present debtors with a united front.[84] This means that they would not only have to agree among themselves not to succumb to the temptation of declaring a debtor in default—an agreement that can play into the hands of debtor-country negotiators who can press for bargaining advantage in restructuring negotiations—but they must also agree to deny future loans in unison, if debtors do not negotiate in good faith. Indeed, they have in general been able to coordinate their bargaining efforts in debt rescheduling by threatening to suspend short-term credit and delaying a debtor's return to long-term credit markets. During the 1980s the cooperative strategy appeared to work; interest on old debt was repaid and the banks cut back on new lending in concert. This solution to the problem of debtor leverage, however, only exacerbates the larger problem of financial instability and can lead to heightened debtor desperation in the face of popular pressure to repudiate the debt.

Finally, then, reducing debtor leverage may actually be a function of reducing the debt as a whole. This was the sense of the Brady Plan in which negotiations between private banks and qualifying debtor governments would be undertaken to actually write down the debt.[85] Governments, too, can decide to write down official debt. In many cases, debt reduction is not only needed to stimulate exports but may be a necessary condition for economic growth that in turn increases the creditworthiness of debtor countries. Debt reduction, combined with sound economic policy to increase investment, helps reduce the internal problems causing financial instability that then lead to debtor leverage. Debt reduction can have a direct impact on the stimulation of private investment: investors will turn away from investment opportunities in countries where banks hold the first lien on their export earnings.

To summarize, the case for debtor leverage as a source of vulnerability in international trade rests on both the instability and uncertainty of the international financial system and on the potential for debtors to exploit the uncertainty for their own bargaining advantage. Large debts, the rise in commercial lending and the global overexposure of an interlocking banking system all exacerbate the vulnerability of lenders. To the extent that vulnerability is mutual and debtors are willing to play "chicken" and make credible threats, the vulnerability of lenders to bargaining pressure is increased even further. To the extent that the debt burden is so great that debtors are faced with negative growth rates and net capital outflows, the debt must be reduced so that among other benefits, the ability of debtors to exercise leverage over creditors will decrease.

The Loss of Market Control

Throughout the Cold War, United States officials worried about a loss of market control on the part of the state over high-technology diffusion as private actors rather than governments appeared to increasingly determine the destination of high-technology exports. They worried that the Soviet adversary would control energy markets upon which their allies depended. And they worried that credit markets would really be controlled by borrowers who would use their control to extract concessions and constrain other foreign policy goals. In short, they worried that Western *states* would lose market control to private actors or that powerful competitor states would gain market control.

In the aftermath of the Cold War, Western nations faced a new set of vulnerabilities in their investment, trade, and finance relations with postcommunist states. Cold War vulnerability fears focused on a strong adversary state; post-Cold War vulnerability fears see weak postcommunist states as a source of concern. It is the former adversary's loss of control over markets that is the chief source of vulnerability across all three issue areas.

With regard to investment and trade, the post-Soviet economic environment of the region is characterized by the demise of state control over the economy and a rise of anarchic economic behavior; production had all but halted as large conglomerates became trading companies, extracting profits from barter. Supplies of goods and services could not be assured; fears of technology exodus *from* the former Soviet Union to potentially dangerous Third World countries replaced fears of technology exodus *to* the Soviet Union from the West, as weak states began to lose control over the resources to support their science and technology institutes. Fears of a disruption in energy supplies because of the loss of state control over energy trade replaced fears of the adversary's control over energy markets.

With regard to finance as well, fears of too little control replaced fears of too much control. During the Cold War, central authorities could pursue a centralized campaign of debtor leverage and use their debtor status to constrain U.S. foreign policy. In the post-Cold War era there has been little central state control over a plan to reduce balance-of-payments deficits; increasing political fragmentation means there is little authority to actually repay debts. The loss of control could lead to even greater debt threats from Eastern Europe than were experienced in the early 1980s.

In order to reduce these new vulnerabilities in old places, Western states can take measures to aid in the efforts on the part of new states to regain market control on the basis of market rational behavior. They should especially be aided in their effort to establish stable property rights; without stable property rights, established and protected by the state, barter cannot be replaced by market exchange and large conglomerates cannot be replaced by competitive enterprise. Thus, ironically, Western assistance may be required to reduce new vulnerabilities caused by old adversaries.

We can now briefly summarize the main arguments in the vulnerability thesis, as expressed in concern over technology exodus, importer dependence, debtor leverage, and loss of market control in East-West trade. These arguments can be stated in the following propositions:

SOURCES OF ECONOMIC VULNERABILITY
IN INTERNATIONAL RELATIONS

- As commercial high technology both increases industrial strength and has increasing military applications, its export to adversaries or trade competitors will increase the industrial productivity of the importer's economy, closing the technology gap between exporter and importer and releasing resources to the importer's military, thereby contributing to the exporter's vulnerability.
- The rise of multinational corporate investment and joint-venture activity has increased the ease of these high-technology exports, reducing the exporting state's control over those exports, thereby contributing to the exporter's vulnerability.
- The importer's trade vulnerability is a function of its dependence on strategic commodities from abroad. Dependence varies with the intensity of the importer's demand for the commodity and the dominance of the exporter's control over supply. Dependent importers are vulnerable to the exporter's attempts to influence its intentions or weaken its capabilities.

- A creditor state's vulnerability varies with the debtor's ability to destabilize the financial system and exercise leverage in debt negotiations. Creditor states are also vulnerable when financial instability constrains their broader foreign policy goals.
- Exporters, importers, and lenders are vulnerable to a loss of market control on the part of their trading partners. Loss of market control is a function of weakening states and results in high uncertainty in the direction of technology transfer, disruption in supplies of resources, and the absence of authority over debt repayments.

SOURCES OF VULNERABILITY REDUCTION:
THE CONSOLIDATION OF MARKET CONTROL

- Vulnerability reduction is a function of the consolidation of market control by those whose behavior and goals coincide with economic and military interests of Western states.
- Western control over markets is a function of the potentially vulnerable state's ability to control a market through trade and finance restriction policies.
- Trade and finance restriction policies will be effective under two conditions: 1) that all private actors are constrained by the policy; and 2) that other exporters, importers, and creditors do not have the ability to undermine the potentially vulnerable state's trade restriction policies. In other words, state control over markets is a function of market dominance of a potentially vulnerable state.
- In the absence of a dominant power, vulnerability can be reduced through the multilateral coordination of policy restrictions on the part of potentially vulnerable states and private actors.
- Multilateral policy coordination to consolidate the control over markets is a function of agreement on the scope and extent of vulnerability among state actors. Agreement on vulnerability helps resolve political disputes and strengthens the norm of trade restriction; strong norms reduce the costs of enforcement of the agreement and help prevent private actors from acting outside the agreement.
- Vulnerabilities associated with the transfer of commercial high technology through direct investment and industrial cooperation agreements can be reduced through the strategies of private corporations whose goals of withholding state-of-the-art technology coincide with the vulnerability reduction goals of the state. These strategies are:

investments in enterprises targeted for domestic production rather than export; investments in extractive rather than manufacturing industries; investments in assembly plants rather than complex business organizations; and contractual provisions to withhold technology from the importer.

- Importer vulnerabilities are reduced through mutual dependence and by switching suppliers, stockpiling materials, substitution, and sacrifice.
- The reduction of financial vulnerability in particular is not only a function of multilateral agreements among states and private actors, but it is potentially a function of sacrifice on the part of vulnerable actors: vulnerability can be reduced through debt forgiveness and other strategies to reduce the total debt.
- With regard to economic relations with the former Soviet Union and Eastern Europe, Western vulnerability reduction is a function of the ability of postcommunist states to establish stable property rights on the basis of market-rational behavior. Western states can promote this "market control" on the part of new states in the region with aid and assistance programs.

Did the vulnerabilities of technology exodus, importer dependence, and financial instability lurk in OECD trade with Eastern Europe and the Soviet Union during the 1970s and 1980s? What kind of vulnerabilities are likely to arise as economic relations between East and West are reordered in the 1990s? In the chapters that follow, I will assess the vulnerability claim in East-West trade and speculate on the future prospects for Western vulnerability in the 1990s.

3

Technology Exodus:
The Impact of Imported Innovation
on the Soviet Economy

By all important indicators of economic performance, the Soviet Union was a "trailing power" throughout the postwar period. Estimates of just how far behind the United States the Soviets were, however, vary widely.[1] In 1976 Soviet GNP was roughly 50 percent of United States GNP.[2] At the same time, the CIA estimated that the Soviet economy would hit a wall in the late 1970s; indeed, between 1976 and 1983, the rate of Soviet economic growth declined and lagged behind every Western country except Britain.[3] Some scholars even argued that Soviet growth actually ceased as early as 1982;[4] by 1990 some estimates had put Soviet growth at less that 30 percent of U.S. GNP.[5]

The vulnerability thesis predicted that the Soviet Union as a trailing power would attempt to acquire leading nations' technology in order to fundamentally change production methods throughout the economy. In general, technology importers hope to use foreign machinery, equipment, and production and management techniques to enhance efficiency and add value to the world economy, and thus gain a higher national standard of living in the future without going deeper into debt. Nations that enhance efficiency in this way can build a strong manufacturing base that gives them increasing long-term advantage over others that are less efficient. Indeed, as we will see, Soviet officials increasingly focused on the import of Western technology as a source of potential strength while the Soviet economic growth rate declined. Patterns of technology acquisition, including orders for machinery, purchases of Western licenses, and expanding industrial cooperation agreements are good indicators of how serious the Soviets were about strengthening their economy with Western know-how.

The Soviet effort to acquire Western technology was not lost on the Reagan administration. Assistant Secretary of Defense Richard Perle argued that, although the Soviet leaders historically engaged in a "systematic program to acquire Western know-how and equipment," they organized an elaborate collection effort in the mid-1970s to dramatically increase both their legal and illegal imports of Western high technology. He claimed that Soviet acquisition of Western technology had resulted in a "qualitative improvement of Soviet strategic and conventional forces based on Western technology in the midst of a massive quantitative buildup."[6] Assistant Secretary for Trade Administration Lawrence Brady stated in an address before the National Association of Manufacturers in January 1982 that

> the USSR has utilized a variety of means to harness the vast energy of the free enterprise system to the engine of the Soviet military machine. The KGB operates a vast covert apparatus in the West, whose function it is to procure, legally or illegally, the most advanced technology available. . . . Over the past ten years, the free world has concentrated its attention on the Soviet military threat, while remaining largely oblivious to the Soviet economic threat.[7]

But evidence of Soviet attempts to acquire Western technology did not provide an adequate test of the vulnerability thesis. For technology exodus to lead to Western vulnerability, Western technology must actually contribute to the adversary's capabilities, narrowing the technology gap between it and the West, and releasing valuable resources to its military. Did Western technology sold to the USSR in the 1970s contribute to Soviet economic power and thereby indirectly bolster Soviet military might? Would the economic situation in the Soviet Union have been worse without Western technology? Will Western direct investment in Russian industrial capacity provide Russia with a new basis upon which to build real economic strength?

The Reagan administration's answer to the first two of these questions was yes. Defense Secretary Caspar Weinberger, in his 1982 annual budget report to Congress, stated that "without access to advanced technology from the West, the Soviet leadership would be forced to choose between its military industrial priorities and the preservation of its tightly controlled political system. By allowing access to a wide range of advanced technologies, we enable the Soviet leadership to evade that dilemma."[8] Lawrence Brady, in a speech before the National Defense Executive Reserve, said, "Because of the [Western-supplied] 'escape valve' the Soviets were able to save billions and billions of dollars in research and development, and to postpone reforms to decentralize political and economic power. In short, thanks in part to foreign trade, the USSR became a much more formidable adversary and a much more repressive society."[9] And Richard Perle argued that

> time and time again, over the last several decades, through legal pur-
> chases, use of open scientific sources, deceptive business practices,
> and espionage, the Soviet Union has amassed American and other
> Western technology at a direct cost to the West of many billions of
> dollars and indirect cost that is virtually incalculable. All available
> evidence points to a Soviet decision, taken in the late 1950s and early
> 1960s to invest heavily in the expansion of Russian military power
> and the Russian military industrial base. . . . At the same time it
> was decided that trade with the West could be helpful to both the
> civilian and military sectors. Despite profound fears of liberalization,
> Soviet policy emphasized the ties between their system and Western
> capitalism. . . . These commercial links with the West were ex-
> ploited by the Soviets principally to develop the industrial base
> needed for the development of a modern military establishment.[10]

These vulnerability beliefs, however, were never supported by evidence. They became, as I have argued in chapter 1, symbolic currency in policy debates with NATO allies over how much trade should be limited and what the instruments of limitation should be. And they contributed to policy confusion between liberals and economic nationalists over the real relationship between commercial trade and security.

This chapter will critically examine the available evidence on Soviet *intentions* with regard to the import of Western technology and Soviet industrial *capabilities* that may have resulted from Western technology imports until 1990. I begin with a discussion of Soviet patterns of industrial technology acquisition from the West and move on to a brief review of the literature on the contribution of Western technology acquired in the 1970s to Soviet industrial productivity and economic growth in the 1980s. Included in that examination is a discussion of the impact of Western technology on the size of the industrial technology gap between East and West and an assessment of the evidence on the "resource-releasing effects" of imported technology that could allow shifts in domestic investment allocation to enhance military power. Finally, through an examination of joint venture agreements between Western firms and Soviet enterprises in effect in 1990, and through an analysis of a series of interviews with Western corporate officials who sold technology to the USSR and are negotiating sales with Russia, I assess the future impact of Western investment in Russia—the establishment of joint ventures and other forms of industrial cooperation in particular—on the potential for Russian economic strength.

The evidence suggests that the positive effects of technology transfer feared by economic nationalists could only have been possible under certain specific conditions that did not obtain in the Soviet economy and are not likely to emerge in the region in the near future. These positive effects are also inhibited by Western corporate strategy designed to withhold key technologies from Soviet and post-Soviet customers. In fact, the future speed of Russian industrial development may be obstructed by Western control of production technology even if the institution of a market economy creates the conditions under which technology can be rapidly absorbed and diffused. Western technology exodus to the Soviet Union, rather than leading to Western vulnerability, actually created dependence on the West that may even inhibit the region's development of a competitive niche in the world economy.

Soviet Intentions: Import Policy and Patterns of Technology Acquisition

Western technology historically played an important role in both the czarist and the Soviet economies.[11] Peter I (1682–1725) imitated Western methods of organization and production when he built a modern military and bureaucratic apparatus for the czarist state. By exporting raw materials, the state was able to import European manufactured goods, weaponry, and technical expertise in order to modernize the economy. After 1815, growth stagnated, and the economy was not revived until the appointment of Count Sergei Witte as minister of finance in 1892. Witte used tariffs to protect infant industries in Russia, but he relied on European companies to develop Russian mining, metallurgy, and machine-building industries; French and Danish firms built the Trans-Siberian Railway. By World War I, 21 percent of textile production, 41 percent of the chemical industry, 63 percent of mining, metallurgy, and machinery production, and 96 percent of shipbuilding were foreign-owned.[12]

The Bolshevik revolution, however, cut these established links between the new Soviet economy and the West. Indeed, the Soviets explicitly avoided policies that would make the Soviet Union dependent on Western capital and technology. The first step in severing relations was a repudiation of all international debts incurred by the czars, an act that severely curtailed the new Soviet regime's access to foreign capital.[13] Second, the new regime placed conditions on foreign firms' access to the Soviet economy; imports were strictly regulated according to planned industrial modernization programs and in accord with policies intended to limit dependence on foreign capital and technology. Nonetheless, within the framework of these restrictions, Lenin brought in a few Western firms to produce certain products that contributed to the development of the new postrevolutionary economy, and under Stalin, Soviet planners bought up Western machinery in large quantities, especially during the first five-year plan. These acquisitions, however, were always sporadic, and they were not reflected in official import policy. Throughout the 1930s Soviet imports from Europe and the United States were "one-shot deals" involving the purchase of entire factories and prototypes of finished products without long-term training, service, or the transfer of improvements.[14]

But in the early Cold War period even these kinds of acquisitions were rare, as the Soviets began to withdraw more completely from the international economic system. Under the policy of economic autarky, Soviet authorities viewed exports simply as the means to obtain the foreign exchange needed to finance the import of goods that could not be produced domestically.[15] The import plans of the late 1940s were an extension of the domestic investment plan; import substitution was the top priority. Concepts of international specialization and comparative advantage were not only ignored but repudiated outright.

As the Cold War intensified, it was Stalin's view that trade with the West should be halted altogether. Imports should be stopped; therefore foreign exchange was not needed and exports were not required. In 1949 Stalin announced the creation of the Council of Mutual Economic Assistance (CMEA) whose purpose was to "exchange economic experience, extend technical aid and render mutual assistance with respect to raw materials, food stuffs, machines, and equipment" among socialist countries.[16] In other words, the purpose was to secure the Soviet bloc from outside influence by encouraging economic cooperation among the Soviet Union and its Eastern European satellites and by cutting old trading patterns with the West. In 1948 trade between Eastern and Western Europe had increased by 50 percent from the previous year; by 1950, the year after the founding of the CMEA and the year the Korean War began, trade had dropped significantly. Although the CMEA was largely a "paper organization" and proved to be absolutely ineffective, Stalin's message to the bloc was clear: as little truck with the West as possible.

Soviet—and, by extension, Eastern European—postwar economic policy under Stalin was based on what planners called a strategy of "extensive" growth. This strategy was grounded in the conviction that an increase in the national product could be achieved and even accelerated through the commitment of increasing resources, i.e., labor and capital, to key sectors of the economy. The sectors singled out were iron, steel, capital equipment, and infrastructure industries like energy, transportation, and construction.

But both the extensive growth strategy and import substitution policy proved a disaster. By 1953 Stalin had died and Khrushchev came to power only to confront severe resource and labor shortages. By the early 1960s a rising capital-output ratio accompanied by tremendous waste was exposed by declining rates of national product increase. Excess demand put pressure on the import substitution policy; imports were increasingly required to fill domestic shortfalls in both capital and consumer goods. By the late 1960s it was clear that the USSR was beginning to engage in a policy reversal that would allow technology trade with the West. A three-step process, it involved expanding imports, switching to a strategy of "intensive economic development," and legitimizing "industrial cooperation," the precursor to joint ventures with Western firms and even Western direct investment in the Soviet economy.

The first step was Soviet awareness that imports from the Western capitalist nations would have to increase. Khrushchev recognized early on that the attempt at autarky had resulted in chronically unsatiated demand for productive inputs and a serious drain on domestic resources. Excess demand caused domestic shortfalls in material inputs, and imports were increasingly required to fill factory orders. Often the needed imports were only available in the West. In the late 1960s these imports were permitted, despite the still-avowed policy of autarky.

Second, the 1966–1970 plan period introduced a new strategy of "intensive" development, a strategy that would eventually come to rely heavily and consistently on foreign technology. The plan's first goal was to step up economic growth by producing more efficiently through domestic technological innovation. Although Soviet economists had always been aware of the role of technology as a growth stimulant, for the first time since their formation of the intensive growth strategy, they emphasized the role of technology as a critical productive factor; technological innovation could lower the amount of resource consumption necessary to produce desired increases in output. Advanced technology could raise the average capital-to-labor ratio, a crucial ingredient of economic growth when the labor supply is inadequate.[17]

Domestic innovative capability, however, was not adequate to produce the changes envisioned in the intensive growth strategy. Under Khrushchev, and in pursuit of "intensive" growth, an ideological shift toward increased trade with the West to acquire advanced technology began to appear. Beginning in the 1960s, Soviet economists started talking about the "advantages of the international division of labor." They even characterized market prices as "socially necessary prices," and advocated joint Soviet production with Western firms. In his report of the eighth Five-Year Plan directives, then-Prime Minister Alexei Kosygin outlined the rationale for increased technology imports from the West:

> Until recently we have underestimated the importance of trade in patents and licenses. Yet this trade is playing an ever more noticeable role in the world at large. . . . Our scientists and technicians can create . . . excellent new machinery and equipment. Therefore we can and must occupy a worthy place in the world market for licenses. And in turn it is more profitable for us, too, to buy a license than to concern ourselves with the solution of this or that problem. The purchase of patent rights from abroad will allow us in the new Five-Year Plan to save hundreds of millions of rubles in scientific-technical work.[18]

This shift was accompanied by important institutional changes and an increasing proportion of Soviet GNP devoted to trade with the West that emphasized the *systematic* import of technology.[19] As part of Khrushchev's "chemicalization" drive, the Soviet Union saw a surge in imports of entire chemical plants from the West, and in 1962 a new foreign trade organization, Litzenzintorg, was created to facilitate the purchase of licenses abroad. In 1965 Moscow became a member of the Paris Convention on the Protection of Industrial Property, and in 1966 the Soviet Union concluded an agreement with Italy's Fiat for the construction of an automobile plant, an agreement that required close and continual contact with the Western firm in the transfer of automotive technology.

In the 1970s a major effort was launched to import Western technology on a continuing basis. For the first time, the ninth Five-Year Plan stated that "consideration is being given to mutually beneficial cooperation with firms and banks in working out a number of very important economic questions associated with the use of the Soviet Union's natural resources, construction of industrial enterprises, and exploration for new technical solutions."[20] In this plan, the Kama River Truck Plant became the focus of Western machinery imports, but by 1975 that focus had widened from chemical and automotive plants to natural gas, oil, timber, metal extraction, processing, and distribution technology, as well as computer-assisted systems design.[21] The plan had projected a 35 percent growth in trade with the West—in fact, however, trade actually grew 186 percent![22]

The tenth Five-Year Plan (1976–1980) was even bolder in its emphasis on the expanded role of foreign technology in the Soviet economy. It stated that the rate of technological change was one of the key problems in Soviet economic development, and it provided for "curtailing the growth of new construction starts in favor of investing in advanced machinery and equipment."[23] A far cry from the early policy of autarky, it called for "measures aimed at the broader participation of the Soviet Union in the international division of labor and at enhancing the role of foreign economic ties in the accomplishment of national economic tasks and the acceleration of scientific and technical progress."[24] As a result, 10–12 percent of all Soviet investment during the latter half of the 1970s in machinery and equipment was spent on imported technology.[25]

To meet the goals of these plans, the spurt in license purchases from the West was impressive. According to Litzenzintorg, the Soviet Union bought only a handful of licenses abroad in the 1960s, but went on a license shopping spree in the West between 1970 and 1977. During the 1971–1975 Five-Year Plan the import of licenses from the West quadrupled, and quadrupled again during the tenth Five-Year Plan.[26] Between 1971 and 1977 the value of Soviet imports of machinery and transport equipment from the West quadrupled, and imports as a share of investment in the production of domestic machinery investment doubled between 1956 and 1977.[27] Furthermore, statistics compiled by Western analysts on industrial cooperation between OECD and CMEA countries show a significant increase in their number during the 1970s. While very few agreements were concluded with the Soviet Union and Eastern Europe in the 1960s, there was an explosion of these agreements in the early 1970s: from 600 in 1973 to over 1,000 in 1975.[28] Joint ventures grew exponentially after Gorbachev's reforms; by mid-1990 the Soviet Union had concluded about 1,250 joint venture agreements with firms from the United States, Western Europe, and Japan.

Clearly, then, the Soviet Union intensified its efforts to *acquire* Western technology throughout the post-Stalin era. The essential question in the vulnerability debate, however, is whether those acquisitions actually contributed to Soviet economic power.

Soviet Policy and Actual Technology Imports

The above evidence on Soviet technology import policy supports both the Reagan administration's arguments about the USSR's elaborate Western technology collection efforts in the 1970s and the prediction put forth by the exporter vulnerability thesis that trailing states will attempt to catch up by importing technology from leading states. Indeed, the Soviet Union moved from a policy of intermittent, ad hoc technology purchases from the West in the 1930s to a systematic policy of technology acquisition in the 1970s and 1980s, and continued that policy under Gorbachev.

Nonetheless, during the 1970s the USSR imported less *advanced* technology than most countries in the world; indeed, the United States imported more. By 1981 Western exports of high technology to the Soviet Union accounted for only 8.6 percent of total Western exports to the Soviet Union, while Western exports of high technology to the world accounted for 12.4 percent of total exports.[29]

High-technology items constituted only a small portion of total Soviet imports of manufacturing equipment and all manufactured goods. In fact, that portion declined steadily throughout the 1970s, from 20.3 percent in 1972 to 15.4 percent in 1980 to 12 percent in 1981. Thus, the bulk of Soviet imports of Western manufactured goods in the 1970s were not advanced technology items at all, but rather run-of-the-mill manufactured goods and production equipment. In 1977 there was a sharp drop in the USSR's technology imports from the West, and Soviet purchases of Western technology fell even further between 1980 and 1981.[30] Despite the significant policy changes, levels of legal Western technology imports measured by the import of capital goods and equipment, never high to begin with, actually declined during the period in which Reagan administration officials compared exports of high technology to the Soviet Union to a "hemorrhaging" of Western technology.

Soviet Capabilities: Western Technology and Industrial Productivity

But does the *volume* of technology exports matter? The import of a few key innovations can make an important difference to the productivity of an economy. In all manufacturing sectors, a central component of productivity is the underlying equipment used to manufacture products. For example, the strategic placement of numerically controlled (NC) machine tools and commercial robots can vastly enhance manufacturing productivity across the industrial spectrum if they can be effectively integrated into the production system. NC machine tools can therefore be considered a critical technological input to a range of user sectors.[31] If imported critical technologies are "diffused" across industrial sectors, productivity increases should result. The industries that produce these critical technologies can be considered *strategic*—that is, they are industries whose goods have broad application in the production of a large portion of a nation's goods and services.[32]

Some critical technologies also act as "drivers," or catalysts, for innovation and productivity increases in a whole host of industries. Because many industries are interdependent, technological innovation in one industry can have a "spillover" effect into other industries. For example, the needs of the consumer electronics industry, which incorporates advanced microelectronics components, in turn shapes the direction of technological developments in the semiconductor industry. Developments in the semiconductor industry, in turn, determine the ability of the computer industry to innovate. Advances in computers, transistors, and microchips feed into one another, triggering further developments in each sector; computers, in turn, become essential components in other products, like machine tools and robots, changing the character of manufacturing in other industries.[33] Many analysts, for example, argue that new technologies needed to bring HDTV to market will determine the direction of major advances across the entire spectrum of electronics, from chips to supercomputers. The import of key technologies, then, have a spillover effect, encouraging technological change in a number of industries and enhancing industrial productivity throughout the economy.

The volume of technology imports, then, is less significant than the particular technologies imported, due to the importance of innovation in a few strategic industries and the technological advances that can be realized as technology spills over from one sector to another. The questions then become: what technologies in which industries did the West sell to the Soviet Union, and to what extent did Western technology *actually sold* in the 1970s and 1980s contribute to the productivity of the Soviet industries that bought them and to the economy as a whole? To answer these questions we would need to know the content of Soviet technology import plans and the precise contribution of technology to the efficient utilization of Soviet factor endowments. We would then have to isolate the contribution of Western technology to Soviet economic productivity and growth.

In the 1970s Soviet technology imports from the West were not targeted specifically at strategic industries. The bulk of those imports went to the energy sector and the chemical industry. Western computer systems were also a high-priority item on the import plan, despite the tight Western export restrictions on state-of-the-art computer technology.[34]

Precise measures of Western technology's contribution to Soviet economic growth are difficult to come by. Nonetheless, attempts have been made to compare the productivity of Western capital goods in the Soviet economy with that of domestic stock, both at the macroeconomic and microeconomic levels. These measurements can be used to arrive at a preliminary assessment of the fear expressed by economic nationalists that vulnerability would result from commercial technology exodus that strengthens the adversary's economy.

Two approaches have been used to measure the impact of those technologies actually imported on Soviet industrial productivity. Each approach, however, leads to different conclusions. First, *aggregate studies*[35] sought to link the USSR's total machinery imports to the rate of growth in the economy as a whole. The aggregated data, however, did not allow analysts to control for possible perturbing variables such as the contribution of domestic R and D to the production process and the impact of capital and labor inputs that contribute to increasing or declining growth rates.[36] It has been tempting for analysts to impute causality to the correlation between a declining Soviet economic growth rate and declining Western technology imports between 1976 and 1990. But it is important to stress that both output and labor productivity grew much more rapidly between 1955 and 1965, when Western technology imports were much lower, than between 1965 and 1975, when technology imports increased.[37] Clearly, factors other than Western technology were decisive in increasing productivity in the earlier period, and decreasing productivity later on.

Second, *industry and sector studies* looked at how fast imported manufacturing technology was incorporated into the production process and the extent to which it contributed to the productivity of a given industry. These studies were particularly good at measuring the impact of imported production technologies on the output and efficiency of a given plant. They did not, however, adequately capture the technology diffusion process, that is, the process by which new production techniques and equipment were replicated in other plants and industries and were assimilated throughout the economy. Technology diffusion is one of the important ways in which technology transfer contributes to enhanced economic performance. Whether productivity improvements are diffused throughout the economy depends on the nature of a nation's industrial structure and whether that structure permits strong linkages and technological spillovers. Because these studies do not focus on the structure that facilitates or inhibits the diffusion process, their results tell us little about the effects of imported technology on the economy as a whole. Furthermore, these studies suffer from many of the same problems encountered in aggregate studies; they do not account for other variables that would retard or advance productivity in a given sector.

Finally, the measure of technology transfer used in this evidence is the sale of Western machinery and equipment to the Soviet Union. This equipment may be targeted for strategic industries and may be a catalyst for innovation; nonetheless, this measure is limited because it cannot encompass other forms of technology transfer, especially those involved in industrial cooperation, for which data is more difficult to obtain.[38] I explore the effects of industrial cooperation agreements in a later section. Here it is simply important to emphasize that the benefit of new technology to the Soviet economy in general, and of Western technology in particular, is difficult to separate out from other factors that impact economic health. Below is a brief examination of the measurement attempts at both the aggregate and industry/sector levels.

Donald W. Green and Herbert S. Levine made the first attempt to measure the macroeconomic effects of imported capital goods on the Soviet economy in an important study published in 1977, when Soviet demand for Western technology was still relatively strong.[39] They estimated that the marginal productivity of capital goods imported from the West was eight to ten times higher than the productivity of domestic stock. But although they argued that Western technology *did* increase Soviet industrial productivity, they calculated that because import levels were so low, variations in Soviet technology imports from the West within any plausible range would affect the annual Soviet economic growth rate by only 0.1 or 0.2 percent.[40] They concluded that although Western production technology had the *potential* for increasing Soviet economic growth, there was little evidence that it had a major impact on the growth of the Soviet economy as a whole.

The findings of many of the industry and sector studies, on the other hand, indicated that, for the most part, Western technology had made an *actual* contribution to the productivity of the plants studied when compared with plants that did not import Western technology.[41] Comparisons of Western- and Soviet-equipped plants in other industries in Central European countries under central planning report that the installation of Western machinery and equipment cut production costs and increased output from previous levels, but compared to the same Western industries, the performance was consistently rated as poor.[42]

Studies of the Soviet chemical industry provide a good example of Western technology's contribution to productivity at the enterprise level. They found that Western-equipped chemical plants in the Soviet Union took three to five years to become operational after orders were placed. Startup times for domestically equipped plants, on the other hand, averaged eight years. Once in operation, Western-equipped plants cut Soviet production costs substantially. Nonetheless, by 1990 the growth of the Soviet chemical industry was even slower than the slow growth of overall industry.[43] Not even an infusion of Western technology could eliminate problems that led to a slowdown in overall growth.

The most detailed and oft-cited microeconomic study is Philip Hanson's analysis of the impact of Western chemical fertilizer production technology on performance in the Soviet agricultural sector.[44]

Hanson estimated that imported technology had a decisive influence on increased agricultural output in the early 1970s. He calculated that the net incremental farm output of 4 billion rubles in the period 1970–75 was obtained by means of 2 billion rubles' worth of imported Western plants installed in the USSR between 1960 and 1975. Nonetheless, in the 1980s Soviet agricultural productivity began to decline, and the decline was widely attributed to shortfalls in the production of chemical fertilizers.[45]

In sum, the evidence on the impact of Western technology on the Soviet economy during the 1970s and early 1980s was contradictory. The macroeconomic studies found little evidence that Western technology had a significant positive impact on Soviet economic performance. The microeconomic studies, on the other hand, found that, with important qualifications, Western technology made a contribution to the productivity of the plants studied, even though productivity lagged behind that of the West. That expanded productivity, however, appeared to have little impact on overall economic growth or even on the long-term health of the industries for which they were targeted.

What accounts for this difference? Aside from the methodological problems of each approach, it is entirely possible that projects based on Western technology were more productive than those based on domestic technology because they were high-priority projects. As such, they received higher-quality domestic inputs, and their technical level was high to begin with.[46] But if technology that had been successfully assimilated in these high-priority plants or industries could not diffuse productivity throughout the economy, the effects on overall economic health would be insignificant. I will now turn to a more detailed discussion of diffusion problems. It is sufficient to note here that, despite the increased productivity of those plants that employed Western technology, the effects of that technology on the targeted sector and the economy as a whole were minimal.

Western Technology Imports and the Industrial Technology Gap

A related theme of the technology exodus thesis is that with the import of foreign technology, trailing states can narrow the gap between themselves and leading technology exporting states. Given the above assessment of the minimal effects of Western technology on the Soviet economy, we would not have expected the gap to narrow significantly with the aid of Western technology; in fact, there is general consensus that the gap widened. Most studies that attempted to measure the gap between technological levels of Soviet and Western industry suggested that while Western technology helped raise production in the Soviet Union to levels slightly higher than they would have been, technological advance in the West was faster and increased productivity even more, thus actually widening the gap.

The most comprehensive and careful of these studies was published by Ronald Amann, Julian Cooper, and R. W. Davies in 1977. They did not measure the effect of Western technology on the size of the technology gap, but rather conducted case studies to compare Soviet and Western attainments in research, experimental development, innovation, and technology diffusion over a fifteen-to-twenty-year period. The gap was thus measured in the years between Western and Soviet attainments in each of these areas. The findings of the study revealed that overall the technology gap between the USSR and the West remained unchanged between 1950 and 1976 across all key industrial sectors including computers, chemicals, machine tools, metallurgy, rocketry, steel, transportation, and communication.[47] R. W. Davies summed up their findings in the following way: "In most of the technologies we have studied, there is no evidence of a substantial diminution of the technological gap between the USSR and the West in the past 15–20 years, either at the prototype/commercial application stages or in the diffusion of advanced technology."[48]

Evidence from the 1980s suggests that the technology gap in these key sectors actually widened. A 1986 study conducted by Ronald Amann and Julian Cooper on Soviet technological progress concluded that there had been a continuous absolute decline in the production of prototypes of new machinery and equipment since the 1960s, especially in the more advanced high-technology industries. Ronald Amann observes that

> the most startling trend to emerge . . . is the relatively steep decline of the impact indicators, expressed in terms of labor savings from new technologies and their annual economic effect. This suggests a growing ineffectiveness of industrial innovation. . . . Incremental improvements at the shop floor level . . . are . . . an important aspect of technical progress in the West. This is where science interacts with production. In the course of fully mastering and modifying a new process, fundamentally new technologies can begin to take shape. In the USSR, however, the long-term statistical trends would

seem to cast some doubt on the vitality of these creative responses. Since the early 1970s there has been a fall in the growth rate of the number of improvements introduced and a similar though less pronounced fall in expenditures on their implementation.[49]

A study of the Soviet computer industry published in 1989 shows that the USSR was nearly ten years late in reconstructing the first American microprocessor and by 1989 had not been able to build a supercomputer similar to the Cyber-203 or the Cray 3 machines. The study further reported that the Soviet Union was fifteen years behind the West in the production of personal computers.[50]

The Resource-Releasing Effect of Western Technology

A final argument for the claim that technology exodus leads to Western vulnerability is that the employment of key technologies that increases the efficiency of industrial production will free resources, which can then be diverted to the military sector, whether or not the economy as a whole would benefit. Western security is threatened when its commercial exports *indirectly* strengthen the adversary's military power by expanding resources available to the military. As we saw above, the Soviet economy was characterized throughout the postwar period by shortages of capital and labor. Although the growth-retarding effects of these shortages were not overcome by the import of Western technology, *any* imports would theoretically free up resources and create some slack in the economy in the short run. Western imports could have enlarged the "bottlenecks" that hamper economic performance; of course those imports would have an immediate cost in terms of the production of exports required for their purchase.

Over time, however, technology imports may have a "resource-demanding" effect; that is, their employment in an economy characterized by chronic shortages exacerbated by weak economic linkages may require substantial material inputs, thus creating bottlenecks elsewhere in an economy where shortages are pervasive. Projects that relied on Western technology in the USSR actually demanded more resources than they released.[51] And because of the high priority that Soviet planners assigned to Western-assisted projects in the 1960s and 1970s, there is evidence to suggest that, over time, scarce resources were actually diverted from other parts of the economy to these projects.

Three examples illustrate this point. In a study of Western technology in the Soviet steel industry, Elisabeth Goldstein found that foreign technology in the high-priority mills became encapsulated and that they actually drew scarce resources away from other mills, thus lowering aggregate steel production levels.[52] A 1973 study of Soviet manpower problems cites examples of five imported chemical plants originally designed to require 91 auxiliary workers for maintenance and repair work. After the equipment was put into operation, the plants required 732 maintenance and repair personnel.[53]

George Holliday's study of the Volga and Kama rivers automobile plants indicates that these operations required increasing high-quality inputs from the economy, such as special plastics and metals, and high-octane gasoline and service facilities. These inputs were drawn away from traditionally high-priority economic sectors, including the military sector, because Soviet officials were determined to make these plants a success.[54]

In sum, this brief review of the literature on the effects of Western technology on Soviet production in the 1970s and early 1980s as a test of the vulnerability thesis provides inconclusive evidence. Macroeconomic studies could not adequately isolate the role of technology in the economic growth process, nor could they separate out the role of *Western* technology in that process. The studies that attempted these measurements found little significant impact of Western technology on Soviet economic performance. Microeconomic studies suggest that the impact of Western technology on Soviet economic growth in the 1980s was not significant because specific production technologies did not diffuse innovation throughout the economy. The evidence on the resource-releasing effects of Western technology on the Soviet economy is largely anecdotal and fragmentary, but the experts suggested that the technology gap between the Soviet Union and the West actually widened.

There are thus only two important conclusions to be drawn from the available evidence on the role of Western technology in the Soviet economy through the 1980s. First, technology itself could not change the set of constraints and incentives imposed by the economic and social commitments of a centrally planned economy; the constraints imposed by the economy's institutional structure obstructed technology assimilation and diffusion. Second, although some of the evidence indicates that imported production technology allowed some plants to use their resources more efficiently by enhancing both labor and capital productivity, the supply of those resources was too limited to have made a difference. New technology in a particular sector may have saved labor in that sector, but the purchase of that technology required capital or labor from either that or another sector to earn the necessary foreign exchange and employ the technology most efficiently. Because shortages were severe, bottlenecks appeared elsewhere.

Clearly, the Soviet economy was not performing well during the entire period under consideration, but the measurement problems discussed above prevent us from knowing how much worse that performance would have been without the import of Western technology. We can conclude with some certainty that the impact of Western machinery and equipment on Soviet growth rates was insignificant, even if the marginal productivity of Western capital goods was greater than the marginal productivity of domestic goods. Although technology acquisition from the West was important to Soviet planners in the 1970s and 1980s, its impact on industrial capabilities was not what the planners had hoped for or what U.S. officials feared. Vulnerability claims due to a technology exodus were clearly overstated and unfounded.

Reassessing the Vulnerability Effects of Technology Exodus

What accounts for the minimal effects of Western technology on the Soviet economy? Foreign technology was utilized efficiently in other nations—Japan, Korea, and Taiwan, for example—to enhance economic growth throughout the postwar period. Why was the impact on the Soviet economy so dismal? Why did the effects predicted by the vulnerability thesis not appear in the Soviet Union? Are they likely to emerge in the 1990s as Russia and other former Soviet states restructure their economies?

Two kinds of argument explain the insignificant impact of Western technology on the Soviet economy. The standard account focuses on the *internal* institutional structure of the Soviet economy that discouraged technology spillovers and diffusion. The second focuses on external constraints on the actual import of needed technologies. The latter suggests that Western corporate strategy and type of investment can inhibit the transfer of technologies needed to strengthen an importer's economy. A brief discussion of each of these arguments can facilitate an examination of the conditions under which vulnerability effects are either strengthened or weakened.

Internal Constraints: Institutional Obstacles to Technology Diffusion, Use, and Acquisition

The conventional explanation for the low impact of Western technology on the Soviet economy is that the institutional structure of the Soviet economic system created obstacles to effective foreign technology assimilation and diffusion, and indeed, the above discussion suggests that the diffusion effects of Western technology in the Soviet economy were low.[55] Low levels of technology diffusion and spillover in the Soviet Union can be attributed to weak and nonexistent linkages among suppliers, producers, and consumers throughout the economy. These weak linkages intensified the development of ad-hoc vertical integration in Soviet factories and fed the "second economy,"[56] both of which further exacerbated the negative effects of central planning on the strengthening of linkages and spillovers.

There was no "wholesale trading system" in the Soviet Union. The formal distribution—or rationing—of industrial inputs to producers was carried out by Gossnab, the central state committee for material and technical supplies, which allocated all industrial inputs and issued supply authorizations for almost a million different kinds of goods. Enterprises had no choice of suppliers and clients; relationships between suppliers and clients were difficult to establish because they were mediated by the central authorities.[57]

To overcome the supply bottlenecks which were the inevitable result of supply centralization, most enterprises had to improvise in order to be certain that critical inputs would be available. They did this in two ways: either by finding ways to produce critical inputs themselves— through ad-hoc vertical integration—or through informal bartering for inputs. Most enterprises were specifically designed to be as self-sufficient as possible. Indeed, 30–40 percent of the value of all Soviet goods were produced on single sites.[58] For example, 45 percent of all metalworking equipment in the Soviet Union was produced in non-machine-building enterprises, and 84 out of 100 machine-building enterprises produced their own forgings; 65 out of 100 produced their own metal hardware; and 76 out of 100 produced their own stock. This kind of vertical integration "at almost any price" was not based on cost calculations showing that these enterprises could produce the goods as cheaply or as well as others, but on intense uncertainty about supplies.[59] Many enterprises thus became "conglomerates" out of necessity: they even raised food and manufactured those consumer goods for their employees that could not be found in retail stores. Indeed, in late 1987 the Presidium reprimanded the Ministry on Non-Ferrous Metallurgy because *only* three out of four Soviet metal-smelting plants had their own herds of cows![60]

Not only were economic linkages created *within* vertically integrated industrial enterprises, but the economic bottlenecks caused by central planning gave rise to a set of informal relationships and unofficial networks in wholesale trade. As a condition for supplying industrial inputs, suppliers often demanded consumer goods—including food—produced by the supplier as payment. If those goods could not be supplied, the input would not be forthcoming. Soviet tractor manufacturers, for example, could not sign direct contracts with metal suppliers in 1990, even though such contracts were legal, because the metal suppliers demanded meat or sausage, vehicles or building equipment in exchange for metal shipments.[61]

These complex but unreliable "private" linkages among industries were initially weakened and in some cases even broken by the reform process because hard currency rather than rubles or bartered goods was often required as payment for inputs. For example, a Soviet joint venture with Britain to produce tampons wanted to export 30 percent of the output and to increase locally produced inputs to 90 percent from 33 percent. But because of cotton shortages, supplies were not available, and when they were available, cotton producers began to demand hard currency for cotton, rather than the bartered wheat that they had received previously. Hard currency was not forthcoming, however, because shortages prevented the raising of production levels, which could have increased output for exports. Therefore, cotton inputs were withheld.[62]

U.S. corporate officials doing business in the Soviet Union for the first time as reform began to open the Soviet economy were astounded at the weakness of economic linkages. "Communication is so bad they don't know what someone else makes in the country. Soviet manufacturing plants set up to produce a given item usually make every component for the end product."[63] Without these linkages, it was not likely that technology would diffuse throughout an industry, nor was it likely to spill over into related industries. When an exporter's technology becomes encapsulated in isolated plants, its contribution to overall economic power of the importer is likely to be weak.

At the enterprise level, too, management had a stronger incentive to push obsolete equipment to its production capacity than to install new equipment that could eat up precious foreign exchange and that could not clearly be integrated into the old production processes. Managers hesitated to install and fully utilize foreign equipment because their goal was to maximize output rather than reduce factor inputs and run efficiently. Furthermore, management was generally risk-averse, since risks were seldom rewarded; and the installation of new equipment involved some risk. It usually demanded a change in inputs from other industries, and weak economic linkages created tremendous uncertainty at the enterprise level: unless the plant was targeted as high priority, management could not be sure that inputs will be available.[64]

Furthermore, decisions to import Western technology often focused on the purchase of *pieces* of machinery and equipment rather than on completely new production systems and how they could be linked to developmental requirements in the rest of the economy. Often the attempt to implant a new technology in an old production system resulted in failure, because the adoption of new equipment required adaptation and change in other parts of the production system as well. The story Western corporate officials told most often was that of a Soviet purchase of this or that piece of equipment, which was never installed and was left outside the factory to rust.

By 1992, the collapse of state socialism had not significantly changed these institutional features of the former Soviet economy that were widely thought to impede the acquisition, absorption, and diffusion of Western technology. True, perestroika was an important step away from state control; Gorbachev moved toward economic decentralization: privatizing agriculture, legalizing the "second economy," increasing investment in industry, gradually chipping away at the power of the economic plan, and tearing down protectionist barriers to trade with the West. He further appointed to positions of power those economists who favored the benefits of a more open economy, attacked the monopoly position of the Ministry of Foreign Trade, and legalized Soviet joint ventures with Western firms.[65]

Yeltsin has moved even faster in the attempt to dismantle state control over the Russian economy in efforts pointed toward monetary stabilization, privatization, price liberalization, and the removal of tariff barriers to foreign trade. Nonetheless, there remain many insurmountable institutional obstacles to the emergence of efficient capitalist production and exchange. And these barriers, discussed below, also promised to obstruct the acquisition and diffusion of Western technology.

The former Soviet economy appeared initially to exhibit a capacity to reproduce the features described above and *resist* successful liberalization. What happened in the Soviet Union under Gorbachev was a *withering away of state control over the economy*.[66] As the state moved away from regulating the supply of industrial inputs, both the vertical integration of industries—the growth of monopolies—and barter were intensified. Thus the institutional obstacles that inhibited the absorbtion and diffusion of Western technology became even more pronounced.

The withdrawal of the state from its previous role in regulating the economy meant that economic power devolved to the monopolistic enterprises described above. In many cases these conglomerates used their power to control supplies to more dependent enterprises; they became, in effect, large trading companies rather than more efficient producers. Furthermore, many key party officials had valuable information about supply sources that allowed them to enter new positions of power where they could maintain their economic control. New cooperative enterprises that mediated trading between enterprises were established by former party secretaries turned capitalist businessmen.[67] These large enterprises and the barter relations they perpetrated also became the economic foundation of nationalism and localism. New states of the former Soviet Union and regions controlled by monopolies within those states increasingly attempted to control markets, formerly controlled by the central party apparatus.

The control of the supply of goods continued to be highly personalized and politicized in the wake of the Soviet Union's demise. The economies of the region were characterized by increasing struggles over control. One effect, of course, was the continued inhibition of technology diffusion. In short, the postcommunist economic transition was, in 1992, marked *not* by a transition to more efficient and innovative production that could lead to long-term economic growth; it was instead characterized by the extraction of "profits" from monopoly control over exchange and more intensified barter relations.

Furthermore, the import of foreign technology continues to be blocked by domestic R-and-D institutes. The careers of those who work at these institutes were (and continue to be) dependent upon indigenous technological advance. The purchase of technology from the West threatens to reduce their funding. Increasing purchases of Western technology also painfully demonstrate the inability of domestic R-and-D institutes to develop technology themselves. Nonetheless, representatives from these institutes were (and continue to be) part of the team that negotiates with Western firms on joint ventures and other industrial cooperation agreements under which Western technology is acquired. In these negotiations, they are often extremely critical of the Western technology in question, and their veto has blocked many technology sales.

External Constraints on Technology Imports: Western Corporate Investment Strategies

But it was not just central planning and institutional obstacles that inhibited Soviet economic development based on foreign technology. It was and continues to be Western corporate strategy as well. Even if the introduction of a market economy does begin to remove the institutional obstacles to economic growth, Western corporate strategy and contractual provisions work to ensure that Russian dependence on Western technology continues and that the stimulation of linkages and spillovers is inhibited. Post-Soviet integration into the international economy does not necessarily mean future economic growth and development. The *way* that the Russian economy integrates into the international economy, and the Western corporate strategies that shape that integration, may portend further economic stagnation. Those same strategies have reduced Western vulnerability in the past.

Both Soviet and post-Soviet officials believed that new foreign investment and new joint ventures with Western firms would create an institutional structure through which the technology gap could be narrowed; Western officials felt similarly. Indeed, one of the most important findings of the "Bucy Report" (discussed in chapter 2) was that joint ventures (as well as other forms of industrial cooperation) would create in the Soviet economy the kind of sustained contact with the West that could permit the Soviets to acquire state-of-the-art production technology, ensuring the highest degree of production efficiency and quality, rather than standardized production techniques transferred through simple licensing agreements or looser forms of industrial cooperation.

Indeed, industrial cooperation as a mode of East-West technology transfer dramatically increased throughout the 1970s (only to level off in the 1980s) and Soviet planners hoped that joint ventures with the West would not only provide a new infusion of capital but also give the Soviet economy modern production equipment, long-term technical training, and management personnel. These would be the keys, they reasoned, to the competitiveness of Soviet exports in global markets and the modernization of the Soviet economic system.

As we saw above, by mid-1990, over 1,200 joint ventures between Soviet enterprises and Western firms had been established in the Soviet Union under the new joint venture law. Although many of those involved little or no transfer of advanced technology, some did involve advanced production facilities, and some involved the transfer of dual-use technology over the entire life of the project.[68] As I noted in chapter 1, some analysts claim that these new efficient modes of technology transfer within a market framework will overcome some of the obstacles that earlier technology transfers met and could trigger new Western vulnerabilities as the Russian economy grows strong.

It is too soon to assess the effects of joint ventures with the West on the post-Soviet economic performance. Nonetheless, studies of direct foreign investment and technology transfer in the United States, Asia, and Latin America suggest that different modes of investment and technology transfer will have differing effects on economic development and growth in these regions. Furthermore, interviews with corporate officials engaging in industrial cooperation or forming joint ventures with enterprises in Russia suggest that corporations themselves can control the locus of technology development and that they can either facilitate or inhibit host country economic growth based on foreign technology imports. As I will demonstrate in more detail below, Western corporate control is exercised through decisions on whether to produce for the domestic market or to produce for export, whether to invest in manufacturing or the production of primary goods, and the type of business organization through which technology is transferred. These decisions determine what kinds of technology are transferred to domestic Russian customers and whether technology will ultimately be withheld from the Russian economy. Although I refer to Russia throughout this discussion, the argument can apply to the entire post-Soviet region, although one should not presume that economic outcomes will be similar in all of the new states.

Production for Export or for the Domestic Market

First, the foreign investor can decide to invest in production for export or for the domestic market. Production for the domestic market is less likely to stimulate technological innovation or bring in the latest technology, especially if import barriers are in place. Purchasing power in the domestic market is limited to certain groups; products are largely protected from global competition, and thus there is little incentive to improve quality or lower production costs with state-of-the-art technology. Under these conditions, the domestic market will show little tendency to expand after its needs are fulfilled.[69] In the Soviet economy, as Joseph Brada has pointed out, the excess demand for downstream products made it difficult to divert supplies away from domestic claimants and toward foreign markets.[70] If the output of foreign technology is not exported, it is less likely to meet the standards that the world market demands.

Production for export, on the other hand, reduces trade deficits and, in the Soviet economy, brought in hard currency to continue the import of technology and needed consumer goods. When production for export is the goal, the producer has a high incentive to build economies of scale and bring in capital-intensive technology to the host country. Most important, the foreign investor is motivated to bring in state-of-the-art technology and to continue to improve the technology so that the output will be competitive on world markets. If Western technology is used to produce manufactured goods for export, it would make a more significant contribution to Russian economic power than if it is used to produce goods for the domestic market.

Production of Primary Products and Manufactured Goods

Not all production for export, however, will necessarily push technological development forward. The export of manufactured goods will, in general, earn higher returns than the export of primary products, because more value is added to the goods in the manufacturing process than in the production of primary goods. For the resource-rich Russian economy, however, the export of primary commodities—like oil, natural gas, and timber—is crucial in order to earn the hard currency needed to buy manufacturing equipment and consumer goods. What is important in assessing the effects of Western technology transferred to

Russia through joint ventures and other forms of industrial cooperation is that technology is relatively stable in most primary industries, while it is dynamic and changing in manufacturing industries.

Business Organization

Not only will decisions to produce for the Russian market rather than for export to world markets, and to invest in commodities production rather than manufacturing, inhibit the transfer of state-of-the-art technology; the form of business organization chosen for the joint venture may largely determine whether and what kind of technology is transferred. Business organizations differ in terms of the locus of decision making, the site where products are designed, their source of inputs, and where research and development activities are conducted. John Zysman has argued that "if the home country of a multinational corporation is where market information and technological possibilities are sifted and basic research strategy developed and implemented, then foreign investment by that corporation may cut off both domestic technology development and implementation of domestic R and D in the host country. The host country's gains from technological accumulation may then be eliminated or limited."[71] On the basis of their study of direct foreign investment in the United States, Todd Hixon and Ranch Kimball have suggested that only those foreign businesses that transfer technology through complex business organizations, demanding a high level of local intellectual content, will be effective vehicles for technology transfer and will make a significant contribution to the importer's economic strength.[72] They consider four models of foreign business organization and their impact on a host country's economy.

First, they found that fully integrated operations that integrate product design, manufacturing, process engineering, and vendor management in one organization are the most beneficial to the host country's economy. By requiring domestic inputs, they create extensive and tight linkages with the potential for technological spillover to the rest of the economy.

Second, they found that individual plant complexes can also be beneficial, but less so than complex business organizations. Plant complexes fabricate product components and use local engineering talent but make more mature products for which the key intellectual elements of the product and production system still remain outside the host country. A good example of such an arrangement is the one established by Reynolds Metals, FATA Corporation of Italy, and a Russian consortium to build a $200 million aluminum foil plant complex in Siberia. Reynolds designed the plant using FATA technology and the venture plans to export 70 percent of the output.[73] The Russians will supply labor and will own 70 percent of the venture. If new factories such as this one, which bring new technologies of production, diffuse that production technology throughout the host economy, they can force out less competitive domestic producers and, by threatening to do so, encourage them to adjust. Nonetheless, individual clone factories will not necessarily demand expertise at a high level. After initial construction of the factory, there will be little learning and transfer of state-of-the-art knowledge.

Third, Hixon and Kimball found that assembly operations that make products locally using designs, processes, and management approaches developed in the home country are less beneficial still with regard to the transfer of state-of-the-art production technology. They may buy some inputs locally but are likely to import key components from abroad. All sourcing decisions are made in the home country, and it is difficult for local companies to become suppliers. A Russian-German joint venture, Aquarius System Integral (ASI), assembles computers in Russia but all parts are imported into the plant. Phoenix Group International of Irvine, California assembles computers in Russia as well. But Bo Denysyk, a senior vice-president of the firm, noted that "they are getting all the major components from different manufacturers and providing a little staff to assemble it there, while the Russians are providing the distribution channel. Almost anyone can do it."[74] Assembly plants like these are unlikely to create a locus of technological development in microelectronics because they demand no engineering skill and no learning.

Finally, importing operations that involve sales, marketing, and distribution and that are set up to win local market share for Western exporters are the least beneficial to the host economy because the engine of economic growth is still located offshore. For example, a joint venture between Germany, Iran, and Russia simply sells German and Iranian consumer goods in the domestic Russian economy. British Overseas Pharmacies has set up a joint venture with the Republic of Georgia Ministry of Health to simply distribute medical products in pharmacies catering to tourists.[75]

An Assessment of Initial Joint Venture Agreements

I examined 168 Western joint ventures and other industrial cooperation agreements within the Russian Republic that were profiled in the Soviet or Western press and were registered or actually operating between November 1989 and December 1990. Although these ventures were initially constructed under Soviet control, most continued in 1992 under the auspices of regional Russian ministries. I categorized these ventures according to the market for which their products were targeted, the sectors in which they were located, and the types of business organizations chosen for the venture. It is important to note, however, that a very low percentage of joint ventures registered were actually operational during that time; the USSR State Statistics Committee estimated that only 184 out of 1,250 joint ventures registered as of January 1, 1990 were operating.[76] Furthermore, the term *joint venture* has been used to describe a variety of business activities. At the end of 1989 Soviet authorities had begun to complain that "many are nothing more than representative offices—i.e., shop windows for products of the Western partner . . . because the Soviet government artificially encouraged the growth of joint ventures, partners have dressed up other forms of cooperation, such as barter, as joint ventures in order to get clearance."[77] One analyst even claimed that many joint ventures in computer production simply imported Western computers for hard currency and resold them in the USSR under the guise of joint production.[78]

Of the 168 joint ventures surveyed, 35 were in the primary sector, 56 were in services and the distribution of Western imports, and 77 were in manufacturing. Of those engaged in manufacturing, 62 were manufacturing for the domestic market and only 15 were engaged in manufacturing for export. Although 45 percent of the Western joint ventures surveyed were in manufacturing, the authorities complained that they were not transferring the technology needed for economic development.[79] At the end of 1989 Soviet authorities estimated that only 30 to 40 joint ventures out of the 1,300 registered had introduced Western manufacturing technology.[80]

I was able to classify only 132 of the 168 joint ventures examined according to their type of business organization. Of these, only one of the joint ventures fit the criteria for a fully integrated business operation. This was a joint venture with Fiat of Italy to produce automobiles. The venture planned to almost double annual car production in Russia from 1.3 million to 2.3 million automobiles by the mid-1990s. Fiat would own 30 percent of the venture and the enterprise Elaz would own the other 70 percent. Key management positions, however, would not be reflected in the 30–70 split. Because of Fiat's more sophisticated management techniques and more highly qualified personnel, the Italians were expected to play a major role.[81]

As the joint venture agreement stood as of early 1990, engines and gear boxes imported from Italy would be used in all of the cars produced in Russia, but all other inputs would come from domestic sources. One-third of the annual output was to be exported for sale in Western Europe. Russian engineering would be utilized on a sustained basis, and the locus of innovative activity would be split between Italy and the domestic enterprises.

Only 52 of the 132 joint ventures classified by type of business organization were plants producing manufactured goods. These were primarily in light industries such as food processing, toys, textiles, and other consumer goods targeted for the domestic market. Investments in this sector tended to be modest. Three of these plant complexes, however, were large ones in the petrochemical industry, and six were formed to produce industrial robots and machine tools. Of the 77 joint ventures in manufacturing, 23 could be classified as assembly plants or "screwdriver factories." The bulk of these assembly operations were in consumer electronics: the assembly of VCRs, TV sets, computers, microwave ovens, audio systems, and TV satellite antennas. The rest were formed to assemble motor vehicles.

By far the majority of joint ventures classified according to type of business organization were in services and marketing. Out of 132 joint ventures examined, 56 were established to facilitate imports or to provide services to Western exporters. These included the establishment of insurance and accounting ventures, film distribution, computer sales, market research, design, and tourism.

Finally, it is important to note that seven of these joint ventures were operating outside the Soviet Union using Soviet technology in high-tech industries such as semiconductors, biotechnology, rocket engines, and the design of space reactors.

This survey suggests future trends in Western technology transfer to the economies of the post-Soviet region: if it is indicative, little state-of-the-art technology will be transferred to strategic industries because Western investment in those industries is largely confined to assembly operations. Production for the domestic market is preferred over production for export, suggesting that the transfer of obsolete technology will suffice to capture local market share. Although almost half of the ventures were in manufacturing, the largest investments were in extractive industries. And the bulk of the joint ventures surveyed were located in services and the marketing of Western imports. For the time being, the engine of economic growth in the postcommunist economies of the former Soviet Union may remain offshore.

Corporate Strategy and Contractual Provisions

Interviews with corporate officials from ten Western firms who signed joint-venture and other industrial cooperation agreements with the Soviet Union in manufacturing industries provide further evidence for these conclusions. The interviews suggest that contractual stipulations in joint-venture agreements ensure that the most advanced Western technologies were withheld from the Soviet economy.[82] In general, the interviews corroborate the above survey findings about Westen corporate preference for the domestic market. They suggest that the strategy of all of these firms was to sell products and expand local market share, not to transfer technology. Western firms used the technology transfer aspect of the venture as a "hook," or a means to foster dependence on their products, thus expanding their market share within the Russian economy. Joint ventures and other industrial cooperation agreements were seen as part of the overall corporate strategy to create local competitive advantage.[83] Corporate officials argued that selling technology did not halt product sales in the local market, but actually enhanced those sales in the long run. A report on a survey of U.S.-Soviet joint ventures conducted in 1989 by the U.S.-USSR Trade and Economic Council found that 73 percent of U.S. partners stated that their main goal was access to the Soviet market.[84]

Firm strategies for technology transfer differed according to whether the firm wished to maintain a market in the region, create a market there, or expand their market share. None of the officials interviewed saw as their primary strategy production for export.[85] When maintaining a market was the main motivation for the Western partner to enter into an industrial cooperation agreement, technology sales would be "passive" and the strategy "defensive." That is, firms would not *initiate* technology transfer agreements and when they sold technology, the sale was seen as a last resort by which a market could be maintained. Often firms who were exporting a product to the Soviet Union were approached by Soviet officials to enter into industrial cooperation agreements in order to produce that product in the USSR. Entering into such agreements was the strategy to stay in the market in the face of competition eager and willing to sell production technology and thus potentially capture the market. For example, one firm foresaw that Soviet authorities would try to limit hard-currency outflow for the import of its products. Therefore, the company envisioned a three-step procedure for easing in the sale of technology.

For this firm, straight sales continued as long as possible. When the Soviets attempted to negotiate a joint venture, the Western firm at first limited the venture to sales, marketing, and distribution. Once Soviet pressure mounted for the acquisition of production technology, the company agreed to an assembly operation, or "screwdriver factory," stipulating that parts and components would be shipped from the West for local assembly. This eventually led to local manufacture with several parts and key components still delivered entirely from the West. All sourcing decisions were made in the West; local suppliers were not used if at all possible. One reason cited for this, of course, is the difficulty of obtaining local supplies due to weak or distorted economic linkages.

This strategy of setting up assembly operations led to problems, as the Soviets themselves pushed for the acquisition of foreign production technology. For example, in a U.S.-Swiss-Soviet petrochemical refining joint venture, Applied Engineering Systems, the Soviets accused their Western partners of refusing to provide technology to manufacture the entire product in the USSR because the Western firms could make more profit by exporting parts to the Soviet Union. Because of this dispute, the Soviets threatened to withdraw from the joint venture.[86]

When Western firms were motivated to *create* a market in the Soviet Union, under the new joint venture laws, they indicated that they were more willing to sell technology first, in order to "hook" the buyer into the firm's product line or gain an entrance into other sectors. This required an active stance toward the sale of technology and an aggressive marketing strategy. One electronics firm, for example, entered into an agreement for cooperation in R and D. The motivation cited was to increase the compatibility of systems in order to open up opportunities for expanded sales of its products and to close sales to other Western firms selling similar but incompatible items. Hyundai Corporation of

South Korea, for example, argued in principle to build a $5 million soap factory in Russia in order to make it easier to get permission from the local authorities to build a ship repair center and to participate in the development of Siberian woods and coal mines.[87]

No matter what the motivation, the chief goal was to sell products within the local economy, not to build a platform in the region to compete in global markets. Western corporations would thus only contribute their production technology to this effort if it were necessary to thwart both Western and Soviet competitors *within* the Soviet market. Product sales were continued as long as possible in order to maximize earnings from sales before a cooperative production agreement was negotiated. All corporate officials claimed that selling technology did not halt product exports to the Soviet Union but actually stimulated exports in the long run.

Four contractual stipulations worked to ensure that the agreement boosted product sales and that the most advanced production technology was not transferred. First, what corporate executives call the "core technology," or the key production components, were generally not included in the contract. This meant that the joint enterprise would continue to *import* the key components that embodied the technologies of interest to the local enterprises. This was particularly true when the Western partner was a vertically integrated firm that made not only production tools but also the final products produced with them. These firms would not sell the proprietary production technology to others who could compete with their own end-products. The sale of technology actually triggered the joint venture's *dependence* on the Western firm's inputs. One executive from a large vertically integrated multinational corporation reported that his firm stipulated that the joint venture must purchase critical components from company factories in the West. In this way, the firm could boost sales and improve its market position within the Soviet Union.

Second, Western companies who actually sold "strong" technologies, i.e., technologies at the beginning of the product cycle that were unique and highly competitive, were able to stipulate in their contracts that the joint venture would obtain the technology in its current stage of development and that no improvements would be passed on. If they were selling weaker technologies, they often agreed to pass on technological improvements. But when they did, they contractually terminated the transfer of improvements two to three years before the contract ended.

Thus the buyer was not informed of the latest technological developments of the product at the time of contract expiration. Corporate officials reported that their own past experience indicated that the local
enterprise managers would not generally upgrade the equipment they
imported because there was no incentive to do so.

Third, companies selling strong technologies usually pressed for contracts of short duration, i.e., two to three years. In this way, no improvements needed to be passed on. Longer contracts (five to twenty years)
were negotiated only in those product lines in which technology was stable and improvements were developed slowly. These long-term agreements were usually made with industries in the primary sector.

Finally, company executives reported that when they sold production
technologies, they feared little domestic competition or third markets
from other domestic enterprises that might imitate the innovation. In
other words, they had no fear of technology diffusion, an effect that was
weak in the Soviet Union. This is especially true if the contract was of
short duration. Western firms often sold technologies produced for a
different user in their own country, and it takes time to adapt a technology developed in one setting to the precise needs of another. Many crucial high-technology products are customized or developed for niche
markets. Most high-technology products are developed through numerous iterations and in close communication with the user. If, for example, a Soviet enterprise bought a specific machine tool from a Western
producer, it would often find itself with a product that was designed for
different customers. The needs of the Soviet user would be different
from those of Western users who adapted the machine in collaboration
with the designers and engineers within an entirely different production organization than that of the user. It is likely that the Western
machine tool would not perfectly fit the task in the local plant, and
therefore its effectiveness in increasing productivity would be reduced.
It was not simply a question of placing new production tools in old factories; some executives argued that the factory must be reorganized
around the production processes that the new technologies opened. As
I discussed earlier, local enterprises were and continue to be reluctant
to pursue the kind of reorganization necessary to use Western technologies effectively.

These interview results point to a central problem that arose in past
technology transfer agreements and is likely to arise in future ones:
Western firm strategies and contractual stipulations actually inhibit the

stimulation of linkages and technological spillovers. When key components are imported or withheld, the local enterprises are denied the capacity to control new advances in design and production, and thus potentially connected industries have little incentive to innovate. Some of the interviewees in vertically integrated Western firms indicated that it would not be to their advantage to make available to the importer technological advances that would threaten their share of the market for their own end-products. The evidence suggests that the kind of technical know-how that does not move through product market channels was rarely transferred from Western firms to the Soviet Union, and Western manufacturing facilities in the Soviet Union were at least a generation behind state-of-the-art facilities in the West.

There are a number of crucial differences between *these* strategies and the strategies pursued by Western corporations that transferred technology contributing to the economic development of Korea and Taiwan. Most important, Western corporate strategy in the 1970s was aimed, not at maintaining or improving a market share within those countries, but at producing goods for *export* back to the home market. At first blush, this difference in strategy would appear to make little difference to the outcome: goods produced were in the mature or standardized phase of the product cycle, and the production technologies initially transferred to the Asian newly industrializing countries (NICs) were not state-of-the-art. Only after the technology was proven and its costs reduced through learning and scale economics in the Western market was it transferred abroad.

Nonetheless, because they were building export platforms rather than simply thinking about local market share, Western firms transferred entire *production systems* to these countries in order to produce goods that would be competitive on world markets. The transfer of an entire production system enables a more efficient technology transfer than the sale of some parts of the system and not others. In Korea and Taiwan, these systems were often upgraded by local engineers; these engineers were able to improve their own skill base through participation in the foreign production system. In contrast, Western firms selling technology to the Soviet Union, although sometimes selling entire production systems, often held back key components, and the systems were seldom upgraded by local engineers or production workers.[88] Despite an initial spurt of "turn-key plant" purchases in the early 1970s, the Soviets themselves resisted the purchase of entire production systems.

The initiative for the channeling of foreign investment was also rooted in the priorities and policies of the developmental state. In Korea, the Foreign Capital Inducement Law of 1965 and its revisions required that a certain percentage of production be targeted for export, and restricted foreign investment in sectors where domestic firms could be competitive on world markets.[89] Also, in both Korea and Taiwan, developmental states enforced domestic content requirements, thereby *creating* backward and forward economic linkages with foreign plants, integrating the Western contribution into the national supply and production system. When such linkages are created, the technology—imported within a particular production system—has a widespread economic impact on users and suppliers.[90] There is little evidence even in the post-Soviet economies of the region that the necessary linkages could be created.

It is likely that these same corporate strategies will continue and intensify in the post-Soviet future. As state control over the economy recedes, there are few actors who have both the interest and the ability to promote the development of *productive* capacities in the local economies. The cases of Korea and Taiwan suggest that external economic actors will not, by themselves, compel industrial transformation based on innovative technologies. That kind of transformation is a function of state-directed development policies and a receptive domestic economic environment. Foreign investors in the post-Soviet Russian economy have found it impossible to operate independently of the conglomerates discussed above, which control the supply of materials and manage barter arrangements in order to extract profits. Foreign corporations, then, continue to work with those conglomerates, not to supply productive technology that would contribute to economic development, but to sell their goods in domestic markets and extract raw materials in order to enhance the complex system of barter that is emerging.[91]

Conclusion

A Soviet economy enriched with Western technology was of concern to economic nationalists who worried about Western trade vulnerability. Their assessments, however, often confused the *goals* of Soviet technology acquisition policy with actual policy *outcomes*. They assumed that if the Soviet Union engaged in a massive effort to acquire Western technology, the effort would be successful. As we have seen, this assumption was unwarranted on two counts. First, new technology, whether domestic or imported, is only one factor contributing to the economic growth of any country. And there are major theoretical and methodological problems involved in any attempt to separate out the contribution of Western technology to Soviet economic performance from other factors that actually may have had more impact. Policy debates did not take into account these problems and assumed vulnerability without specifying what it would take to make the West vulnerable through commercial technology exports.

Second, the successful application of technology within any country depends on the extent to which the technology and its positive effects can be diffused throughout an industry, sector, or the economy as a whole. As represented in the political debate, vulnerability arguments assumed that the purchase of foreign high-technology goods would have spillover and diffusion effects, spurring the importer to innovate in related products and processes. But there is much debate over the process of technology diffusion and the conditions under which it will succeed; future debates over economic vulnerability in international relations must take diffusion effects into account. The success of commercial technology transfer depends on the nation's industrial structure and whether that structure provides for strong linkages among related industries through which the positive effects of innovation can spread.

In sum, this chapter began with a survey of data employed to measure the impact of Western technology on the Soviet economy and technological level of Soviet industry through the mid-1980s. If that data had shown that Western technology enhanced Soviet industrial productivity, released resources to the military sector, and contributed to a narrowing of the technology gap, we could argue that vulnerability was present, even if not especially high. What the available measures show is that, although foreign technology imports may have allowed the Soviets to use their scarce resources more efficiently in isolated industries and particular factories, those imports could not overcome the detrimental effects on the economy of factor shortages, economic inefficiencies, and the dependency-creating effects of Western corporate strategy. Even though key Soviet industries importing Western technology through new modes of technology transfer may have been more productive than they would have been without those imports, their technological levels were well behind those same industries in the West. And none of the evidence surveyed could support the argument that Eastern acquisition of

Western technology narrowed the gap between those technological levels. Soviet policies of Western technology acquisition did not appear to have affected the lag, since it remained constant, even after imports had increased. And contrary to an important claim of the vulnerability thesis, licensing of U.S. technology to the Soviet Union did not result in the erosion of the Western technology lead.

The discussion of Western corporate strategy in the former Soviet Union suggests the near-term future will be little different from the past. We can therefore conclude that because Western technology did not make a decisive contribution to Soviet industrial strength, Western vulnerability to the *indirect* effects of technology trade with the Soviet Union was low throughout the 1980s, and will continue to be low through the 1990s and beyond. The recent evidence presented here suggests that if direct foreign investment continues to flow into the former USSR (assuming markets become stable), economic relations between the former Soviet Union and the West in the 1990s may in many ways replicate the features of the czarist-Western relations in the nineteenth and early twentieth centuries.

Recall that under Count Sergei Witte, czarist Russia's industries were supported by direct foreign investment. Timothy Luke has persuasively argued that during this period, foreign firms retained considerable decision-making power in the Russian economy. In particular, they controlled technological resources, managed by their own experts for the firm's corporate interests. Luke suggests that Russia's technological dependence on these firms actually inhibited economic development. Both firm strategy and Russian trade policy focused on the export of raw materials, food, and semi-manufactured goods, rather than the export of advanced manufactured products, and the Russian economy came to be characterized by its dependence on the continuing influx of foreign technology.[92] By 1913 a small Russian technical intelligentsia had emerged, but there were proportionally more foreign-born technical personnel than any other profession. Therefore, Luke argues, by not undertaking the costs of domestic innovation, czarist Russia missed out on the key long-term benefits that domestic innovation brings: the creation of a domestic pool of scientific, engineering, and technical know-how.

Because a technologically proficient intelligentsia did not develop, indigenous innovation was slowed down, and because the locus of innovative activity remained outside the country, Russia's economic development was inhibited. Russia was thus situated in a disadvantageous position in the global division of labor as a producer of raw materials and importer of manufactured goods. The Soviet government exacerbated this situation by instituting central planning and virtually withdrawing from the world economy. The lesson may be that a nation cannot simply purchase foreign high-technology products over a long period of time without running the risk of losing the capability to innovate domestically.

4

Western Technology
and Soviet Military Power

In the spring of 1987 the Reagan administration disclosed what it considered to be one of the most serious security breaches of the postwar era: a subsidiary of the Toshiba Corporation had sold powerful submarine-quieting technology to the Soviet Union. The sale was blamed for undermining America's anti-submarine warfare advances and threatening Western security at sea. It was a bold violation of the rules of COCOM, the multilateral export control regime, and was widely publicized as a clear-cut example of what can happen when lax export restraints permit what Reagan administration officials called the "hemorrhaging of Western high technology." Secretary of State George Shultz called the Toshiba affair the most serious incident affecting U.S.-Japan relations since 1945.

In June 1990 the Bush administration denied a license to U.S. West, Inc. to build a fiber-optic cable communications system across the Soviet Union. The proposed cable was to link the Soviet Union, Japan, and Europe for civilian phone service and business data communications. Opposition to the project was based on the fear that a transfer of fiber-optic telecommunication technology to the Soviet Union would threaten the security of the United States, because it would impair the ability of the United States to monitor Soviet military communications. Current Soviet communications systems rely heavily on microwave beams that can be tapped by Western satellites. Fiber-optic cables, on the other hand, are more secure and are even less vulnerable to electromagnetic pulses from a possible nuclear blast. Fiber-optic cables in the hands of the Soviets, opponents feared, would impair the West's ability to destroy the USSR's communications system in the event of a war.[1]

In February 1991 reports of Western participation in Iraq's acquisition of weapons of mass destruction led the Bush administration to announce that, for the first time, it would restrict all exports of manufacturing facilities, plant designs, and processing equipment associated with the manufacture of chemical and biological weapons. All goods—even vehicles and office equipment—that might be destined for weapons facilities would require an export license. The export of fifty chemicals used in the manufacture of chemical weapons would be restricted—even those used to make fertilizer and flame retardants.

These incidents illustrate the economic nationalist's view of the most dangerous effects of technology exodus: the export of dual-use technologies to the Soviet adversary, which can endanger Western security by closing the military technology gap and negating the effects of the West's advanced military systems. The vulnerability thesis raises two concerns with regard to the direct impact of Western technology on a potential adversary's military power. First, it claims that Western technology can upgrade or introduce specific weapons systems into the adversary's arsenal—like chemical, biological, and nuclear weapons—which can increase the military threat. There are those who claim, for example, that Soviet development of nuclear weapons was dependent on the illegal acquisition of U.S. nuclear "secrets."[2]

Second, economic nationalists argue that "dual-use" production technology will be employed in the defense sector to upgrade weapons capabilities. It is widely acknowledged, for example, that Iraq's ability to produce weapons of mass destruction were bought from the West. With regard to the Soviet case, economic nationalists argue that even if the transfer of commercial technology has done little to enhance the health of the Soviet economy, the transfer of dual-use technologies can increase Western vulnerability if these technologies find their way into the military sector. This is because the military can more effectively utilize Western technology than the civilian sector; it is more highly developed with more resources devoted to it.[3] The most frequently cited case in this regard is the legal purchase of 164 Bryant Centalign grinders in 1972, which were allegedly used to produce components to upgrade the accuracy of Soviet ICBM guidance systems deployed in 1975.[4] Both of these claims support the argument that as technology acquisition efforts increase, the military technology gap will close, and exporters will be forced to spend more on defense, simply to keep ahead.

If we apply the criteria of the exporter vulnerability thesis to an assessment of the contribution of Western technology to Soviet military power, two related questions are paramount: first, what direct contribution did Western technology make to Soviet military strength in the 1980s, both to weapons capabilities and to the strengthening of the military production base? Second, how effective was the Western strategic export embargo during the 1970s and 1980s?

In this chapter, I examine historical patterns of Soviet acquisition of foreign defense technology, acquisition of both the design of specific weapons systems and defense production technology. I then look specifically at the technology gap with regard to those developing and deployed technologies claimed to provide a strategic advantage in future warfare. These are the same technologies that were said to be the target of Soviet acquisition efforts. Was the gap closing? And what was the contribution of Western technology to its size? Third, I examine the effectiveness of the COCOM regime in the 1980s by focusing on its changing degree of legitimacy among its members. Finally, I turn to an assessment of Western vulnerability in the 1987 case of Toshiba's illegal export of strategic submarine-quieting technology to the Soviet Union.

Soviet Patterns of Foreign Military Technology Acquisition

In the 1920s the new Soviet government found that it had inherited a fairly strong arms production industry. This industry had developed important ties with Western European arms producers.[5] A shortage of trained engineers led the Soviet state to directly adopt foreign designs for more advanced weapons systems, such as aircraft and engines. By 1930, for example, most of the 900 Soviet planes were copied from foreign models, but during the 1930s the Soviets began to purchase licenses from Western European and American aircraft firms in order to introduce more advanced production methods. By the end of the decade, however, design changes in these production technologies were required, because unskilled Soviet workers could not learn to use the more sophisticated production techniques. In fact, design changes were always required to adapt Western production methods to the simpler Soviet production technology.

This pattern was repeated with the development of tanks. First foreign licenses were acquired in the early 1930s. At the same time, the Soviets attempted to develop an independent design capability. Foreign production capability was significantly modified to meet Soviet specifications and, over time, original Soviet versions of foreign designs evolved. British tanks were purchased in the early 1930s and modified over time to become the Soviet T34 tank, which was highly successful in World War II. Much the same pattern developed in the Soviet shipbuilding industry.

In the postwar development of missiles, jet aircraft, and radar, domestic research programs introduced before and during the war were accelerated by the introduction of Western technology. But in all of these areas, Soviet self-reliance was achieved by the early 1950s. To a much lesser extent this is also true of Soviet development of nuclear weapons technology. The Soviets were leaders in nuclear physics at the onset of the war, and accelerated R-and-D efforts after 1945. American technology acquired through intelligence channels may have speeded up that effort by about a year if at all.[6]

A clear pattern emerges in all of these cases—a pattern that diverges significantly from that established in the civilian economy. The Soviets have been dependent on foreign technology in early stages of weapons development, and throughout the postwar period Western technology was always integrated into an independent Soviet R-and-D program. Western designs were always modified to meet Soviet specifications, and later original weapons designs and production technologies evolved.

Given this pattern, one would expect fairly long time lags between the introduction of an advanced weapons system in the West and the introduction of the Soviet version, which was generally the case. For example, the Boeing 747 was introduced in 1969 and the Soviet version, the Il-76, was introduced in 1976. The Sidewinder air-to-air missile was developed in 1953, and the Soviet version, the AA-2 Atoll, was introduced in the early 1960s. The Law M72 anti-tank weapon was in production in the U.S. in 1962 and the Soviet counterpart, the RPG-18, was not introduced until the early 1980s.[7] What is significant, however, is that all of these advances were achieved through *imitation* rather than import of Western technology. And the long time lags between Western and Soviet introduction of these systems reduced the Western vulnerability that might otherwise have resulted.

The one example in which it is claimed that Western security was directly threatened by legal technology exports is the case of the ball-bearing-production technology transfer mentioned above. Certainly a

Western contribution to the development of more accurate Soviet nuclear weapons would enhance Soviet first-strike capability and be a clear case of the kind of vulnerability that technology exodus can trigger. In fact, however, the claims in this case were grossly exaggerated. Direct connections between the technology transfer and the missile deployment were never established; similar technology was available from other foreign sources, and the technological level of the Soviet defense industry was high enough to have enabled the Soviets to produce the bearings independently. Indeed, most analysts argue that the grinders were purchased too late to have made a difference in the Soviet fourth-generation missiles.[8]

In the 1980s the Reagan administration issued a new onslaught of charges that the USSR was dangerously enhancing its military power with the aid of Western technology. In 1985 the U.S. Department of Defense claimed that "Warsaw Pact exploitation of Western technology has saved them billions of dollars, drastically reduced their weapons development times, greatly enhanced their defense industrial productivity, and allowed quick Warsaw Pact response to Western weapons and tactics."[9]

Most information used to back this claim, however, rested on evidence of Soviet *acquisition* of Western technology rather than on evidence of the actual employment of that technology in the defense sector. For example, the CIA's influential 1983 study, *Soviet Acquisition of Western Technology*, focused *only* on the ways in which the Soviets succeeded in acquiring Western technology "by blending acquisitions legally and illegally acquired by differing government organizations."[10] It argued that the Soviet Union devoted vast amounts of its financial and manpower resources to the acquisition of Western technology that would enhance its military power and improve the efficiency of its military manufacturing technology in the 1980s.

This study's conclusions that the USSR had begun a systematic effort to acquire Western military technology were bolstered by the 1985 "Farewell" affair in France in which a KGB official provided documents to demonstrate how the Soviet Military Industrial Commission (VPK) acquired significant Western military technology. This case was used as evidence in the 1985 update of *Soviet Acquisition of Western Technology* to argue that the Soviet technology acquisition program "accords top priority to the military and military-related industry, and major attention is also given to the civilian sectors of Soviet industry that support military

production."[11] In 1987 a study by the National Academy of Sciences (NAS) argued that "the Soviet technology acquisition effort was massive, well financed, and frequently effective."[12] The 1988 Defense Department report, *Soviet Military Power*, stated that "although much of the technology acquired from the West has been gained through entirely legal means, the Soviets are gathering significant amounts of information through surreptitious and illegal means. As a result of aggressive exploitation and pursuit of technology wherever available, the Soviets are rapidly achieving higher levels of capability within their military forces with a consequent impact upon the military balance."[13]

Did these acquisitions bolster Soviet military power? Did they increase the West's vulnerability to the Soviet military threat? As we have seen, information on technology acquisitions alone is not evidence of the impact of Western technology on Soviet military strength. Intentions are not the same as capabilities acquired with Western technology. One way to address these questions, then, is to examine evidence on whether the gap between the U.S. and the USSR narrowed in those military technologies that the USSR targeted for acquisition.

Technology Transfer and the Size of the Military Technology "Gap"

Recall that gaps are usually measured by comparing the years in which certain key technologies are employed in industry and weaponry in leading and trailing states. As argued in chapter 3, however, measures of the gap tell us nothing about the contribution of Western technology to its size. A narrowing of the gap may be due to rapid Soviet advances in defense innovation, as well as a slowdown in Western defense technology innovation. Many American officials, however, claimed throughout the 1980s that both the overall military technology gap was narrowed and that it was narrowed through Soviet acquisition of Western technology. The 1985 CIA study cited above stated that the Soviets were able to "narrow the Western lead in nearly all key technological areas, particularly microelectronics." The study tacitly linked this assertion with Soviet technology acquisitions from the West by stating that the Soviets had achieved great success "in supplementing their military research and manufacturing capabilities and in narrowing the technology gap with the West, thereby eroding the technological superiority on which U.S. and Allied security depends."[14] Surprisingly, the report did not show

how or even *if* the technology gap was narrowed. Nor did it present evidence that Western technology contributed to the gap's size.

Evidence on the size does exist, however, that disputes the arguments of economic nationalists and the claims of the authoritative 1985 CIA study, *Soviet Acquisition of Western Technology: An Update.* Throughout the 1980s the Department of Defense issued a series of reports on the control of technology transfer that compared Soviet and U.S. capabilities in those high-technology areas that had the potential to change military capabilities over a period of ten to twenty years. With only slight variation, they are the same technologies that the CIA reported as targets of USSR technology acquisition efforts.

The technologies examined in those reports were chosen because they had the potential to significantly change military capability in the next ten to twenty years. These technologies would enhance the performance of existing weapons systems, provide new military capabilities, strengthen the industrial base, and contribute to the availability, dependability, reliability, and affordability of weapons' systems.

By comparing the CIA and DOD reports, we are able to see that they essentially deal with the same technologies that are targets of the USSR's technology acquisition efforts.[15] They are technologies that increase missile speed and accuracy (propulsion, guidance, and navigation) and enhance ballistic missile defense and are related to the Strategic Defense Initiative (electro-optical sensors, signal processing, signature reduction, telecommunications, and super minicomputers, sensors that are part of Homing Interceptor Technology, and directed energy), and ASW (submarine detection). They are also related to C3I (telecommunications, including fiber optics, signal processing, VHSIC, and optics) and stealth technology (aerodynamics and signature reduction). Other technologies chosen for comparison are those that enhance biological and chemical warfare capabilities (life sciences, including genetic engineering and conventional warheads with chemical explosives).

Secretary of Defense Caspar Weinberger noted in his 1984 report to Congress on the technology transfer control program that in fifteen out of twenty military critical technologies in the experimental stage (those that promise to provide a strategic military advantage) the U.S. had a significant technological lead. In the remaining five, the U.S. and the USSR were equal, but the U.S. was gaining a lead.

Similar reports issued in 1985 and 1986, however, did not compare U.S. and Soviet capabilities in these technologies. The next set of offi-

cial comparisons came in the 1987 issue of *Soviet Military Power*, which reported that the West led the Soviets in sixteen military critical technology areas; the USSR was equal to the West in three, and the USSR was a world leader in one type of specialized power system, magnetohydrodynamic power generation.[16] The 1988 edition of *Soviet Military Power* was more pessimistic. It argued that "the technological advantages enjoyed by the West have been threatened if not eroded."[17] It reported a Soviet lead in a number of military technology areas: certain areas of pulsed-power technology used in the development of laser weapons and other high-powered weapons and sensors, radio frequency, charged-particle-beam-directed energy sources, and some composite materials R-and-D and processing techniques. The U.S. and the USSR were reported as being equal in laser technology, but in all other military high-technology areas, the U.S. was reported as being ahead.[18]

In 1988, in recognition of the United States' declining lead vis-à-vis its allies in many high technology areas, Congress passed legislation requiring the Department of Defense to compare the technological position of the U.S. with both the Soviet Union *and* America's allies. The first edition of this report issued in 1989 disputed some of the more pessimistic claims of the previous year's *Soviet Military Power*. It stated that the Soviets were only "on par" with the United States in pulsed-laser technology, although they possessed a "significant lead" in specific important aspects of the technology. Furthermore, the USSR was on par with the United States in hypervelocity projectiles and biotechnology, but they were generally lagging in composite materials technology. In all other technologies, the United States had a clear, if not growing lead.[19]

The 1990 edition of this report cited only one military technology area in which the Soviets held a clear advantage: pulsed-laser technology. The USSR continued to be on par with the United States in some areas of materials technology and in undersea acoustic research and integration of remote sensing data.[20] From an examination of these reports, then, it would appear that the U.S. lead over the Soviets in areas of military critical high technologies was growing, not diminishing, throughout the 1980s.

The gap also widened in favor of the United States in deployed military systems. In 1988 the USSR led in six; the U.S. and the USSR were equal in ten, and the U.S. was superior in fifteen.[21] A comparison with 1982 data shows that this lead grew during those six years. In 1982 the DOD reported that the U.S. led in only twelve deployed systems, the

U.S. and the USSR were equal in eleven, and the USSR was superior in six.[22] A 1981 Department of Defense report asserted that the Soviets had reduced the U.S. lead in virtually every important military technology.[23]

The comparisons published in these reports do not conform to the predictions of the vulnerability thesis that the technology gap would close with increased Soviet acquisition of Western technology. The critical issue, however, is the contribution of Western technology to the gap's size. Would the gap be larger without the acquisition of Western technology? Is Western technology responsible for the narrowing of the gap in those areas where the Western lead is said to be declining? Did the West have to spend more on defense to stay ahead because the Soviets were subsidized with Western technology?

None of the available evidence shows that Western technology contributed to a potential closing of the gap in those areas in which the Soviets were ahead or on a par with the U.S. Nor has it been demonstrated that Soviet imports of Western technology subsidized Soviet defense spending and caused the West to spend more. This kind of evidence would be necessary to support economic nationalists' vulnerability claims. The two CIA reports cited above provide examples of Western technology benefits to Soviet research projects.[24] But they do not provide estimates of the contribution of Western technology to the size of the technology gap or of the costs to the U.S. of staying ahead.

Furthermore, the Department of Defense reports that compared the technological positions of the United States and the Soviet Union clearly stated that Soviet leads in certain technological areas were due primarily to indigenous Soviet efforts. For example, the 1987 edition of *Soviet Military Power* states that "the Soviets have a significant R and D effort committed to developing specialized power systems for military applications, including all types of directed energy weapons, high-power radars, and jamming systems. Soviet physicists have made major accomplishments in magnetocumulative generation R and D as well as in areas such as thermionics and inductive stores."[25] The 1988 edition of the report states that "many of the world's high-power radio frequency and high-power microwave sources were developed by the Soviets and they lead the West in this area."[26] *All of the studies admitted that, where the Soviets had obtained a lead, no links to the acquisition of Western technology could be found.* The 1987 NAS study even went so far as to state that Soviet acquisition of Western technology "may have resulted in maintaining or perhaps even widening their lag due to dependence on generally outdated Western equipment and technology."[27] It concluded that the huge influx of Western technology documented by the CIA and DOD reports on Soviet acquisition of Western technology would not enable the USSR to substantially reduce the current gap as long as the West continued its own rapid pace of innovation.

In sum, the evidence on the direct contribution of Western technology to Soviet military power indicated that, measured by time lags in the development of similar weaponry and the size of the military technology gap, Western vulnerability through technology exodus was not high in the 1980s. And the official claims of high vulnerability remain unsupported. In light of massive Soviet illegal technology acquisition efforts (and lesser efforts to acquire technology through legal trade channels), we would expect the military technology gap to have been closing. Yet the West appeared to be years ahead of the USSR in its development of important military technologies. Historically the Soviets had acquired foreign technology in early stages of weapons development, but it had taken time to modify that technology to Soviet specifications. Meanwhile, innovation in the West created new "gaps" that need to be filled. Exports of dual-use technologies had made little difference in the Soviet case. All of this speaks directly to the question of the effectiveness of the Western strategic embargo. Was the embargo responsible for maintaining and even increasing the military technology gap between the Soviet Union and the West?

The Effectiveness of the Western Embargo

The vulnerability thesis claims that, with the rise of dual-use technologies and the even greater ease of international technology transfer, the embargo effort would become increasingly unsuccessful. The CIA reported that "the worldwide diffusion of advanced products and high technology . . . clearly has increased Soviet collection opportunities."[28] The study strongly suggests that because much of the technology acquired by the Soviets had been acquired through espionage, trade diversion, scientific conferences, and the acquisition of unclassified scientific documents, the control efforts of the 1970s were ineffective because they restricted only trade in machinery, equipment, and technical data and did not restrict other kinds of technology transfer.[29]

The technical case for an embargo's effectiveness or ineffectiveness, however, is difficult to make. As we have seen, technological progress and widening or narrowing technology gaps were primarily due to domestic innovative capabilities, not technology transfers. Even if Western technology was of minimal importance in ensuring Soviet military might in the 1980s, we cannot assume that the Western multilateral embargo was successful with regard to both what it restricted and how well it enforced those restrictions. An examination of cases in which dual-use technology was transferred but made little difference to Soviet military potential could support the argument that it is the Soviets' lack of success in assimilating, diffusing, and using Western technology rather than the Western embargo that prevented Western vulnerability in the face of technology exodus.

The assessment of the embargo's effectiveness becomes even more difficult when we consider changes in the mode of technology transfer. The vulnerability thesis predicts that the rise in dual-use technologies and industrial cooperation permits new modes of technology transfer that were not restricted by national export controls or the multilateral control regime. If the Soviets were able to successfully employ *legally* acquired Western technology in order to increase their military power, we must ask whether the Western embargo was restricting the export of the wrong technology or not restricting enough. To evaluate the embargo's success in this context we would need to understand the relationship between Soviet economic and military growth and activities of specialists attached to embassy staffs, Soviet and Eastern European attendance at scientific conferences where information on dual-use technologies was available, Soviet access to Western technical literature, and long-term training contracts. Given the difficulty of collecting this kind of data and the multiplicity of causes for enhanced or declining military power, obtaining such measures of an embargo's effectiveness is not feasible.

The assessment is thus necessarily a political one and focuses instead on the strength and stability of the Western multilateral embargo regime. The analysis in chapter 2 suggests that the increasing ease of international dual-use technology transfer would make embargo efforts—both unilateral and multilateral—less effective. As we saw in chapter 1, and as we shall see shortly, the U.S. response to that belief was to increase its own unilateral governmental controls over technology transfer and to pressure its allies to do the same, so that private firms—the agents of technology transfer—could be reined in.

The consequence of this effort to unilaterally consolidate state control over dual-use high-technology markets was political conflict between the United States and its allies. That conflict threatened to make the regime less effective by reducing its legitimacy, which in turn increased the chances of cheating on the part of private firms. Let us now consider the political disputes that emerged among COCOM in the 1970s and 1980s, assessing COCOM's effectiveness and the sources of its effectiveness, and then examine the Toshiba incident in terms of both vulnerability claims and the political debates surrounding the vulnerability arguments.

High-Technology Trade in the 1970s and 1980s

In chapter 1 I argued that unresolved vulnerability claims led to an ongoing tension between the United States and Europe in East-West trade. That tension was exacerbated by the prominence of different institutions in Europe and the U.S. leading policy formulation, and by coercieve strategies on the part of the United States to extract compliance. Even during the Cold War thaw and detente, U.S. decision makers continued in their uncomprising belief in the vulnerability thesis, while Europeans clung to liberal views and relentlessly expanded their non-strategic trade with the East. While trade between the superpowers remained stagnant, trade between Western Europe and the countries of the Warsaw Pact increased dramatically;[30] U.S. officials were determined to halt it, as high-technology trade emerged in the 1970s as an issue in the Western alliance. To gain the allies' compliance with a broad-based embargo, the U.S. as the dominant power pursued the strategies discussed in chapter 2: offering rewards for cooperation, threatening punishment for noncooperation, and all the while attempting to persuade its allies that the American view of vulnerability should provide the basis for regime norms.

First, the United States enticed Europeans to comply with its own policies by offering rewards for strict controls. It was the Carter administration's policy to share technology in order to persuade the Western European allies to tighten their export control policies. Second, the U.S. reserved the right to impose extraterritorial export controls on goods manufactured abroad with its technology; this involved sanctions on sales by foreign subsidiaries of American companies and independent foreign companies that used products, components, services, and technology of American origin. While administration officials preferred the use of the former, they were not adverse to using such extraterritorial sanctions if multilateral efforts failed.

Third, U.S. officials tried to reason with COCOM members. Using the logic of the vulnerability thesis, they argued that more dual-use technologies should come under the Western embargo, that technology should be more broadly defined, and that the vehicles of technology transfer—multinational corporations—should be more strictly controlled. Because more and more high technologies had military significance, a broader range of technologies, called military-critical technologies, should be restricted.

In 1979 an 800-page "military-critical technologies list" was drawn up by the Pentagon that included: 1) high technologies that when applied to existing military or weapons systems improve upon them; 2) high technologies that could lead to the development of military or weapons systems; and 3) high technologies that could make existing non-weapons systems into military or weapons systems.[31] In short, they listed technologies that have increasingly important military consequences, as military environments have expanded and as weapons systems have become more integrated. The Defense Department urged COCOM members to adopt the approach taken in the list as a basis for the COCOM embargo.

Furthermore, the U.S. argued that the definition of technology should be expanded from simple machinery, equipment, and technical data to include knowledge, skill, and information, as well as industrial goods. And, finally, the U.S. pushed for COCOM control over certain "active" technology-transfer mechanisms, such as joint ventures, turnkey plants, and long-term technical training. In short, based on vulnerability claims, the U.S. was asking its allies to control all forms of industrial cooperation with the Soviet Union and its allies, and to restrict the kinds of production, marketing, and research agreements necessary to carry on normal economic relations with the East in much the same way it had done in the early Cold War period.

In fact, it was disagreement over these very issues that threatened to further erode the legitimacy of the embargo regime in the eyes of other members and thus lead to more violations of COCOM rules. The 1979 review of the list of embargoed items saw the U.S. and Europe sharply divided on three issues. First, European members and Japan argued that technology should continue to be narrowly defined as "machinery and transport equipment." Second, they rejected the "critical technologies" approach and refused to restrict "active" technology-transfer mechanisms. Finally, they sharply opposed the extraterritorial application of American export controls. To avoid U.S. extraterritorial controls, Europeans began to bypass American components by "designing them out" of their own products.[32] This became increasingly easy to do as U.S. technological dominance declined.

As the 1980s began, the debate over the source and scope of vulnerability and related technology-control norms further weakened support for a broad embargo. Requests for exceptions to the embargo list grew rapidly and there seemed to be little uniformity with regard to the interpretation of COCOM rules.[33] Most important, there was little consensus about what constituted a dangerous dual-use technology transfer and whether and how dual-use technologies would be controlled. Critics pointed out that the COCOM list was kept secret, not only because of the strategic sensitivity of the embargoed items, but also because "some of the items are so archaic that revealing their inclusion on the list would expose the COCOM authorities to ridicule."[34] Out-of-date embargo lists tempted business to ignore them altogether and thus made the task of enforcement daunting. In this acrimonious policy-making environment, both intential and unintentional violations and diversion were bound to proliferate.

The 1982 list review opened in the midst of tension over these issues, but the meeting concluded with a set of compromises. Although Europeans continued to balk at the "critical technologies approach," they did agree to embargo "high-priority items" containing technologies that U.S. officials deemed critical. These included materials, optics and sensors, floating docks, spacecraft and space launch vehicles, computers, and telecommunications.[35] COCOM further moved to strengthen enforcement measures; national governments were responsible for enforcing COCOM decisions but a subcommittee on enforcement established in the 1950s to pool information on possible violations of the embargo was revitalized.[36]

At home, however, the Reagan administration found little resistance to its arguments for tighter technology-export controls. To halt what it considered the "hemorrhaging" of high technology, the administration and many in Congress tried to bolt the door to U.S. technology exports even tighter with unilateral restrictions. Assistant Secretary of Defense Richard Perle claimed that the elaborate Soviet technology-collection effort in the mid-1970s had resulted in a "quantitative improvement of Soviet strategic and conventional military forces based on Western technology in the midst of a massive quantitative buildup."[37] Under Reagan, for the first time, the Defense Department was permitted to scrutinize domestic industry's R and D for possible militarily significant commercial technologies, and government approval was required for publication of even *unclassified* scientific research with potential military application. Government sanctions on foreign participation in scientific conferences held in the United States were imposed, and a much broader application of U.S. extraterritorial export controls took effect.[38]

Under renewed pressure from the Reagan administration, COCOM members accepted a more stringent set of controls on dual-use technologies to be withheld from sales to Eastern Europe in 1984. These restrictions were designed in part to halt the export of large computers and sophisticated software. In order to ensure continued acceptance of these more stringent controls, COCOM established a military advisory committee. And to further ensure acceptance, a major Department of Defense directive issued under President Reagan stated that the department would "facilitate" sharing of military technology "only with allies and other nations" that "cooperate effectively" in safeguarding that technology from potential adversaries.[39] The pattern was thus repeated: coercive measures by the U.S. were continued in order to extract compliance with regime norms, but little consensus on the validity of those norms was reached.

The next four years saw mounting pressure from the Europeans to relax COCOM restrictions on dual-use technologies. In January 1988 Western European governments demanded a 40 percent reduction in the list of industrial items embargoed by the regime. The Reagan administration, however, immediately rejected this demand and the negotiations ended with a bland revision of 25 percent of controlled dual-use items. Nonetheless, the U.S. allowed restrictions to be lifted on articles such as non-state-of-the-art personal computers and other goods whose sale to the East could no longer be controlled because they were already widely available outside COCOM countries.

The 1980s ended with a compromise which largely reflected European preferences for liberal trade norms restricting a narrow range of clearly military goods, embodied in a control list that dropped superfluous items without military significance in exchange for tougher enforcement measures. As we shall discuss later, agreement to the tougher enforcement was largely a result of publicity around Toshiba Corporation's illegal sale of submarine-quieting machinery to the Soviet Union. In short, the technology transfer issue that emerged in the 1970s and 1980s renewed the U.S.-European conflict over the definition of vulnerability. While the United States employed the extraterritoriality principle and again attempted to use COCOM as the instrument of trade denial, the Europeans pushed for their own preferred changes in COCOM in order to expand trade with the East. From the beginning, the U.S. government used two kinds of strategies to extract its allies' compliance with its goals and thereby enhance the legitimacy of the multilateral embargo. First, the U.S. attempted to control the agenda *within* COCOM. This meant ensuring that U.S. preferences were reflected in the multilateral lists of embargoed goods, the definitions of strategic items, and strategic technology. Strategies to achieve this goal entailed efforts ranging from simple diplomatic pressure in COCOM negotiations to proposed changes in organizational structure.

Second, U.S. policymakers pursued unilateral strategies *outside* COCOM, using both incentives and coercive threats to persuade European governments to halt trade with the Soviet bloc. Washington offered to reward both European firms who suffered export losses from the embargo and European governments who complied with U.S. preferences. Finally, it offered to share technology with those countries who complied with its policy.

The U.S. also threatened coercion to extract unilateral compliance. These threats ranged from laws that would curtail aid to all states exporting strategic and even nonmilitary goods to communist nations to the imposition of the extraterritoriality principle—in which the U.S. would extend its own export control policy to cover the reexport of goods and technology from European firms. If these firms engaged in reexport, they would be denied goods and technology from the United States. Europeans balked at these compliance strategies, however; the balking grew more intense as U.S. dominance declined. They were also unpersuaded by broad vulnerability arguments and agreed to restrict only a narrow set of militarily significant technologies.

An Assessment of COCOM's Effectiveness

Did these tensions make the COCOM regime weak, unstable, and therefore ineffective in binding members to restrain themselves from selling embargoed goods? Did an ineffective COCOM trigger the "hemorrhaging" of Western high technology to the East?

Three sets of conclusions about COCOM's effectiveness can be drawn from this analysis. First, on East-West trade issues, Europe has always demonstrated a commitment to restricting goods with military significance. European leaders, however, disagreed with the U.S. interpretation of the vulnerabilities associated with technology exodus and therefore attempted to pursue liberal policies when it came to non-strategic East-West trade. If COCOM was weak in the 1970s, it was not because European members defected from their obligations but rather because acrimonious debate over definitional issues weakened the regime norms and provided firms with little incentive to comply. The Toshiba case illustrates this point.

Second, Europeans preserved independence in trade with the Soviet Union by pursuing a multilateral approach to export controls. They shielded themselves from American pressure by acting within a narrow definition of the norms, rules, and procedures of the multilateral export control regime. In doing so, the multilateral process may have actually been strengthened, albeit not along the lines that more hard-line economic nationalists would have preferred.

Finally, and ironically, despite public pronouncements on the part of the Reagan administration to the contrary, studies conducted by the administration judged the COCOM embargo to be effective in the 1980s in restricting the sale of *militarily significant* technologies.[40] The Defense Department reported that the embargo saved the United States $20–50 billion in defense spending in the 1980s by preventing the transfer of high technology to the Soviet Union. In part, the embargo accounted for the lower than average level of legal Soviet high-technology imports and the massive illegal efforts to acquire the technology.[41] Thus, even though the U.S. was not able to plug what it considered to be a "leaky" set of multilateral controls, the chief harm to the embargo effort was in fact that caused by the political stalemate triggered by these demands. Ironically, heavy-handed U.S. efforts to expand the embargo due to U.S. perceptions of vulnerability triggered disputes that threatened to render it politically irrelevant. Nonetheless, its apparent effectiveness as a test of European definitions of vulnerability may hold lessons for future technology-restriction regimes. I will return to these later.

The political disputes and COCOM's fragile legitimacy go a long way to explaining the type of violations illustrated by the Toshiba case. Intense competition among firms for exports, the rising trade frictions among Western industrial countries. and definitional disputes within COCOM created an environment in which "involuntary regime defection" was bound to occur. The blatant illegality of Toshiba's sale of submarine-quieting technology was clear, and the sale illustrates problems in building and maintaining an effective export control regime in the future.

The Toshiba Case

In late autumn of 1980 a Soviet trade official contacted a small Japanese trading house, Wako Koeki, about a possible technology purchase. He explained that he was looking for a company that could manufacture a sophisticated milling machine capable of making large ship propellers. Not readily acquainted with such a firm, Wako Koeki enlisted the help of C. Itoh, a large trading house. Together they arranged a deal with Toshiba Machine Co., a subsidiary of Toshiba Corporation, and a leading producer of semiconductors, to sell the four room-sized industrial robots.

The sale was typical of the industrial cooperation agreements that had sprung up between the Soviet Union and Western firms throughout the 1970s. The twelfth Soviet Five-Year Plan placed heavy emphasis on modernizing production and reequiping ailing manufacturing plants. The Japanese had proven themselves to be the world's leaders in industrial application of machine tools. The Soviets focused on the Japanese machine tool industry as a source of supply; machine tools and industrial equipment were the single largest Soviet import from Japan. The agreement included installation, training, and the transfer of technological improvements for five years.[42] It was this type of agreement that economic nationalists believed were the most effective technology-transfer vehicles and thus the most threatening to Western security.

Japanese trade officials gladly did business with Eastern bloc countries; at a time when trade frictions were impeding exports to the West, the Soviet Union and Eastern Europe were virtually crying for Japanese manufactured goods. For Japan, trade with communist countries had begun to decline in the early 1980s, but by 1986 it represented 7 percent of all exports, more than three times the volume of U.S. trade with the Eastern bloc.

Like most Japanese firms doing business with the USSR, Toshiba Machine had made a handsome profit on the sale. The average price of

Japanese machine tools sold to the USSR was considerably higher than those sold elsewhere. The Soviets had paid almost three times more for lathes, similar to those sold by Toshiba Machine, than other buyers.[43] Toshiba Corporation sales to Eastern bloc countries represented about 13 percent of total exports and brought in $36 million a year (1986 figures).[44]

The deal was a special coup for those Toshiba Machine officials who remembered how their company had lost a similar milling equipment sale in 1974 to the now-defunct French machine tool company Forest Line. Forest Line won the contract, they argued bitterly, because Japanese export controls laws had forbidden Toshiba Machine from exporting the equipment. French officials, they charged, had not been so strict. They vowed that this time they would not be suckers. Kongsberg, the Norwegian weapons manufacturer who supplied sophisticated software to steer the intricate cutting heads on the Toshiba machines, and the third party to the deal, depended on its consummation for its financial solvency. It had suffered seven consecutive years of losses and the deal promised to put them in the black again.

From the beginning, however, the technology sale was suspicious. The Toshiba machine centers could mill the complex surfaces of submarine propellers up to forty feet across. The machines would be guided by sophisticated computer programs, knwon as numerical control systems, purchased from Kongsberg. These machines would produce a much higher degree of propeller smoothness and symmetry than was possible with Soviet equipment. Smooth propellers make less noise when they churn the water, making them harder to detect.[45] This was exactly the kind of technology transfer to the Soviet Union that economic nationalists believed would lead to the West's increasing vulnerability.

All long-range and some short-range submarine-detection devices, or sensors, rely on passive sonar equipment that listens for the noise radiated by a submarine. U.S. Navy officials argued that as Soviet submarines become quieter, in response the Navy would be required to turn to active sonar, which broadcasts sound and listens for echoes from nearby submarines. Using active sonar would therefore put the U.S. at a considerable tactical disadvantage, since approaching submarines can "hear" active sonar from further away than the sonar can detect an echo from the submarine.[46] This advanced warning would allow the submarine to either escape detection or move into an advantageous attack position.

The Toshiba milling machines thus had unmistakable military significance. The sale violated COCOM limits that allowed only the transfer of small machine tools—those that could turn a maximum of two and a half axes and make propellers of only ten feet in diameter, too small to make the large propellers necessary for quiet Soviet submarines.

Toshiba Machine was in a bind: in order to close the deal, it was obliged to obtain MITI's permission. MITI officials in the Trade Administration Bureau, in turn, would have to ensure that the sale did not violate Japan's export controls laws and COCOM's strategic embargo. MITI, however, is not organized as a regulatory bureaucracy; its chief mission is to nurture Japanese industry, not restrict exports. Therefore, it was woefully understaffed when it came to export control.[47] Furthermore, given the absence of a highly developed defense industry in Japan, MITI did not have access to the kind of expertise needed to competently assess the military significance of dual-use high technologies. For these reasons, Japan's export control system has relied heavily on "self-regulation"—the expectation that firms would not try to export items on the list of embargoed goods.

Apparently Toshiba Machine managers tried to conceal the sale by misrepresenting the machine's capabilities. Without notifying officials at the parent company, Toshiba Corporation, they changed the machine's name to an unrestricted "vertical lathe" and submitted it for export licenses. Given MITI's limited ability, and willingness, to police sales to the East, it seemed that Toshiba had no reason to fear that the transaction would be discovered and prosecuted.

What no one counted on was a disgruntled whistle-blower, Kazuo Kumagai, chief of Wako Keoki's Moscow office. Embroiled in a dispute with his employers, Kumagai resigned from Wako Koeki in 1985 and then informed authorities of the transactions and the falsified export control application. Not only did Kumagai single out the Toshiba sale as a dangerous violation of export controls, he listed eight deception techniques commonly used by firms trading technology with the Soviet Union.[48]

The Toshiba case was clearly one of "involuntary defection" from COCOM rules. Both the Japanese and Norwegian governments acted swiftly to punish the offenders. The Japanese government banned Toshiba from exporting anything to the Eastern bloc countries for one year, the stiffest penalty ever imposed on a Japanese concern violating export controls.[49] Norway's prime minister, Gro Brundtland, personally assured President Reagan that Norway's export controls would be significantly strengthened and began to reorganize Kongsberg Vapenfabrik, a state-owned company.

The U.S. government, however, was not impressed and took unilateral action. The Commerce Department immediately suspended Toshiba's and Kongsberg's blanket authority to ship U.S. product to third countries until they demonstrated that they had adopted internal controls that would prevent them from again shipping militarily sensitive goods to the Soviet bloc.[50] Both Toshiba and Kongsberg agreed to let the Commerce Department review their internal procedures for guarding against diversions of sensitive products.

But Congress had harsher measures in store. After the sale's revelation, the Senate voted by a wide margin (95–2) to ban all Toshiba and Kongsberg products from the United States for three to five years, and prohibit contracts between the two companies and the U.S. government.[51] The impact on Toshiba would not have been insignificant: in 1986 Toshiba's American sales of $2.6 billion accounted for more than 10 percent of its worldwide revenue of $22 billion.[52] The Senate ban came on the heels of tariffs imposed on imports of Japanese electronic products, the semiconductor trade sanctions imposed by Reagan a few months earlier,[53] and was tacked on to a trade bill already laced with anti-Japanese measures.

The Senate voted for the ban despite Japanese and Norwegian offers to help the United States to improve its antisubmarine warfare capability as partial compensation for the alleged damage caused by the sale. Congressman Duncan Hunter (R-Cal.), a sponsor of the punitive legislation, estimated that it would cost the West $330 billion to regain the superiority lost from the sale, and that with the new propellers, the Soviet submarines could get within ten minutes of missile flying time from the U.S. coast.[54] Clearly Japan was the chief focus of congressional outrage; no one in Washington was asking for an embargo of wheat sales against the Soviet Union or a ban on Norwegian sardine imports.

On the day following the Senate vote, the president and chairman of Toshiba resigned, saying that they felt "gravely responsible for straining the already strained Japan-U.S. relations further,"[55] a move that Toshiba proclaimed to be "the highest form of apology" in full-page ads splashed across U.S. national media. Toshiba's stock plunged immediately and analysts reported that a ban on exports to the United States could wipe out the entire pretax profits of $340 billion expected in

1988. The chairman of Toshiba American stated grimly that he would probably lay off some of the company's 4,000 employees in Tennessee, Texas, and California.[56]

Assessing the Vulnerability Implications of the Sale

The Toshiba sale openly violated COCOM rules and the reaction of U.S. officials was clearly based on vulnerability fears. Throughout the 1980s the United States had held the technological lead in the essential elements of antisubmarine warfare capability: submarine quieting, antisubmarine weapons, and weapons platforms (ships and planes that can reach the places where enemy submarines are operating). In the early 1980s, however, the U.S. Navy reported that the American lead in the field submarine quieting had begun to decline.[57]

The Soviets had long been attempting to engineer quieter submarines and they had had some success. Indeed, from the late 1970s to the mid-1980s the rate of Soviet submarine quieting accelerated due to better propeller design and manufacturing techniques. But what role did Toshiba's technology sale play in the Soviet achievement?

The new quieter submarines were the Akula, Sierra, and Mike class nuclear-powered attack submarines. Presumably, future Soviet missile submarines would benefit from the quieting technology used by attack submarines in ways that would affect the U.S.-Soviet military balance. First, quieter Soviet attack submarines would be better able to stalk and sink U.S. missile submarines. Second, quiet Soviet attack submarines would be better able to stalk and sink U.S. surface vessels during an extended conventional war. Of particular concern was the increased vulnerability of aircraft carriers, merchant vessels carrying supplies and troops to Europe, and expeditionary troop movements and the movement of their supply ships. Finally, quieter Soviet missile submarines would be harder for U.S. antisubmarine warfare forces to detect and sink in the event of a first strike or an extended attrition attack against SSBNs during a limited war.

The central issue in this case was whether the Toshiba sale contributed to this vulnerability. Indeed, Pentagon officials never confirmed whether the Toshiba-milled propellers had actually been installed in Soviet submarines. Most Pentagon planners admitted that the Soviets had not had enough time to put the technology to use. Most U.S. military analysts argued that the "improvements in the Soviet submarine force were the result of long-term, evolutionary, broad-based engineering and scientific development efforts, not overnight break-throughs."[58] Furthermore, the timing of the sale and the launching of the quiet submarines that had worried the Defense Department made it unlikely that these submarines were launched with Toshiba-produced propellers. As of 1985 only one of each of these classes had been launched: the Mike was launched in May 1983, the Sierra in July 1983, and the Akula in mid-1984.[59] Yet, according to the whistle-blower Kumagai, the Toshiba machines were not delivered to the Soviets until June 1983 and they were not installed and fully tested until the fall of 1984.[60] The timing of the sale, then, ruled out the possibility that Toshiba propellers had been installed when these submarines were launched.

Nonetheless, the possibility of long-term vulnerability effects was still worrisome. The advantage of importing the Toshiba machines was that they provided the Soviets with the capability to produce large propellers in higher volume than had previously been possible. The "gap" in quiet-ing was closing; the Toshiba sale may have helped it close more quickly. But it was clear that Toshiba was singled out to take the blame for what was really a long-term overall decline of U.S. superiority in submarine-quieting technology. After the revelations of the illegal sale, the Penta-gon and congress argued that the U.S. should respond with an increase in spending on research, development, and deployment of more sophis-ticated antisubmarine warfare sensors. The Pentagon pointed out that this effort would cost about $30 billion, while other sources put the fig-ure at $100 billion.[61] Again the argument that the hemorrhaging of Western high technology was closing the gap and that it would cost the U.S. more to stay ahead was rearing its head.

Opposition in Japan

Inside Japan opposition to these claims had begun to spread immedi-ately. Japanese commentators raised two arguments in defense of Toshiba. First, many questioned the link between quieter Soviet sub-marines and the Toshiba sale. Private Japanese military specialists argued on national television that Toshiba's illicit sales could not have been responsible for a reduction in Soviet submarine propeller noise. A spokesman for the Defense Agency, Masanobu Ohtsuke, said: "It is true that in the last decade, Soviet submarines have become quieter, but

there are many sources of noise besides propeller sounds—engine, auxiliary pumps, the shape of the submarine itself. Of course Toshiba
Machine's equipment is capable of manufacturing with high precision,
but just having the machine does not mean the Soviets can make a quieter propeller. In order to be able to do that, they have to be able to
draw the design of the propeller shape."[62]

The second objection focused on U.S.-Japanese trade relations; the
United States was simply using the Toshiba affair to discourage Japanese
exports to the United States. To many commentators, the Senate ban
looked especially convenient because Toshiba happened to be the leading producer of sophisticated semiconductors. Throughout the early
1980s Japan had surged ahead in semiconductor production, leaving
American producers to close their manufacturing plants and lay of
65,000 workers. In July 1986 Japanese chip makers, including Toshiba,
consented to charge more for their chips in the United States so that
American producers could again compete. Chip buyers then began to
shop abroad so that their computers, telephone networks, and cars
could be priced competitively with Japanese electronic products. Again,
semiconductor companies began to flounder, congressional protection
notwithstanding. Against this background, Japanese observers argued,
Congress could tout the case as a compromise of military security and
ban at least one Japanese company's chips and possibly score some
points with American chip producers.

Skepticism and doubt abounded. Could it be that Washington's
harsh response had been aimed at making Toshiba a scapegoat for
an alleged diminishing U.S. technological lead over the Soviets and
the U.S. trade deficit with Japan? Could congressional outrage simply
reflect American fear of Japanese competition? Could the U.S. response
to the Toshiba affair be evidence of an American effort to bully Japan
into technological subservience since it had not been able to win
in commercial competition? Japanese critics claimed that U.S. policy
was aimed at one thing—bringing Japanese technologies under U.S.
control.[63]

Privately, Japanese business grumbled about the tighter controls.
A representative of Toshiba Machine America expressed clear displeasure at the ban on Toshiba products to the East and argued that it
was simply necessary to please the United States and not necessary to
protect Western security. He described American pressure on Toshiba
as "zuru," or cheating or underhandedness. He went on to say that

violations would continue if companies saw their competitors getting away with them.[64]

Negotiating with Japan: Sanctions as a Bargaining Chip

Sensitive to Japanese opinion, pressured by lobbyists, and caught in a series of negotiations with Japan on both trade and security issues, the Reagan administration recognized that the threat of sanctions could be used to achieve other goals. At the same time, however, they also recognized that the threat must not be carried out, lest it sour relations with Japan—and consequently its European allies and trading partners—and destroy the chance to extract concessions in other areas.[65] For their part, the Japanese recognized that any sanctions would endanger the already beleaguered trade relationship; after all, Japan depended on the American market to absorb almost 50 percent of its exports.[66] The Reagan administration pursued simultaneous domestic and international negotiating strategies: urging Japan to tighten export controls in order to gain bargaining leverage with Congress to soften sanctions, and using the sanctions threat to gain bargaining leverage with Japan in related negotiations over SDI and the F-16 fighter plane.

First, Japan would have to tighten its export controls. Commerce Department officials told the Japanese that if they could produce a tough export control law, the administration would seek to water down the Senate-passed bill aimed at barring Toshiba exports to the United States. The Pentagon proposed a bill that would retain penalties against violators of allied export control rules but would drop specific mention of Toshiba or Kongsberg.[67]

Indeed, by September, Japan's parliament had approved legislation to stiffen penalties for illegal exports of militarily sensitive technology to communist bloc countries.[68] With Japanese promises of tighter export control—and strict punishment for violators—the Reagan administration could stall sanctions deliberations in Congress but still use the threat of sanctions in two separate sets of negotiations with Japan.

The Toshiba case also presented an opportunity in negotiations with Japan on SDI research. Ironically, at the same time it permitted the Pentagon to block congressional opposition to Japan's participation. The Defense Department had already negotiated agreements with some American allies to participate with the United States on SDI research. Japan would have been the fifth country to sign a participation agreement, after the United Kingdom, West Germany, Italy, and Israel. Defense Department officials perceived Japan as a treasure trove of sophisticated technologies for SDI: a list drawn up in the Pentagon set out sixteen areas, including radar transmitters, superconductors, software systems, optical systems, and semiconductors, where Japanese technological prowess could further the administration's goal of creating space sensors and weapons to detect and intercept ballistic missiles.

The Toshiba affair could not have come at a better time for Pentagon officials in charge of negotiating the SDI research agreement with Japan. Three issues were at stake. First, Japanese business had been reluctant to participate because it risked corporate profits. Why divert 80–100 researchers to a project of unknown destiny to obtain findings of unknown utilization? Second, during earlier negotiations, Tokyo had pressed for more openness in the agreement than similar pacts between the U.S. and Israel and the European allies. The Pentagon was opposed, fearing that the Soviets would have more access to the technology if the contracts were not strictly confidential. Third, the Federation of Economic Organizations in Japan (Keidaren) had pressed for a clause in the agreement which would assure that U.S. companies would not have access to Japanese participants' technological secrets. Once again, the Pentagon was opposed; U.S. access to Japanese technology would provide the infusion of technological capability needed to offset the vulnerability effects of dependence and strengthen the U.S. technological base.

Linking the Toshiba case with SDI negotiations, the Reagan administration hinted that it could influence Congress to ease Toshiba sanctions if Japanese negotiators could quickly meet U.S. requirements for an SDI participation agreement. Ironically, Toshiba's illegal high-technology sale and the outrage it triggered gave U.S. negotiators the upper hand in securing Japanese SDI participation and realizing their preferences on confidentiality. In the end, the Japanese government guaranteed participation, promised to restrict the transfer of SDI-relevant technologies, and Keidaren dropped its demand for secrecy vis-à-vis U.S. firms. "The Toshiba incident facilitated our reaching an agreement on a strengthened security regime," said one official. He added that the terms in the SDI accord would also be extended to other defense-related U.S. contracts with Japanese companies.[69]

The agreement was signed on July 21, 1987. Although the details were secret, U.S. officials stated that the outcome was a triumph over two sets of opponents: the Japanese negotiators and a group of U.S. congressmen opposed to any foreign participation in SDI research. With regard to the Japanese, the administration reported that the agreement was packed with special provisions to ensure that U.S. technological secrets would be protected from the Soviets and that Japanese export controls would indeed be tightened.

Linking the Toshiba case to SDI negotiations also expedited the final agreement, allowing the Reagan administration to overrun congressional opposition to Japan's participation. In the aftermath of the Toshiba affair, Senator John Glenn (D-Ohio) reintroduced a bill to exclude Japan from SDI research altogether. Media accounts reported that the bill would surely pass, with the Toshiba case so fresh in the minds of congressional leaders. If passed, it would have prohibited SDI awards to foreigners unless the Pentagon could certify that the work could not be done as effectively by U.S. companies. The bill would have exempted contracts already awarded under the four earlier SDI pacts, and it would have applied to all those signed after the bill's enactment. Senator Glenn clearly wanted to exclude Japan but the administration, reminding Japanese negotiators that the bill had been reintroduced, managed to get an agreement before he could make his move.[70]

Second, the Toshiba case strengthened the Pentagon's hand in negotiations over Japanese cooperation with the United States in its building of a new fighter plane. Early in 1987 Japan announced that it was going to design and build its own fighter, the FSX. Japanese business and government leaders were united in the view that Japan should have an independent aerospace industry; the issue was one of national pride. The American aerospace industry, however, viewed the plan as a Japanese effort to build a competitive aircraft industry and take away the market share of one of America's few remaining technological giants.

Again, American negotiators hinted at the threat of sanctions against Toshiba in order to nudge the Japanese toward compliance with U.S. preferences. If Japan did not cooperate, they suggested, the Toshiba sanctions would most certainly become law. In the end, Prime Minister Nakasone and Defense Agency Minister Yuko Kurihara stood up to their domestic forces of "technological nationalism" and announced on October 2, 1987 that Japan would enter into a joint venture with an American company to develop the plane. By April 1988 Japan had agreed to join with General Dynamics Corporation in a $1.33 billion project to develop an upgraded F-16 fighter plane.[71]

The Toshiba Example and Efforts to Strengthen COCOM Enforcement

The Reagan administration hoped that the Toshiba case would provide them with further ammunition in their battle to persuade not only Japan but the European allies to tighten export controls. Because no American citizens, companies, or technologies were involved in the case, the State Department argued that it symbolized U.S. dependence on strengthening international agreements to keep sensitive equipment from reaching communist hands. Assistant Secretary of Commerce for Trade Administration Paul Freedenberg remarked that revelations of Toshiba's illegal technology sale would "inspire our allies to commit more resources to export controls and enforce them more rigorously."[72] Revelations of the earlier illegal sale by the French added even more ammunition to U.S. export control fire directed at the allies. U.S. officials had not forgotten that in 1982 Europe had defied U.S. requests for a technology embargo against the Soviet Union in the wake of the Soviet invasion of Afghanistan. That denial had led to the infamous Urengoi pipeline dispute (discussed in the following chapter) in which U.S. technology control demands had not been met.

Investigations by Kongsberg and Toshiba revealed deeper problems in enforcing the multilateral control of technology transfer. Toshiba's allegation of the 1974 illegal French sale of similar milling equipment was confirmed, and Kongsberg's investigation revealed illegal sales by American, British, and Italian companies. On October 16, 1987, L'Express and American officials reported that between 1983 and 1985 a French company had shipped tons of machinery aimed at giving the Soviet Union the technology to make high-speed integrated circuits. Defense Department officials said that the sale would enable the Soviets to produce a special type of radiation-resistant computer memory frequently used in fighter aircraft and guided ballistic missiles.[73]

Shortly after these revelations, a team of American export control officials toured fourteen European capitals, hoping to convince the Western allies to beef up their systems for punishing COCOM violators. In exchange, they said that they were prepared to eliminate license requirements for dual-use technologies shipped from the United States to COCOM countries.[74] The Europeans clearly opposed the sanctions legislation, arguing that if Toshiba were barred from the American market, it would dump its products in Europe.[75] They thus accepted U.S. conditions and agreed to tighten their enforcement procedures on export controls.

COCOM Effectiveness and Western Vulnerability

The lesson of Toshiba is that tighter U.S. export controls would be ineffective in a policy environment characterized by the conflicting definition of norms. Disputes within COCOM over norms increased the clout of private actors in the export-control policy arena. First, the weakened regime norms increased Toshiba Machine's incentive to cheat, as others had cheated before. Cheating was made easier because export control conflicted with the preference for expanding exports of high technology. The vicious circle was then reinforced: when export control enforcement was sacrificed to other policy goals, COCOM's norms suffered. Furthermore, norms suffer when member states find themselves in fundamental disagreement over what should be controlled. For example, as we have already discussed, COCOM nations have long debated the control of dual-use technologies. The restriction of dual-use technologies, some members argued, would hamper the process of technological innovation so vital to industrial competitiveness, yet unrestricted diffusion of those same technologies was seen by some factions as harmful to Western security. The Toshiba case illustrates how the international debate over dual-use technologies weakened COCOM's control norms and led to the proliferation of regime violations, causing Japan's involuntary defection. As this debate continued to plague COCOM, member states' obligation to place security above commercial gain in technology trade became increasingly vague. As the obligation clouded, punishments were more difficult to apply, even in the case of a clear-cut violation. When sanctions are not forthcoming, norms decay further. Hence, this process of norm decay largely explains why private actors like Toshiba were willing to defy the regime rules.

Nevertheless, the sale apparently did not bring about the short-term vulnerability effects long feared by economic nationalists. More important, U.S. officials used *vulnerability arguments as political bargaining chips* in negotiations with Japan over collaboration in SDI research and cooperation in building the FSX fighter plane. Both sets of negotiations illustrated problems for the United States associated with Japanese dominance in key high technologies with both commercial and military significance. The political events surrounding the Toshiba case clearly illustrate increasing American dependence on Japan for high-technology components for military goods. Arguments about Western vulnerability vis-à-vis the Soviet Union were used to manipulate and control perceived vulnerabilities vis-à-vis Japan.

Implications for the Future: Old Vulnerabilities in New Places

What does this analysis tell us about the future of Western economic vulnerability in international relations? Recall the argument at the outset that vulnerability was a function of an adversary's market control, or the loss of market control by those whose interests are consistent with Western security objectives. Throughout the Cold War, U.S. vulnerability fears were focused on the Soviet Union out of concern that its "all-powerful" state was able to manipulate dual-use technology markets in order to increase its military power. With the demise of the Soviet state, and the emergence of a fragmented region governed by many weak governments, these particular fears have vanished. Dependence on the West for aid and attempts to impose liberal democracy throughout the region have led to increased transparency and have greatly simplified the task of determining the end-use of technology transfers.

In place of the concerns of the Cold War, however, two new, and related, vulnerability fears have emerged: 1) concern over *Soviet* technology exodus to dangerous countries in the absence of state control over technology in the former Soviet Union; and 2) concern over the exodus of *Western* technology to developing states capable of absorbing Western technology, thereby increasing their relative power.

The economic crisis in the former Soviet Union and the inability of the state to establish stable property rights and market rationality has led to fears of an exodus of Soviet military and dual-use technology to the Third World. For example, a group of former party elites in Russia with good connections to the state bank—promising easy credit terms— bought dual-use technology in early 1992 and planned to sell it in the global market.[76] Although President Boris Yeltsin threatened to impose sanctions on such activity, it was not entirely clear whether his government had the power to do so. Furthermore, uncertainty over control of economic forces and the disintegration of the Soviet state increased the likelihood that Soviet scientists trained in building nuclear and chemical weapons would sell their expertise to states such as North Korea and Iraq.[77]

In order to prevent this technology exodus *from* the former USSR to other potentially dangerous countries, the Bush administration initially provided $25 million to help finance an international science and technology center supporting former Soviet scientists and engineers so that they could redirect their talents to nonmilitary endeavors.[78] At the same time, however, the United States blocked the purchase of missiles, rocket engines, satellites, space reactors, spacecraft, and other aerospace technology from the former Soviet Union in order to force the decline of the Russian space and military industry so that it would pose no further threat to the U.S. Many argued that this embargo would further force former Soviet scientists to sell their knowledge to potential military rivals in the Third World.[79]

Although dangerous, this consequence of the demise of state power in the Soviet Union pointed to a more pervasive problem: an intensified diffusion of dual-use technology to the Third World. Throughout the 1980s several Third World powers sought to develop chemical and biological weapons capabilities. Traditional Western export controls were targeted on the Soviet Union, and the technology became increasingly available from non-Western suppliers whose export controls were lax. Even when controls were in place, private firms often claimed that they were selling commercial, not military technology. Most firms knew that in Third World transactions there were no legitimate institutions monitoring what was being sold and for what purpose, an example of which is the German sale of a chemical plant to Libya.

On January 1, 1989 the United States accused the German firm Imhausen-Chemie of playing a central role in designing and constructing a chemical plant in Rabta, Libya. Once complete, this plant was scheduled to produce between 22,000 and 84,000 pounds of mustard gas and nerve agent daily. The company denied these claims, rebutting that they were only supplying pharmaceutical products. The German government initially backed Imhausen-Chemie, claiming that the United States had provided no solid evidence on the military significance of the sale. Indeed, the familiar political debate over vulnerability emerged. Völker Rühe, deputy head of West Germany's Christian Democratic party, stated that "the government has a right to protect itself against unfair attacks and media campaigns from the U.S." The German Foreign Ministry conducted its own investigation but found no solid evidence that Imhausen-Chemie had sold militarily significant technology.

The United States stepped up efforts to provide evidence of dual-use technology exodus to Libya. When the vulnerability evidence was finally presented, it was so overwhelming that Chancellor Kohl was forced to admit that German companies were involved in chemical weapons proliferation. Leaks published from German intelligence sources claimed that Bonn had known months before about Imhausen-Chemie's involvement in Libya and had ignored warnings of Libya's effort to produce gas since 1980, thus contradicting Bonn's claim that it knew nothing until the American accusations were made public. Extremely embarrassed by this turn of events, Kohl adopted new export controls prohibiting German companies from helping make gas outside the aegis of NATO.[80]

What this illustrates is a need for the future multilateral consolidation of control over dual-use high-technology markets to prevent exporter vulnerability. The postwar history of such efforts in East-West trade, however, suggests that for multilateral vulnerability reduction efforts to be successful, they must be grounded in a clarification of vulnerability claims and consensus on the scope and extent of vulnerability. If these claims are clarified, political disputes among exporters that can weaken the regime may be avoided. In Cold War East-West trade, Europe readily agreed to restrict the export of technology that had clear military significance. If that history is a guide for the future, it should not be difficult to gain agreement on clarified vulnerability claims. But if there is intense dispute over vulnerability among governments, private firms often believe they have the license to "cheat," in much the same way that Toshiba and Imhausen did.

Conclusion

I have addressed two questions in this chapter: First, what direct contribution did Western technology make to Soviet military strength in the 1980s? Although the Soviets historically imitated Western military technology and engaged in massive illegal technology acquisition, Western innovative capabilities ensured a lead in the development of important military technologies and in the deployment of advanced weaponry. The Soviets could not successfully use Western technology to upgrade their weapons to the point where the effects of Western weaponry were negated. Nor could they effectively employ Western production technology to significantly upgrade their weaponry. Vulnerability claims made in the 1980s, then, were grossly exaggerated.

Second, how effective was the Western embargo in preventing Soviet acquisition of militarily significant technology? That question is essentially a political one and its answer depends on an assessment of the strength and stability of COCOM. An examination of struggles within COCOM throughout the postwar period suggests that disagreement over the appropriate scope of the embargo weakened COCOM's norms. This was especially severe as U.S. technological hegemony declined, while the U.S. continued to insist on a broad embargo of dual-use technologies. The Toshiba case illustrates how "involuntary defection" can occur when conflict over norms weakens the legitimacy of the regime in the eyes of those private actors who are the "agents" of technology transfer.

The lesson of the case was that enforcement is easiest when real agreement on norms is reached, and real agreement is best reached when the scope and extent of vulnerability is clearly specified. Europeans stipulated a very narrow definition of vulnerability, despite U.S. protest, and then enforced controls based on that definition. Thus, the Reagan administration agreed that despite these weak norms, COCOM was largely effective in preventing the sale of militarily significant technologies to the Soviet Union, thereby underscoring the legitimacy of European preferences for a narrow embargo of truly militarily significant technology. COCOM was effective in controlling select military technology and *did* contribute to the consolidation of Western control over high-technology exports.

These examples hold lessons for the future. In a new era marked by the global diffusion of high technology, the reduction of vulnerabilities associated with technology exodus will be a function of both helping to ensure that technology exporters can establish stable property rights on the basis of market-rational behavior and on multilateral agreements based less on coercion and more on the careful specification and testing of vulnerability claims.

5

Resource Dependence
and Natural Gas Trade Between
the Former Soviet Union and Europe

In 1982 the United States imposed an embargo on all U.S. technology bound for the USSR to be used in the construction of a natural-gas pipeline from Siberia to Western Europe. Western European firms had contracted to build this pipeline with U.S. technology and equipment in exchange for increased supplies of Soviet natural gas. With the embargo of equipment, the U.S. attempted to halt the construction of the pipeline, arguing that its supply of gas to Europe would create unacceptable NATO dependence on Soviet energy supplies. The embargo triggered bitterness and discord within the Western alliance because European allies refused to comply with U.S. embargo requirements and stubbornly refused to halt the pipeline construction. After acrimonious debate and grudging agreement to study the issue further, the embargo was lifted.

American opposition to the pipeline hinged on the argument that Western Europe was becoming dangerously dependent upon the Soviet adversary's supply of energy. The vulnerability thesis contends that dependence on the adversary for vital materials is a threat to national security. In wartime the supply of those materials will be curtailed. In peacetime, threats of supply disruptions can be a tool of diplomacy, a means to exert leverage over the importer. That leverage can be as subtle as sending a signal of approval or disapproval of the importer's policies. Or it can be as direct as an attempt to influence the importer to change its policies. Dependence that permits such potential weakness or influence is unacceptable.

Was the West subject to the vulnerabilities of resource dependence in its natural-gas trade with the Soviet Union? What are the new vulnerabilities in the post-Soviet future? In energy trade, the "threat" has reemerged in a new form. Now that gas flows through the Trans-Siberian pipeline, neither Russia nor any other former Soviet republic is likely to gain the political and strategic advantage that the Reagan administration feared before the Urengoi pipeline construction. But the disintegration of central power and the new states' rising economic separatism may create new vulnerabilities for Western nations if they are dependent upon the region's energy resources. Control over energy supplies in the former Soviet Union was fragmented with the death of the central state, but energy supply grids built in the Soviet era were tightly integrated. Conflict over control of pipelines, refineries, and sources of raw materials has slowed down the flow of goods and commodities between the independent states. And if economic conflict among the new states intensifies, the delivery and supply system is likely to break down, disrupting the flow of resources to the West. Energy-exporter policies may be no longer disruptive by design but they may be so in practice as supplier states lose market control.

In its energy trade in general and natural-gas trade in particular, Eastern Europe faces both old and new vulnerability problems. Indeed, Hungary, Czechoslovakia, and Poland continued in the 1990s to be engaged in joint efforts to explore and develop ex-Soviet natural-gas fields in exchange for natural-gas supplies. Does Eastern Europe continue to be vulnerable to economic influence and even dominance from the new states of the former Soviet Union? The transition to a market economy is not in itself a reason to neglect potential Eastern European vulnerabilities in relations with the former Soviet Union. The immediate postcommunist period brought political and economic instability in which the delivery of energy supplies was uncertain—indeed deliveries to the West were preferred over deliveries to the East in a desperate search for hard-currency earnings. The future may bring new vulnerabilities: a successful transition to the market will enhance the economic capabilities of some of the newly independent republics and their control over energy sources upon which Eastern European countries depend.

The vulnerability thesis yields a set of criteria by which to assess both Western and Eastern European resource dependence. This chapter employs a case study of natural-gas trade between the Soviet Union and

Europe to examine those vulnerabilities. If we apply the criteria of the argument for resource dependence, the following questions must be answered: 1) How intense was Western Europe's need for Soviet natural gas both before and after the pipeline crisis? 2) How much control did the Soviets exercise over Western Europe's natural-gas supply in the 1970s and 1980s? 3) What channels of influence were open to the Soviet Union within the export-import relationship? 4) How dependent was the Soviet Union on natural-gas exports to Europe? 5) To what extent did European countries diversify natural-gas supplies and initiate contingency plans in the event of a supply cutoff? In general, the account presented here will also consider the following questions: Was the Reagan administration needlessly worried about Europe's natural-gas security? Or did the crisis itself trigger Western European governments to consolidate market power and take vulnerability reduction measures discussed in chapter 2? What are the energy vulnerabilities faced by the newly sovereign states of Eastern Europe?

The chapter begins with a brief account of the U.S.-European debate over the Urengoi pipeline construction and the central arguments at stake. It then uses the arguments about "resource dependence" discussed in chapter 2 to assess vulnerability, both before and after the pipeline crisis. When the analysis addresses the post-Soviet period, it will disaggregate the evidence on the supply of natural gas from the former Soviet region and focus on individual states; clearly, however, the bulk of the region's natural-gas reserves are in Russia; only 12 percent of the natural-gas output of the former Soviet Union comes from Turkmenistan, and 5 percent or less come from Uzbekistan, Ukraine, Azerbaijan, and Kazakhstan, respectively. Furthermore, Russia supplies most of the natural gas produced for export to the West.

What the evidence suggests is that Western Europe's resource dependence in this case was and continues to be significant if it is considered in isolation from the former Soviet Union's perceived dependence on its hard-currency earnings, Europe's ability to diversify natural-gas supplies, and the robustness of contingency arrangements to assure gas in the event of a supply cutoff. But the confluence of Soviet dependence on exports and Western European contingency plans—in place before the pipeline crisis—reduced the vulnerability effects of dependence both before and after the Cold War's end. Eastern Europe's resource dependence on the Soviet Union, however, was and continues to be much higher: the former Soviet Union is the dominant supplier of energy to Eastern Europe, and as of mid-1991, supplies were not fully diversified and contingency arrangements were neither planned nor in place.

In short, I will put forth three arguments in this chapter: first, the Reagan administration's fears of Western Europe's resource dependence on the Soviet Union were not grounded in evidence, and the available evidence shows that vulnerability was low, both before and after the pipeline crisis. Levels of dependence projected before the crisis were simply codified as "acceptable" in the agreement to end the crisis. Nonetheless, the agreement may have acted as an additional deterrent to the potential "dumping" of Soviet gas on the Western European market. Second, I suggest here that the coercive measures taken by the U.S. with regard to its European allies in order to control markets to reduce perceived vulnerability were both unnecessary and counterproductive; joint consolidation of Western market control could have been more productively based on the kind of normative consensus and agreement on vulnerability before the crisis that was achieved in its aftermath. Finally, I argue that the vulnerability of resource dependence on the former Soviet Union will be low in the 1990s for the same reasons it was low in the 1980s, despite the change in the source of vulnerability from international threats of supply cutoffs to the loss of market control by supplier states. Eastern Europe, however, will continue to be vulnerable.

The 1982 Urengoi Pipeline Dispute[1]

Expressing interest in energy cooperation with the West, Soviet leaders in 1973 proposed joint East-West development of the Western Siberian natural-gas fields. By 1978 Soviet planners had entered into negotiations with Western firms to develop the Urengoi field, the largest gas field in the world. It was here that the disputed pipeline would originate. From the beginning, the Soviets had planned to construct it with turbines, compressors, pipes, and auxiliary equipment manufactured in and purchased from the West.

The U.S. position was that Europe would become permanently dependent on Soviet gas, assuring the Soviets hard-currency flows and political dominance, while Western Europe denied these allegations, refuting dependency claims. European officials argued that only 6 percent of their entire energy mix would be imported from the Soviet Union and that European contingency plans mitigated any fear of a

Soviet embargo on gas exports. These contingency measures included dual firing capabilities and contracting with alternative suppliers.

American officials were not satisfied with these claims of low vulnerability and with plans for vulnerability reduction. The Reagan administration argued that an increase in Soviet natural-gas supplies to Western Europe would create unacceptable dependence. Dependence on an adversary would open a window of energy vulnerability that would, in turn, weaken the Western democracies. At the Ottawa economic summit in October 1981 the U.S. expressed reservations about the pipeline construction, claiming it would cause vulnerability due to two factors: gas is difficult to replace on short notice; and certain regions would become especially vulnerable. In congressional hearings regarding the pipeline construction held the following month, Assistant Secretary of Defense for International Security Policy Richard Perle argued that "the revenues available to the Soviets will help to forge an economical link with Europe that will inevitably increase Moscow's influence among our allies. . . . A centrally controlled economy like the Soviet Union can place orders where it likes, and where jobs and profits in Europe emanate from Moscow, it would be naive to believe that politics will stay far behind."[2] A few months later, Lawrence Brady echoed this concern about Western vulnerability to Soviet influence: "Soviet firms and trade ministries have cultivated a vast network of influence in the capitalist nations that they can rely on to maintain continuity in U.S.-Soviet commercial relations, even when security needs in the West demand policy adjustments." In even stronger language, he asserted that "the Siberian pipeline . . . throws an energy noose around the economies of Western Europe that can gradually be tightened as the USSR attempts to gain greater control over the energy resources of the globe. Today Eastern Europe depends on the USSR for a critical share of its energy needs. A dependency which is readily manipulated by the Soviets for political purposes. The parallels are clear."[3]

Not only would energy dependence create deeper channels of Soviet influence in Europe, but it would give the adversary the power to weaken European economies. Perle warned that "Europe will incur dangerous vulnerability to the interruption of supplies of natural gas from the Soviet Union. . . . We have to anticipate that in a crisis, the Soviets might interrupt the flow of gas to achieve political purposes. They have done so before, as the Israelis, the Yugoslavs, and the Chinese have learned, to their regret."[4]

What kind of evidence was used to support these claims? It is important to note that opponents of the project admitted they had very little empirical support for their arguments. Anthony Cordesman, a fellow at the Woodrow Wilson International Center for Scholars, and an opponent of the pipeline claimed, "We do not have useful data on several major risks which go beyond the immediate issue of European dependence on this particular pipeline."[5] John Gibbons, director of the Office of Technology Assessment stated that "it must be recognized . . . that many aspects of the pipeline project and of its consequences involve matters subject to interpretation."[6]

To counter these assertions, Roger Hormats, assistant secretary of the Bureau of Economic and Business Affairs, Department of State, used CIA projections to demonstrate the extent of Western European reliance on Soviet gas by the 1990s, and submitted them as evidence of Western European resource dependence in the hearings.

These projections (see table 5.1) were quite accurate. Actual figures for 1990 indicate similar percentages for Soviet imports. Germany increased to 31.6 percent; France, 28.4 percent; and Italy, 26.4 percent. For the European Community as a whole, Soviet exports actually exceeded projected figures. Hormats estimated that total Soviet gas exports to Western Europe would grow to 1.46 trillion cubic feet per year by 1990. By 1988, however, this figure had almost already been reached at 1.43 trillion.[7]

This evidence, however, did not demonstrate enough vulnerability in the eyes of Western European governments to stop construction of the pipeline. With the negotiation of the final contracts for equipment, gas deliveries, and financing for the construction of one gas pipeline in

TABLE 5.1

Dependence on Soviet Gas as a Percentage of Total Gas Consumption and as a Percentage of Total Energy Consumption

	1979		1990 (est)	
	Gas	Energy	Gas	Energy
West Germany	14	2	29	6
France	0	0	23–28	4
Italy	29	5	29	5

SOURCE: "Proposed Trans-Siberian Natural Gas Pipeline," Hearings in the Committee on Banking, Housing, and Urban Affairs, U.S. Senate, November 12, 1991 p. 113: original data furnished by the CIA.

1981 and 1982, the divergence between American and European positions became unambiguous and irreconcilable as Europeans continued to insist that they were not vulnerable. The debate over dependence erupted into a full-blown dispute when, on December 13, 1981, martial law was declared in Poland. The Reagan administration immediately imposed unilateral sanctions on U.S. oil and gas technology and equipment bound for the Soviet Union and earmarked for the now controversial pipeline.

Western Europeans, however, did not support the United States by initiating sanctions of their own. The EC's response to the imposition of martial law in Poland was to bar only luxury goods from the Soviet Union some two months after the American sanctions were imposed. In response, Reagan administration officials suggested that if the Europeans could not be persuaded by example, the U.S. was prepared to use coercion. Thus, in the spring of 1982 the United States gave warning that sanctions would be extended to European firms if there was no voluntary compliance with the embargo. But the Europeans refused to halt construction of the pipeline, holding fast to their position that the Soviet energy it would supply would in no way make them vulnerable. The Reagan administration disagreed, and sanctions were extended in June.

The firms hit by the extension of the sanctions were caught between a rock and a hard place; they were barred by their governments from adhering to the embargo, but they were not given governmental protection from American retaliation. As the United States stepped up its coercive efforts to gain compliance, tensions increased; the only thing on which there was general agreement was that the dispute must be settled for the sake of alliance unity.

In November 1982 an agreement was reached between the U.S. and Europe to lift the sanctions, which revealed the utter failure of the American coercive efforts. The essence of the agreement was consent by all parties to generate more technical information about the dependency issue. The formal document stated that, in return for lifting the sanctions, studies to be conducted at the international level would be used to coordinate Western policy on East-West trade. European governments agreed not to negotiate further contracts to purchase natural gas from the Soviet Union until a study by the International Energy Agency on European dependence on Soviet gas had been completed.

The study was published in March 1983 and European natural-gas contracts with the Soviets were resumed. IEA forecasts indicated that the Soviet Union and Algeria would supply 35 percent of Western Europe's natural-gas needs (excluding the United Kingdom) by 1990. The IEA thus recommended that no single European country depend on one gas supplier for more than 30–35 percent of its annual gas needs, simply codifying the projections. Therefore, although Hormats had used similar projections to demonstrate unacceptable vulnerability and as evidence to convince Europeans to lower their volume of Soviet gas imports, this agreement stated that no further vulnerability reduction measures were really necessary. The agreed level of Soviet gas imports was based on European contingency plans in place by 1983.

The agreement to end the dispute was important in that it suggested that the level of dependence the U.S. had argued would lead to vulnerability was now safe, and that a thorough examination of vulnerability and required levels of Western market control could have attenuated the conflict. I will now turn to a more detailed assessment of the central vulnerability issues both before and after the pipeline crisis. The assessment proceeds according to the criteria of "resource dependence" elaborated in chapter 2: the intensity of the importer's demand, the exporter's degree of control over supply, the channels of influence opened to the exporter by the relationship, and the extent and effectiveness of vulnerability-reduction measures, i.e., diversification of suppliers and contingency measures, including fuel-switching capabilities, stockpiles, and sacrifice.

An Assessment of Resource Dependence

European Demand for Soviet Natural Gas

Western Europe proved itself politically vulnerable to the Arab oil boycott of 1973. Bowing to OPEC pressure as a result of an intense need for OPEC oil, the EC issued pro-Arab statements and instituted a Euro-Arab dialogue to work out disputes between Europe and the Middle East. To the United States, this served as an indication of what political concessions Europe might make when threatened with an embargo by an important energy supplier.

Yet in the aftermath of the 1973 embargo, the OECD countries, both individually and collectively, took steps to reduce their dependence on

OPEC oil. An "energy security system" emerged through the institutions of the International Energy Agency (IEA), bilateral agreements, and within the European Community.[8] An important focus in each of these forums was the formulation of policy to diversify energy supply and thus reduce the intensity of Europe's need for OPEC oil. Two policies in particular became salient: the diversification of energy sources to reduce dependence on oil, and the diversification of energy suppliers to reduce supplies from the Middle East. Increasing natural-gas supplies from the Soviet Union was a central objective of that strategy. Yet, as the above discussion pointed out, the United States feared that this policy would create an intense need on the part of Western European countries for Soviet natural gas. How intense was that need, both before and after the pipeline crisis?

The intensity of both Western and Eastern European demand for Soviet natural-gas imports can be roughly measured by looking at trends in the energy mix of OECD and former Council for Mutual Economic Assistance (CMEA) countries, the volume of Western European and Eastern European natural-gas imports, and the volume of Soviet natural-gas exports to Europe. These are essentially the measures used by Hormats during the pipeline crisis and by the IEA in its aftermath.

First, natural gas was of some importance in the European energy mix before the pipeline crisis. In 1980 it represented 13–14 percent of total energy demand in the EC, and in 1990 natural gas accounted for 15.5 percent of Western Europe's primary energy sources and 17.5 percent of EC energy use.[9] In the Eastern European countries, which were formerly members of the CMEA, natural gas represented roughly 17.1 percent of total energy consumption throughout much of the 1980s.[10]

Second, despite the fairly constant share of natural gas in Western Europe's energy mix, imports, which were fairly static in the 1970s, grew throughout the 1980s. According to 1988 figures, the European Community produced 50 percent of its own supply in that year, down from 77 percent in 1978.[11] In 1982 imports accounted for 15 percent of total gas consumption in Western Europe, but by 1988 natural-gas imports into Western Europe from outside the OECD area (Algeria and the USSR) had more than doubled, accounting for 33.7 percent of total gas requirements.[12] In 1983 the EC estimated that by 1990 gas imports would meet 44 percent of total natural-gas demand and only one-third of these imports were expected to come from the Soviet Union.[13] In fact, however, in 1989 gas imports met 50 percent of the total natural-gas demand in the European Community, and almost 40 percent of those imports came from the Soviet Union. French imports of Soviet natural gas increased 270 percent between 1979 and 1990, German imports grew 100 percent during that same period, and Italy's imports grew 42 percent.[14]

After 1990 a united Germany inherited the energy trade of the former DDR. Natural-gas consumption in East Germany had been only one-fifth that of West Germany, but imports from the Soviet Union were over 50 percent of total East German consumption. German unification meant that over 50 percent of all imported natural gas would now come from the USSR.[15]

Despite the fact that the Soviet share of imports in Western Europe was higher than expected when it was calculated during the controversy over the construction of the Urengoi pipeline, the USSR held the same share of the West European gas import market in 1990 as it did in 1979, when its share of total imports was 39.8 percent. Nonetheless, between 1979 and 1990, the Soviets maintained significant share in the growing Western European natural-gas market, and supplied almost 20 percent of Western Europe's total natural-gas requirements.

Virtually all of Eastern Europe's natural-gas imports still came from the former Soviet Union in 1992. From 1970 to 1987, Eastern Europe experienced a 136 percent increase in natural-gas consumption, but a 1700 percent increase in gas imports, all from the Soviet Union. By 1987 imports represented 40 percent of natural-gas consumption by the Eastern European members of the CMEA. As the 1980s came to a close, however, overall energy consumption in Eastern Europe declined dramatically in the wake of economic crisis; natural gas represented only 11 percent of total energy consumption. Nonetheless, most of Eastern Europe's oil was imported from the Soviet Union and gas and oil together made up almost 30 percent of energy consumption there in 1991. Soviet control over the East's energy supply was, and continues to be, significant into the 1990s.[16]

Soviet share of the European natural-gas market did not, by itself, indicate the vulnerability due to resource dependence. For vulnerability to be present, the USSR would have needed a near-monopoly over supplies and the ability to supply gas to Europe under terms that would have made it extremely difficult to switch suppliers. Therefore, we need to assess the extent to which the Soviet Union exercised control over supply, and the extent to which exporters in the region exercised control after the Soviet collapse.

Control over Supply

Throughout the postwar period, the Soviet Union periodically used its control over energy supply to influence intentions or weaken the capabilities of some of its most dependent customers.[17] Before 1948, when the rift between Stalin and Tito dramatically reduced commerce between Yugoslavia and the Soviet Union, Yugoslavia had received 60 percent of its oil from the USSR and Romania. When Tito began to pursue independent policies, Stalin applied pressure on him to return to the Soviet line by cutting the supply of oil in half; indeed, in 1949 Soviet exports of oil to Yugoslavia were only 10 percent of their 1947 level. The Soviet Union, however, did not have a monopoly over Yugoslavia's energy supply; Soviet oil was quickly replaced by supplies from the West, which was only too eager to lure Yugoslavia away from the Soviet orbit. The Soviets found that they needed the Yugoslav market, and by 1954 the USSR resumed oil trade with Yugoslavia.

During the Suez War in 1956 the USSR cut all oil deliveries to Israel in support of the Arab nations. Nonetheless, Soviet oil supplies were still delivered to Israel through black-market routes, with full knowledge of the Soviet authorities. These deliveries continued until 1967 when all diplomatic relations between the USSR and Israel were severed.

The Finnish case is one in which the mere threat of a supply cutoff determined the direction of domestic politics. In 1958 elections in Finland brought in an anti-Soviet government. In response, the USSR refused to renew trade agreements between the two countries. Because Finland relied heavily on Soviet oil, Prime Minister Fagenholm was forced to resign, and President Urho Kekkonen went to Moscow to reassure the Kremlin that Finland would remain on friendly terms with the Soviet Union. Normal trade relations were subsequently resumed.

The rift between the Soviet Union and China also led to a Soviet embargo of oil, oil equipment, and oil engineers in 1960, which did indeed cause a short-term energy crisis in China. Nonetheless, China marshaled its domestic resources to withstand the crisis and refused to bow to Soviet pressure. In 1968 the Ghanaian government seized two Soviet trawlers on suspicion of transporting arms to antigovernment rebels. The USSR subsequently cut all oil deliveries to that country; two months later the trawlers were released and the oil trade resumed. In chapter 2, I described the cases of Cuba and Lithuania; in both cases, the cutoff of energy supplies forced political changes favorable to Soviet interests in the short run, but in the Lithuanian example, independence was achieved despite Soviet manipulation of energy supplies.

At first glance it appears that three conditions were present that allowed the Soviet Union to dominate the supply of both Western European gas imports and, to a greater extent, Eastern European imports: ample reserves, high opportunity costs of contracting with alternative suppliers, and the necessity of contractual provisions that "lock" supplier and consumer into a trading relationship difficult to break. These conditions made Soviet supplies more accessible, cheaper, and more reliable than those of other potential natural-gas exporters, and continued to exist even after the Soviet collapse.

First, 40 percent of the world's proven gas reserves are in the former USSR. This is equivalent to the magnitude of Saudi Arabian oil reserves, and even if the analysis is confined only to Russia, Russia's share represents potential dominance in the natural-gas market.[18] Between 1968 and 1979 the Soviet Union had established itself as a major natural-gas exporter, tripling its exports to the European Community between 1975 and 1979.[19] Production also grew steadily throughout the 1980s. In 1983 the Soviet Union produced 633.2 million tons of natural gas; in 1988 it produced close to 890 million tons,[20] an increase of about 70 percent.

Second, despite its deepening internal economic crisis in the late 1980s and early 1990s, the Soviet Union was an attractive supplier, when compared with other alternatives. Potential alternative suppliers to Western Europe are the Netherlands, Norway, Algeria, Libya, and Iran; all have ample natural-gas reserves and have constructed pipeline networks for gas transport. The Netherlands, however, was reluctant to use up its reserves, and had therefore signed no new contracts with other Western European countries during the 1980s. In fact, production of natural gas in the Netherlands decreased throughout the 1980s.[21] Norway supplied 44.5 percent of EC gas imports in 1979, but by 1989 its share had dropped to 31.1 percent, coinciding with a rise from 9 percent to 27.9 percent during the same period for Algeria. But although Algerian exports grew faster than any other exports from 1979 to 1989, most of those exports came in as liquefied natural gas (LNG). LNG is expensive when compared with gas shipped through pipelines, and there is much dispute over its safety. Accidents to LNG tankers and storage facilities could cause catastrophic explosions and fires.[22]

Libya and Iran are not considered reliable sources of supply, due to political instability and hostility to the West.[23] Other suppliers, chiefly from among OPEC nations, would have to export natural gas to Western Europe in ships in liquid form. And if Europe expanded its gas imports from the Middle East, OPEC would gain increasing control over Europe's energy supply, an outcome that Western European energy-diversification policies discussed above attempted to avoid.

Third, the most important source of vulnerability may lie in the unique dependence created by the necessity of pipeline supply. There is no world gas market and no world gas price. Unlike oil, which often changes destinations a number of times during transport, gas must flow from point of production to point of consumption through a capital-intensive, fixed-transport medium. The pipe and compressor stations, once constructed, are investments that cannot be easily directed to alternative uses without excessive costs. Thus, the trading relationship usually involves firm contractual commitments on volume, with the gas utility matching consumption to gasline load through storage. There is little flexibility for entering spot markets or finding ready alternative supplies. Thus, when the Soviet Union built pipelines for deliveries to Western Europe, it insisted upon contracts of long duration, which were costly to break. It is this unique trading relationship that was feared would provide a channel for Soviet influence in both Western and Eastern European politics. Nevertheless, despite the unique conditions of the natural-gas market, the Soviet Union was never able to meet other market conditions that would have allowed it to fully control supply. New competitors emerged and potential competitors existed throughout the period under examination. Between 1970 and 1990 natural-gas supplies were still abundant in Western Europe; in 1988 the reserve-to-production ratio was at least forty-seven years.[24] Prospects for the import of natural gas from Norway also began to improve. In the late 1980s Norway constructed the "Zeepiep," the longest underwater natural-gas pipeline in the world, in order to transport new supplies from the Troll and Sleipner fields. Contracts for the sale of gas from these fields were negotiated with Spain, France, Belgium, Italy, Austria, and Germany. In 1988 sales were projected to average 2 billion cubic meters (bcm) per year to Belgium, 6 bcm per year to France, and 1.1 bcm per year to Spain. And Norway's reserve-to-production ratio as of 1987 was well over one hundred years.[25] It is important to note here that these new competitors did not emerge until the late 1980s, and that the lack of competitors in the market increased U.S. perceptions of Western European vulnerability during the pipeline crisis.

It should also be noted that Eastern Europe began to diversify its energy supplies and its natural-gas suppliers after the revolutions of 1989. For example, in 1991 Poland entered into negotiations with Norway as a natural-gas supplier. Both political incentives to reduce dependence on the Soviet Union and pressure from the Scandinavian countries on Poland to reduce its dependence on coal in order to diminish pollution prompted this move. Hungary, too, planned to reduce its dependence on Soviet energy sources by increasing its use of lignite and nuclear energy.

Throughout the 1980s the Soviet Union attempted to increase its own flexibility as a supplier, thereby weakening the third source of vulnerability. In 1982 it began to create a type of spot market for gas in Europe in order to fill excess pipeline capacity. France and Germany were offered spot gas sales in low quantities far below the contractual price.[26] The possibilities of developing an important spot market for natural gas, however, continue to be slim, and we can only expect them to appear under conditions of excess supply.

Contractual commitments played an important part in keeping the price of Soviet gas consistent and low in both the West and the East. Although gas prices were linked to the price of oil, throughout the 1970s there were contractual lags in the price escalators. When oil prices increased fourfold in 1973, gas prices remained stable, thus increasing the attractiveness of Soviet gas in Western European energy markets. Although new contracts signed in the 1980s had shorter lags, oil prices dropped, keeping the price of gas low.[27] This gave European importers a bargaining advantage; the Soviet Union had to give in to lower prices if they wished to increase gas exports.[28] Theoretically, the Soviet Union could have "dumped" natural gas on the Western European market in order to force out other suppliers. But, as discussed earlier, OECD countries codified projections based on "normal" market conditions in their agreement that Soviet natural-gas exports would be capped at 30 percent of consumption. Therefore, dumping and its pernicious effects were unlikely, and there was no evidence to indicate that the Soviet Union had any intention to "dump" energy supplies. Note that, in addition to the vulnerability reduction measures taken before the pipeline crisis, this agreement added a further instrument of market control.

Although the USSR did not control natural-gas supplies to Western Europe, it was clearly the most attractive supplier to the Western European gas market. Despite vast reserves, however, its production potential was limited. Western European countries knew in 1982 that by the mid-1990s they would be forced to augment cheaper Soviet gas supplies with more expensive supplies from other countries. More significant, however, was the fact that the opportunity costs of depending solely on alternative natural gas suppliers were high, and the trading relationship was difficult to break. It is understandable, then, that these conditions created perceptions of Western European dependence on Soviet natural-gas supply and, during the pipeline dispute, invoked memories of previous Soviet energy embargoes.

A second look at those embargoes, however, reveals that most failed to achieve clearly desired results. The rifts with Yugoslavia and China were never healed; in fact, in the case of Yugoslavia, the embargo pushed Tito to initiate ties with the West. Israel was able to buy oil on the open market after 1967; Fidel Castro continued to snub his nose at Soviet reforms, and Lithuania was not deterred from the path of independence.

But even if these embargoes had been successful, the same conditions between supplier and customer in these embargo episodes did not obtain in Western Europe either before or after the pipeline crisis. In all of the cases in which the Soviet Union initiated an embargo, the countries or regions were relatively weak, clearly dependent on Soviet energy supplies, with few ties to the West. Furthermore, the Soviet Union did not depend on their exports. But, as we shall see, increasingly throughout the 1980s Soviet dependence on trade with and aid from the West created conditions under which a cutoff of energy to manipulate political relations was deterred. I return to a discussion of this "exporter" dependence below.

In post-Soviet Europe, Eastern Europe's dependence on natural gas from the former Soviet Union is more pronounced. The weak economies of these countries and the fragility of their new democratic institutions put them in a category with those countries that experienced energy supply cutoffs from the Soviet Union in the past. Whether their growing bonds to the West would create conditions that reduce incentives for any future curtailment of energy supplies is indeed a matter of concern. Energy dependence can have both blatant and insidious effects. Importing states can be subject to threats of supply cutoffs in the event of future political disputes between the struggling states of the former Soviet Union; consumers might become a political constituency that would pressure their governments to avoid policies that might provoke a supply cutoff. Precisely because of these fears, negotiations have begun to diversify energy supplies in order to reduce the kind of dependence under which Russia or any other exporting state could continue to exercise dominance over Eastern Europe.

Channels of Influence

What about these more subtle influence effects under which domestic constituencies are created in order to pressure their governments not to provoke suppliers? Roger Hormats stated the potential problem clearly: "Certain regions will be very heavily dependent on Soviet gas and might apply strong pressure on national governments to avoid actions which could result in an interruption. . . . Users of Soviet gas would be likely to urge their governments to avoid action which could provoke a Soviet cutoff or sharp price increases. It is this sort of leverage which, even without a direct Soviet threat to cut off flows, could have an impact on Western European political behavior."[29]

Who were those users of Soviet gas who would have acted as Soviet "agents" within Western European polities? In Germany, the country believed to be the most vulnerable to Soviet influence, the largest percentage of gas is consumed in the north, which is (and will continue to be) supplied by Norway and the Netherlands. The industrial Ruhr region—which was not supplied by Soviet natural gas—consumed 37.5 percent of total gas supplies in 1982. Bavaria, the state where Soviet gas entered the country, consumed only 11.4 percent of the total.[30] This region would have been the most vulnerable in a scenario in which the Soviet Union attempted to influence political outcomes, yet it was traditionally the most conservative, anti-Soviet region in all of the BRD.[31] It was highly unlikely that consumers in this region would be channels of Soviet influence in West German politics. Household consumers who would have been the most vulnerable to Soviet influence are generally a diffuse group and not organized politically and their channels of influence are weak.[32]

In the eastern part of the BRD, before German unification, the major gas consuming sectors were industry (47 percent of the total), households (26 percent of the total), and power stations (11.6 percent of the total). This is important to note because it signifies that the majority of gas users (industry and power stations) had and continue to have the flexibility to handle supply interruptions. This is because they installed dual-fired burners, which allowed them to switch fuels both before the pipeline crisis and after.[33] (In general, households do not have that flexibility; nor do industrial users in the former DDR.)

Furthermore, the history of the Soviet-Western European energy trade relationship during the Cold War built the reputation of the USSR as a reliable supplier even in periods of greatest political tension. Jonathan Stern goes so far as to claim that "it could be argued with respect to oil and gas . . . Soviet deliveries have proved both more reliable and more market responsive than their competitors."[34] As we shall see, shortfalls only occurred during the severe winters of 1979, 1981, and 1985, when technical difficulties halted supplies for brief periods. The only Soviet postwar attempt to cut off the supply of essential material to Western Europe was during the Berlin blockade of 1948. In that case, the Soviet Union controlled access to all vital supplies coming into Berlin by land. Even then, however, the Berlin airlift continued to provide basic supplies, and the blockade was lifted without significant damage to West Berlin and without achieving the Soviet objective: to prevent the creation of a West German state.

Again, Eastern Europe was and continues to be more vulnerable in this regard. Throughout the region, the legacy of the old political culture, and its embedded institutions, still exists in different degrees of intensity, constraining the liberalization process. In some cases, for example, privatization schemes have bolstered the power of entrenched former communist elites. Taking advantage of the absence of realistic pricing mechanisms and other institutions that could establish the value of industrial assets, former managers were able to acquire enterprises for little or nothing, and emerged in many places as the new capitalist owners of the means of production. Conservative political forces maintain positions of power and influence throughout the bureaucracies and industrial organizations of the region. They quickly looked West when the Soviet Union was no longer willing to keep them in power, but it is probably safe to suggest that without full integration of these countries into the international economy to create alternative suppliers, many of these conservative opportunists could again yield to

Russian political pressure and become channels of foreign influence within their own political systems.

Soviet Dependence on Natural Gas Exports

If the "channels of influence" in the dependent relationship were weak in Western Europe, then Soviet capability to exert leverage in the relationship was also weakened. Furthermore, Soviet perceptions of its own dependence on trade also reduced its incentive to use the importer's dependence as leverage in a political crisis. That "dependence" can be assessed by examining Soviet energy export policies in the 1970s and 1980s.

Soviet planners believed that cheap, readily available energy supplies were the key to Soviet economic strength. Yet in the late 1970s production of coal and oil faltered, and planners were faced with a shortfall in exports, which had to be met with stock drawdowns. Planners were surprised at the fall in energy production rates. To meet the crisis, they decreased their energy supplies to Eastern Europe, contributing to economic stagnation in the late 1970s and to social and political instability there in the 1980s. At the same time, they began to sink huge investments into energy production and transport equipment. In the 1981–85 economic plan, investment in the total fuel-energy complex increased 50 percent while overall investment increased only 10 percent. Energy was clearly the highest priority sector in the Soviet economy. While energy's share of total investment in 1983 was up almost 19 percent from 1976 to 1980, all nonenergy investments rose only 4 percent. In 1983 energy claimed 67 percent of the increment to investment in the total economy.[35]

While subsidized energy exports to Eastern Europe fell dramatically throughout the 1980s, Soviet planners made it clear that they intended to continue to expand energy exports to the West. In 1985 80 percent of the value of Soviet exports to the West and 40 percent of its exports to Eastern Europe were in the form of energy; by 1989 half of all the oil exported went to the West and was paid for in hard currency. Soviet natural gas exports were about equally divided between Eastern and Western Europe; by 1991 all trade between the Soviet Union and Eastern Europe was on a hard-currency basis.

By the mid-1980s energy sales to Western Europe provided four-fifths of all Soviet hard-currency earnings. These earnings were used to purchase grain and capital goods. Although most of the grain came from the United States, Western Europe was the chief hard-currency supplier of machinery and large-diameter pipe.[36] Hard-currency export earnings paid for about 10 percent of Soviet food consumption and 10 percent of investment in equipment.[37]

This focus on energy as the key to export earnings was not new. Since the late 1950s the Soviet Union looked to the West as a market for its vast energy supplies. Soviet planners had originally encouraged the production of coal and promoted fuels with proven reserves.[38] In the 1960s, however, the massive gas reserves of the Soviet Union were discovered in the search for new sources of oil. Subsequently, the promotion of the natural-gas industry became a priority in Soviet economic development plans.

This became evident in the 1970s when energy production rates began to decline and the energy mix in the USSR shifted dramatically. First, oil and natural gas began to supplant coal as the key fuel for power generation. From 1971 to 1980 Soviet natural-gas production more than doubled.[39] In 1982 natural gas accounted for 28.6 percent of Soviet energy production; by 1990 it accounted for 35–40 percent of the total.[40] Throughout the 1980s, coal production stagnated.

By the late 1970s the decline in Soviet oil production appeared increasingly serious. Initially, this decline led to a decrease in the volume of oil exports to Western Europe. Soviet leaders recognized that if the situation persisted, and if the USSR became a net oil importer, its main source of hard-currency earnings would be eliminated. Furthermore, the USSR would have needed more hard currency to pay for imported oil.[41] Thus, throughout the 1970s and 1980s the Soviet Union pushed for the increase in natural-gas exports to supplant oil as the key hard-currency earner.

Soviet leaders recognized as early as 1971 that indigenous gas pipeline production capability would be the central constraint on the production of natural gas, and looked to the West for steel pipe imports. Between 1973 and 1979 half of all the large-diameter steel pipe exported by the BRD went to the Soviet Union; pipe exports became the largest single export item in West German trade with the Soviet Union.[42] With the increase in pipe exports throughout the 1970s, production of natural gas rose, and Soviet gas exports increased dramatically. Between 1970 and 1980 Soviet natural gas exports to Western Europe increased from 1.8 bcm annually to 30 bcm.[43]

Indeed, these trends indicated that Soviet planners saw natural gas as a central component of a stable energy future for the Soviet Union; its exploration and production was a top priority in Soviet investment plans, and natural gas played a vital role in meeting both domestic energy needs and in export prospects. In 1984 Ed Hewett argued that "Soviet leaders will be induced by the consequences of their energy production strategy to seek expanding markets for their gas exports. As a practical matter, those markets will have to be primarily in Europe because trade with other countries would involve expensive transportation systems and large capital investments."[44] In this sense, the Soviets were dependent on Western Europe, both for the import of natural-gas production technology and as a market for the export of natural gas. As I suggested in chapter 3, Soviet export of natural gas was thought to be a crucial earner of the hard currency needed to buy manufacturing equipment and consumer goods.

Despite this "exporter dependence" to reduce the odds of supply cutoffs, in the post-Soviet period the odds of unintentional disruption and curtailment of energy supplies increased. By 1990 the existing gas pipeline network—208,000 kilometers throughout the former Soviet Union—was showing signs of age and was slated for extensive repair. Soviet demise and conflict among the members of the fragile Commonwealth of Independent States (CIS) began to cast doubt on the region's ability to develop new fields and new delivery systems, from such prospective regions in Turkmenistan and Kazakhstan. Turkmenistan has a very poorly developed transport system and economic structure; as it emerged as an autonomous state, the economy was in severe crisis. Gas deposits could only be developed if investments on a broad scale were available. While Kazakhstan has a better chance to develop its resources, its population is very heterogeneous, and it will be difficult for its various ethnic populations to agree on a common policy. Even if these regions do develop their gas fields, the building of pipelines across the various republics would present tremendous economic and organizational problems. In 1992 Russia and Ukraine were engaged in a protracted dispute over ownership of the gas and oil pipelines that traversed their countries. Under these conditions, supply disruptions to Western Europe are even more likely than they were during the Cold War.

Western European Contingency Plans

Certainly European economies would be weakened if gas utilities could not supply critical users with available resources over an extended period of time. The key to vulnerability reduction, then, is a set of alternatives if a supplier should cut off or even threaten to cut off its exports. During debates over the construction of the Urengoi pipeline, Western European officials identified six ways in which this flexibility was already provided for the future; a seventh measure was added after the crisis was over.

First, as discussed above, critical industrial users were supplied by the most reliable exporters and by domestic producers. The cost of the gas from these suppliers was higher, but it included the cost of providing the security of supply.

Fuel switching provided a second means of vulnerability reduction. Fuel switching requires interruptible supply contracts and dual-firing burners. Both before and after the pipeline crisis, gas utilities contractually provided for the interruption of their supplies with certain customers. These contractual provisions varied among countries. In West Germany, for example, industries had to find alternative gas supplies for up to fifty days if the utility decided to interrupt supplies.[45] These contracts were designed to balance the gas load on a seasonal basis, but they also provided flexibility in the event of a supply cutoff. In the 1980s 9 percent of West Germany's industrial supply contracts were interruptible, as were 15 percent of all French gas contracts. In addition, Italy mandated interruptible contracts for the imports that came from the Trans-Siberian pipeline.[46]

Industries with interruptible contracts often install dual-firing burners that allow them to switch from gas to oil or coal in a short period of time. In the event that this switch is necessary, supply and demand of the alternative fuels must be considered. In the event of a supply disruption of two fuels, e.g., gas from the former Soviet Union and OPEC oil, this safety measure would lose its effectiveness, however. Although a deliberate simultaneous embargo by gas and oil suppliers is unlikely, it is not impossible, and EC governments must recognize conditions under which there will be little flexibility to switch between fuels.

A third security measure involved enlarged storage capacity for stockpiles. Gas is more expensive to stock than oil, and thus stockpiles were never as large for gas as they were for oil. Although gas storage capacity was only developed commercially, to balance demand, it could be used to provide reserves in the event of a curtailment of supplies.[47] In 1982 West German storage capacity was 2.4 bcm. This represented 4.5 percent of total 1982 consumption and 23 percent of 1982 Soviet gas imports.[48] Whereas France's stockpiles covered 100 percent of Soviet annual imports, West Germany's stockpiles were planned to cover only 50 percent and Austria reported that it had stocks equal to six months' consumption.

A fourth security measure was the provision for the reallocation of gas from alternative suppliers. Usually gas flows are designed to reduce transportation costs. This means that they flow from the source to the nearest user. In the BRD, customers in Bavaria and in the five new states used Soviet gas while customers in the north used Norwegian and Dutch gas. The grid is not designed, however, to transport gas from north to south. Nevertheless, the pipelines are in place to do so, and there is no technical reason why gas cannot be pumped from the northern to the southern regions. In all European countries, gas networks allow for reallocation of supplies.[49]

The feasibility of reallocation was actually tested in the early 1980s. In the coldest months of 1979 and 1980 the USSR reduced deliveries to the BRD by 25 percent because of technical problems in the pipelines. In 1981 the Soviet Union announced a cutback of 30 percent. During those periods, Soviet customers were supplied with lower-BTU gas from other sources, and they experienced very little difficulty.[50] Shortfalls were then made up in the summer months. If a supply disruption is prolonged, however, additional contingency plans must be made to balance the supply/demand load.

Fifth, measures were taken to increase "surge production capacity." The Gronigen gas field in the Netherlands was earmarked for increased production in case of an emergency, and the Dutch government adopted a policy to conserve its gas as a strategic reserve. Since the early 1980s, no new gas export contracts were signed in order to conserve supplies. West German reserves were not so flexible, because half of the domestically produced gas has high levels of sulphur and nitrogen that had to be removed before use. Furthermore, production levels were decreasing in domestic gas fields.[51] France and Italy produced even less natural gas domestically than Germany.[52]

Sixth, governments planned to mandate conservation measures in case of emergency. The state could raise the price of natural gas in order to reduce consumption or legislate a reduction in the volume of consumption. The West German government used this vulnerability reduction measure duringthe Arab oil boycott of 1973; the population was mobilized to sacrifice consumption, sending an important signal to the energy supplier that the embargo would ultimately not achieve its goals.

Finally, international agreements codified projections of Soviet imports into Western Europe and capped them at the projected level, a measure which—if pressures to import more arose—created an incentive to find alternative suppliers and increase domestic gas production. The IEA based its projections on contingency plans in place by 1983 in Europe, well before most contingency plans had been fully implemented. Thus the 30–35 percent figure could actually be even more flexible in the 1990s when the "threat" of a curtailment of natural-gas supplies from the former Soviet Union is even higher than it was in 1982.

A combination of all of these measures provides a "safety net" that guards against vulnerability to a disruption of ex-Soviet natural-gas supplies in Western Europe. Such a safety net sent a signal to the Soviet Union that a gas embargo would have little damaging effect. It could thus provide an important disincentive for supply cutoffs and threats of supply disruptions. As of 1992, however, similar safety nets did not exist in Eastern Europe, and the region remained more vulnerable.

Conclusion

The vulnerability argument focusing on resource dependence claimed that an importer's vulnerability to the influence of exporters over its political choices or capabilities varies with the intensity of the need for imports and with the degree of the exporter's control over the needed good. Exporters rarely have an absolute monopoly on supply, but they might create conditions under which it is difficult to switch suppliers. The IEA in 1983 set the level of "dependence" on natural gas at 30 percent of consumption; imports of Soviet natural gas now approach 40 percent of all imports. Nonetheless, given the characteristics of natural gas trade under which the opportunity costs of switching suppliers is high, competition is emerging among alternative suppliers. As the 1990s began, Soviet incentive to manipulate its control over supply for political purposes had been drastically reduced both by the need to export and the decline in the political power of the Soviet state. But as the Soviet Union itself disappeared and fragile new states were born, the odds of supply disruptions drastically increased.

This assessment suggests that the United States did not have a strong case for arguing that Western Europe was vulnerable in its natural-gas trade with the Soviet Union before the pipeline crisis. U.S. fears of resource dependence before the end of the crisis hinged on the erroneous assumption that there were few alternatives to Soviet imports and little flexibility to switch suppliers. But the analysis here suggests that both domestic and foreign alternative sources of supply did exist, and that contingency plans—known to the Reagan administration—increased flexibility and decreased vulnerability. Furthermore, there were few channels of domestic political influence created by natural-gas imports from the Soviet Union; its ability to exercise political influence as a result of the relationship was minimal. In West Germany, the country most dependent on Soviet gas, the channels of influence simply did not exist. Furthermore, the USSR had a good track record as a reliable supplier to Western Europe, and even though they grew, Soviet natural-gas exports represented a small percentage of total energy demand in Western Europe during the 1980s. Projections of that demand during the crisis were actually quite accurate. Ironically, the increase in Western European natural-gas imports that so worried the Reagan administration had been part of a conscious effort to reduce dependence on OPEC oil. Finally, the degree of Soviet dependence on its natural gas exports reduced its incentive to link those exports to political or strategic aims. The IEA agreement reached in 1983 provided an additional brake on resource dependence, but was not in itself the key to vulnerability reduction; the essential vulnerability reduction measures had been taken earlier. And the fact that new competitors entered the market in the late 1980s reduced vulnerability even further. Therefore, although the IEA agreement and market conditions reduced Western Europe's vulnerability in the late 1980s, it was minimal to begin with. Contingency plans and alternative suppliers mean that Western Europe's vulnerability will continue to be low, despite the new uncertainties in the post-Soviet period.

In sum, Western Europe's vulnerabilities of resource dependence in this case were low before the pipeline crisis and were reduced even further thereafter. Coercive measures threatened by the United States could not be implemented in a multilateral setting, and policy coordination among importers could only be achieved through agreement on the level of dependence that would cause vulnerability. That agreement resolved the disputes and strengthened Western market control.

The Eastern European case is somewhat different, and its resource dependence on the former Soviet Union is exacerbated by economic crisis and hard-currency shortages. Eastern European countries experienced serious interruptions in oil deliveries beginning in 1990, when short supplies led the Soviets to serve their Western customers first. Eastern Europeans are beginning to switch from coal to other energy sources, and are looking to the West for natural gas supplies. Cash shortages, however, will constrain these efforts. Thus, in the near term, Eastern European resource dependence on the former Soviet Union is still high.

6

Financial Instability and Debtor Leverage in East-West Economic Relations

Throughout the 1970s, and the latter part of the 1980s, Eastern Europe and the Soviet Union stepped up their borrowing from Western banks to finance their growing demand for Western imports. Increased borrowing was essential to finance these imports, because these countries' currencies were inconvertible and their exports were uncompetitive. And as Western exports to the East soared, so did Eastern Europe's debt to the West. By 1982 the combination of rapid unregulated debt expansion and the shift in the lending burden to European private banks led to an Eastern European debt crisis. By that time, the bulk of Polish and Hungarian export revenues were spent on debt service. The question of default, especially in the case of Poland, began to loom large in the minds of bankers. All of Eastern Europe seemed to be in a precarious position. The Polish debt crisis sent shock waves throughout the international banking system, causing funds to dry up, deposits to be withdrawn, and credits to be curtailed in other CMEA countries.

During this period of rising Eastern European debt, the United States stepped up pressure on its Western European allies to tighten credit to the East. The U.S. government demanded multilateral policy coordination among NATO countries to curtail export financing of manufactured goods to the adversary. In support of this pressure to cut the amount of Western lending to the East, U.S. officials made three arguments. First, they argued that Western banks would be vulnerable to unstable economic conditions in Eastern European countries. Second, they claimed that overextended commercial banks would become channels of Soviet influence with their own governments. And third, they feared that the East would have a bargaining advantage in the debtor-creditor relationship. Assistant Secretary of Defense Richard Perle stated the fear simply: "The creation of a community of interest between Western banking circles and the Soviet Government is hardly what is needed to arrest the troubling neutralist intent that we detect in some European countries. Moreover, the fact that Western banks, rather than the Soviet Government will bear the risk will put the Soviets in a commanding position with respect to any renegotiation of terms in the outyears. My bank has rather a lot of influence on me, as one of its smaller customers. Its largest industrial borrowers have rather a lot of influence on it. This is a commonplace that we understand at home, and it applies as well abroad."[1]

This statement was not born in the anti-Soviet hysteria of the Reagan era; it echoed beliefs voiced by almost every U.S. administration since 1917 about financing trade with the Soviet Union.[2] Beginning in the 1920s, successive U.S. administrations viewed the new Soviet regime as an international outlaw. Presidents Wilson, Harding, Coolidge, and Hoover all advocated nonrecognition of the Soviet Union. Hoover, however, placed particular emphasis on the Soviet regime's international economic behavior as the basis for his position. He believed that the new Soviet state had demonstrated its unwillingness to abide by the accepted principles of international relations through its refusal to repay pre-Soviet czarist debts to U.S. citizens. Soviet refusal to meet its debt obligations proved to him that the USSR did not respect international rules associated with property rights and the sanctity of contracts. If the Soviets could not recognize those rules, he argued, the U.S. could not recognize the Soviet Union.[3] Furthermore, during his tenure as secretary of Commerce, the U.S. government initiated a ban on long-term private financing of exports to the USSR if that financing required the public sale of securities.

In 1934, Congress passed the Johnson Debt Default Act, forbidding governments in default on their debt payments to float bonds in the United States. The disputed Soviet debt put them in default. In that same year, the Export-Import Bank was created to finance U.S. exports abroad, but its board of trustees refused to grant credits to the Soviet Union for the same reason. For the next thirty-nine years, Ex-Im Bank credits went unused in U.S.-Soviet trade.

In the postwar period, however, Western European export credit agencies liberally financed Soviet purchase of capital goods, leading the U.S. to take steps to curtail East-West trade finance. The *political* goals that pushed U.S. policies toward continued denial of trade finance to the East were clear in the climate of anticommunism and the Cold War, but vulnerability claims were never grounded. And with the collapse of communism, fears of financial vulnerability have emerged in a new form: by 1991 the Soviet Union's external debt had become a matter of concern to the financial community. In the face of rising Soviet debt and hard-currency shortages, nervous commercial bankers were increasingly unwilling to lend to the USSR and most of its newly liberated Eastern European neighbors. With private banks withdrawing as lenders, Western governments were asked to significantly increase financial assistance to the Soviet Union, increasing the amount owed to Western governments from $12 billion in 1989 to $21.5 billion in 1990.

To what extent was the West vulnerable in its financial relations with Eastern Europe and the Soviet Union under state-socialist regimes? To what extent is the West vulnerable in the 1990s as those regimes have collapsed and as these countries struggle to achieve open economies and political democracies? The vulnerability thesis makes two claims: first, lending nations are vulnerable if an infusion of their capital into an adversary's economy redirects funds to the military. Second, creditor nations are in a vulnerable position when debtor nations face insolvency.

This second kind of financial vulnerability takes three distinct forms. First, the prospect of default can have a destabilizing effect on the international financial system; both creditors and debtors are vulnerable to a collapse of that system. Second, within financial negotiations to avoid default, debtor nations can have the upper hand, and creditors face the prospect of debt restructuring that offers more favorable terms for the borrower than the lender; that is, debtors can exercise *leverage* in debt-restructuring negotiations. Third, both the prospect of default and the potential for debtor leverage places important constraints on creditor nations' foreign policy goals toward debtors. Economic and political sanctions will be difficult to implement because other creditor nations and commercial bankers apply pressure to maintain trade in order to prevent default. And if one creditor nation wishes to ease a debtor nation's financial burden for political reasons, it may face intense opposition from bankers and creditor nations who wish to present a unified front to apply pressure for repayment on their terms. A central aspect of financial vulnerability, then, is that it limits a creditor state's ability to use trade as an instrument of either positive or negative political leverage.

This chapter focuses on the second argument of vulnerability: financial instability, debtor leverage, and constraints on other foreign policy goals. Because of the extremely difficult economic situation Eastern Europe faced in the early 1980s and both Eastern Europe and the Soviet Union face at the beginning of the 1990s, these vulnerability arguments far outweighed those that claimed that these loans could increase Western vulnerability. In order to assess the extent of vulnerability, we must examine the volume of these countries' debt, the underlying causes of its growth, the prospects of insolvency according to the traditional indicators of indebtedness, the kind and degree of leverage debtors exerted in negotiations, and the actual foreign policy constraints that creditors faced.

I will also examine the kind and extent of financial vulnerability in two periods. The first section analyzes vulnerabilities that accompanied the Eastern European debt crisis of 1982, while the second section examines debt problems and vulnerabilities that have arisen since the collapse of communism in Eastern Europe and the Soviet Union. The evidence suggests that in the first period, because instabilities in the international financial system raised the prospect of insolvency in Eastern Europe, lenders were vulnerable to debtor leverage that borrowers did not exercise. In the current period, despite more intense regulation by governments, the Paris Club, and multilateral lending institutions, the sources of vulnerability have changed, but both lenders and borrowers are vulnerable to a financial crisis in the region that can destabilize the international financial system and constrain Western foreign policy choices.

The Eastern European Debt Crisis of 1982

In 1970 CMEA debt to the West was only $8.3 billion. The first large-scale CMEA borrowing began in 1973, and by the end of 1974 it had reached $24 billion. Table 6.1 shows that one year later, in 1975, the total debt had reached $35 billion. By 1980 the debt was over $80 billion, and by 1985 the gross debt was $100 billion. By 1980 Poland's gross hard currency debt of $24 billion was the highest of all of the CMEA countries. The Soviet Union followed with $23 billion and the GDR was third, with $13 billion.[4]

TABLE 6.1

Growth of Gross East European Debt ($ million)

	1975	1980	1985	1986	1987	1988	1989	1990*
Bulgaria	2640	3509	3739	4955	6218	7915	9133	10400
Czechoslovakia	1132	4896	4608	5567	6657	7281	7915	7900
DDR	5188	13896	13000	15300	18400	20300	20000	N/A
Hungary	3929	9090	13804	16914	19592	19625	20605	21700
Poland	8388	24128	29806	33587	38800	37746	41400	48200
Romania	2924	9557	6861	6984	6515	2799	582	2300
USSR	10577	23512	28900	31400	39200	43000	54000	52000
Total	34778	88588	100718	114704	135382	138666	153635	142500

*preliminary   N/A = not applicable.
GDR data for 1975 and 1980 do not include West German imports.
SOURCE: 1975–80 Vienna Institute for Comparative Economic Studies, *Comecon Data 1989*, New York: Greenwood Press, 1989, p. 261; 1985–90: *Financial Market Trends*, "The International Financial Situation of the Central and Eastern European Countries," vol. 48, Paris: OECD, February 1991, p. 20; DDR data from 1985–89: *Business International*, "East Germany Country Report," no. 4, 1989, p. 17 (this source includes government lending). Data from 1989 is from March 1989.

Between 1970 and 1982 the Eastern European debt had increased eightfold. This dramatic growth, although not as explosive as that of the LDCs, resulted from a confluence of four important forces: increased import demands beginning in the late 1960s; difficulty in finding export markets in hard-currency countries; Western firms' eagerness to find export markets; and private banks' eagerness to finance those exports.

Until 1970 these forces were weak in East-West trade, and CMEA countries had avoided borrowing in the West. Rapid decline in their rates of economic growth, however, led planners to attempt productivity increases by importing Western technology. Western banks and their governments were only too eager to provide balance-of-payments financing and additional export credits. Because of its spotless record, bankers saw Eastern Europe as a reliable credit risk. The accumulation of petrodollars in Western banks, combined with the 1974 recession, freed loan capital, as lenders scrambled to compete for business. Eastern European borrowers had little difficulty in arranging loans on excellent terms in a financial environment marked by excessive liquidity and "overcompetition" among lenders. In the political climate of detente and the economic climate of a recession, Western European governments liberally extended credits and credit guarantees to the East in an effort to promote both good will and exports; commercial banks followed suit.

Although Western imports into the CMEA countries greatly increased during this period of easy finance, Western demand for Eastern goods did not grow at the same pace. The recession that began in 1974 closed Western markets to the East, and increasing EC agricultural protectionism exacerbated the problem, especially for Hungary, Bulgaria, and Romania, countries whose chief exports were farm products. In 1978 30 percent of Eastern Europe's exports went to Western industrialized countries, while 38 percent of their imports came from the West. The debt continued to grow as imports outpaced exports. And as imports grew faster than exports, repaying the debt in convertible currency became increasingly difficult. New loans were needed to service old ones. Evidence of a debt "problem" can be detected in the debt-export ratio.

Rapid growth in the volume of debt is not a significant indicator of debt problems, unless there is also a change in the debt-export ratio. In fact, growth in volume can be expected, given the policy changes in CMEA countries and the decision to borrow in the West in the early

TABLE 6.2
Net Debt/Export Ratios (Percentage)

	1975	1980	1985	1986	1987	1988	1989	1990*
Bulgaria	241	84	50	135	157	173	254	468
Czechoslovakia	35	74#	89	101	111	112	105	111
DDR	116	154	N/A	N/A	N/A	N/A	N/A	N/A
Hungary	N/A	211#	275	352	358	331	302	343
Poland	N/A	288#	546	570	556	442	452	418
Romania	77	146	103	107	73	27	−21	38
USSR	95	43	62	72	91	92	128	139

*preliminary #1979 figures N/A = consistent data not available.
SOURCE: 1971–1980 U.S. Congress, Joint Economic Committee, *East-West Trade: The Prospects to 1985,* (Washington, D.C.: U.S. Government Printing Office, 1982, pp. 41, 94, 154, 173, 227, 264, 308; 1985–1990: (excluding DDR): *Financial Market Trends,* "The International Financial Situation of the Central and Eastern European Countries," Paris: OECD, February 1991, p. 24.

TABLE 6.3
Net Interest as a Percentage of Exports

	1985	1986	1987	1988	1989	1990*
Bulgaria	3	6	9	11	20	43
Czechoslovakia	8	6	7	7	9	10
Hungary	18	29	22	24	26	35
Poland	49	42	39	36	42	41
Romania	9	8	6	4	1	1
USSR	4	4	5	6	9	14

*preliminary
SOURCE: 1985–1990 *Financial Market Trends,* "The International Financial Situation of the Central and Eastern European Countries," Paris: OECD, February 1991, p. 25.

1970s. Such a rapid debt expansion only leads to lender vulnerability if the borrower finds it increasingly difficult to service the debt. The higher the proportion of a country's income devoted to debt service, the more that country's capacity to repay is in jeopardy.

The debt-export ratio and the interest-export ratio are the most widely employed indicators of a borrower's creditworthiness. The less creditworthy a borrower, the more vulnerable the lender to insolvency and debtor leverage. The debt-export ratio is the net debt (gross debt minus reserves) divided by annual exports. Usually, a ratio of less than 100 indicated a country with a light debt burden; between 100 and 200 indicated a moderate debt burden; and over 200 signaled a heavy debt burden. The interest-export ratio is the annual interest and principle payments on total long-term debt divided by annual export earnings. The ratio shows the percentage of earnings that go to pay off the debt. The higher the proportion of export earnings devoted to debt service, the more a country's capacity to repay is in jeopardy. Table 6.2 shows that the debt-export ratio for Poland and Hungary demonstrated high vulnerability for creditors by 1980.

When countries have difficulty servicing the debt, banks may be willing to roll over principal payments as long as interest payments are faithfully met. Because, beginning in the late 1970s, banks consistently rolled over their loans to Eastern Europe, it was the interest service ratio that came to be the best indicator for bankers of CMEA countries' ability to repay their loans. In 1981 the interest service ratio for Eastern Europe as a whole (excluding the USSR) had reached 22 percent.[5]

The debt-service ratio is a fourth indicator of vulnerability. It includes amortization payments on medium- and long-term debt as well as interest payments. Claiming vulnerability on the basis of the debt-service ratio is often a subjective issue. Bankers may express confidence in countries with a ratio of 40 percent; other countries are considered to be in trouble with a ratio of 10 percent. Table 6.4 shows that in 1980, Bulgaria's debt-service ratio was 35 percent, Czechoslovakia's 22 percent, the DDR's 39 percent, Hungary's 45 percent, and Poland's, 86 percent.

Not only did a burdensome debt grow significantly during this period, but CMEA countries also increased their commercial borrowing faster than their official borrowing. As discussed in chapter 2, this was part of an overall trend in private international lending in the 1970s and the growth of the Eurodollar market, but it is an indicator of

Table 6.4
Debt Service Ratio (Percentage)

	1975	1980	1985	1986	1987	1988	1989	1990*
Bulgaria	44	35	14	31	30	35	48	77
Czechoslovakia	11	22	20	20	21	18	23	25
DDR	26	39	N/A	N/A	N/A	N/A	N/A	N/A
Hungary	24	45	58	67	52	57	49	65
Poland	23	86	96	63	79	68	76	71
Romania	N/A	N/A	28	28	26	20	19	10
USSR	N/A	N/A	20	23	24	22	26	29

*preliminary **1971 figure N/A = consistent data not available.
SOURCE: 1975–1980: For Bulgaria, Czechoslovakia and the DDR—David Driscoll, "East European Hard-Currency Debt to the West," in *Congressional Research Service*, Library of Congress, May 5, 1982, pp 14, 17; for Poland—David Driscoll, "Sovereign Debt: The Polish Example," *Congressional Research Service*, Library of Congress, January 4, 1982, pp 14, 17; 1985–1990: *Financial Market Trends*, "The International Financial Situation of the Central and Eastern European Countries," Paris OECD: February 1991, p. 26.

vulnerability, because it is usually unregulated and unguaranteed. In the mid-1960s it was estimated that 80 percent of all short- and medium-term credits extended to CMEA countries were backed by official credit guarantees.[6] Table 6.5 shows that by the 1980s, most of the CMEA debt was held by private banks.[7]

The combination of rapid debt expansion, growing current account deficits, and the shift in the lending burden to private banks led to the Eastern European debt crisis of 1982. By that time, both Poland and Hungary were unable to expand their export earnings to meet their loan payments; Poland's debt-service ratio reached almost 90 percent and Hungary's debt service ratio was 57 percent. Poland's economic problems led creditors to question the wisdom of their lending to all of Eastern Europe, and lending institutions appeared highly vulnerable to a breakdown in the financial system.

The Polish Debt Crisis

The Polish debt crisis provided the first indication to Western bankers that Eastern European debt had reached dangerous levels. By 1977 Poland had begun to reduce imports in order to service the existing debt. But rising interest payments on Eurocurrency loans began to worsen the current account deficits after 1978. Table 6.1 shows that between 1975 and 1980 the Polish external debt nearly tripled from $8 billion to $24 billion. The Polish government lacked both the export potential and the hard-currency reserves to meet even its interest payment obligations.

In April 1980 the Polish central bank attempted to put together a syndicated loan of $550 million, but banks refused to participate in new loans unless the Polish government implemented strict economic reform measures. In response, the Gierek government enacted an austerity plan that supressed wage increases. The austerity measures taken were crucial in creating widespread support for the general strike in August 1980 under the leadership of the Solidarity union.

Even with these new measures, however, Poland had only been able to raise a $325 million loan for seven years.[8] This, Polish officials admitted, would not be enough to even service the existing debt and the Polish economy continued to decline. One year later, in April 1981, Poland was forced to negotiate with its major creditors on debt relief. Fifteen major Western government creditors agreed to reschedule 90 percent

TABLE 6.5
Hard-Currency Debt by Category of Lender (Percent Share of Total)

	1971	1976	1980	1985	1986	1987	1988	1989
Bulgaria								
Commercial	60	90	94	64	67	71	73	78
Official	40	10	6	36	33	29	27	22
Czechoslovakia								
Commercial	59	85	N/A	60	57	63	66	69
Official	41	15		40	43	37	34	31
DDR								
Commerical	61	86	89	78	76	77	77	76
Official	39	14	11	22	24	23	23	24
Hungary								
Commercial	90	N/A	99	72	68	73	74	72
Official	10		1	28	32	27	26	28
Poland								
Commercial	37	N/A	59	36	35	36	31	31
Official	63		40	64	65	64	69	69
Romania								
Commercial	N/A	63	70	43	38	36	26	57
Official		23	18	57	62	64	74	43
USSR								
Commercial	23	65	57	45	47	60	71	75
Official	77	35	43	55	53	40	29	25

N/A = consistent data not available.

SOURCE: 1971–1980 U.S. Congress, Joint Economic Committee, *East-West Trade: The Prospects to 1985*, (Washington, D.C.: U.S. Government Printing Office, 1982, pp. 41, 94, 154, 173, 227, 264, 308; 1985–1990: *Financial Market Trends*, "The International Financial Situation of the Central and Eastern European Countries," Paris: OECD, February 1991, p. 23; DDR data: *Business International*, "East Germany Country Report," 1989, no. 4. p. 17.

of the Polish official debt, and agreement was also reached later to reschedule commercial loans.[9] Meanwhile, Poland requested membership in the IMF, in the hope of a major loan to ease the crisis. IMF membership would also raise the incentives of commercial banks to continue lending. Benjamin Cohen argues that the United States was in favor of easing Poland's debt burden at this time in order to support the political efforts of Solidarity in its opposition to the Communist regime.[10]

The declaration of martial law on December 13, 1981, however, led the United States to seek a major policy change among Western countries. One faction within the Reagan administration, led by Defense Secretary Casper Weinberger and supported by right-wing groups headed by the Conservative Caucus, sought a declaration of default on Poland's official debt to the U.S. government.[11] Those in favor of this option made two arguments for it. First, a declaration of default would put financial and political pressure on the Soviet Union and deprive the communist bloc of the infusion of credit it had enjoyed in the 1970s and the Soviet Union would have to use its own precious hard currency to bail out Poland.

Second, a declaration of default would put pressure on the recalcitrant Western European allies who were flaunting their "business as usual" policies in the face of increasing tensions between the Soviet Union and the United States. A particular thorn in the side of the Reagan administration was the Trans-Siberian pipeline construction, which the administration had attempted to block. Responding to the Polish declaration of martial law, President Reagan imposed sanctions on American oil and gas technology destined for the Soviet Union. The U.S. had hoped that the Europeans would follow Washington's lead and impose their own sanctions on the export of energy equipment, but they refused. One way to coerce Western Europe, conservative forces argued, would be to declare Poland in default. Because of the interlocking nature of the world banking system, a declaration of Polish default would trigger cross-default agreements that would dry up future loans earmarked for the pipeline. Western European governments, supported by the U.S. Treasury and State departments, strongly argued against a U.S. declaration of default, stating that such an option would trigger an international financial crisis. Default would force Western governments to make good on their commitments to honor credit guarantees and lead to massive writeoffs of the nonguaranteed portion of the debt. This would drastically reduce the banks' assets and interrupt their stream of profits.[12] In this way, the threat of financial instability constrained U.S. foreign policy options. As Benjamin Cohen aptly suggests of this case, "Rarely . . . have the complex connections between high finance and high politics been quite so manifest."[13]

Ultimately, Western European governments were able to strike a tacit bargain with the U.S. to avoid a declaration of Polish default. Throughout 1981 it became clear that the Polish crisis was part of a much larger international debt problem. Within the IMF, the U.S. lobbied for support for a debt-restructuring package for Mexico, which was also tottering on the edge of default. Western Europeans, particularly the West Germans, would not support the loan for Mexico until they had assurance that the U.S. would not place Western European banks in danger. The U.S. backed down and agreed not to declare Poland in default.[14] The default option was simply not viable, given the interests of Western European banks and governments in Eastern European stability and solvency, and U.S. interests in protecting its own banks, and its interest in Mexico's solvency and stability.

Since default was now out of the question, the Reagan administration sought alternative means to pressure Poland's military government through the instrument of Western trade finance. Four unilateral measures were quickly decided upon: a freeze on all new official credits, suspension of debt rescheduling negotiations, opposition to Poland's membership in the IMF, and suspension of Ex-Im Bank's line of credit insurance for Poland. The U.S. hoped for policy coordination among the Western allies in pursuit of these goals. As a symbolic act, other NATO governments agreed to suspend negotiations on further official debt rescheduling. And because Poland's creditworthiness was now in question, they cut by half all new official credits to Poland. The United States wanted these measures to remain in effect until the Polish government put an end to martial law, released all political prisoners, and resumed talks with Solidarity.[15] European officials, however, stated that because the suspension of restructuring negotiations was purely symbolic, they would resume, even if these demands were not met. And credits would be granted on the basis of financial decisions, not Polish "political concessions."[16] U.S. foreign policy options were again constrained.

Clearly the situation had become desperate for Poland; indeed, vulnerability was mutual. In order to meet the terms of a previous rescheduling agreement, Poland attempted to borrow $350 million in the

Eurocurrency market, but to no avail. In January 1982 the Reagan administration ordered the Commodity Credit Corporation (CCC) to offer reimbursement to U.S. banks for $71.3 million in interest that the CCC had guaranteed. This was a touchy situation because legally the CCC was supposed to require a formal declaration of default before it could make good on its guarantees. The Reagan administration hesitated to do this, however, because a formal declaration would trigger cross-default agreements and a possible domino effect, with other CMEA countries following suit. Private banks, too, hesitated to take up the administration's offer, because the CCC would only pay 6 percent interest on the debt, which was 10 percentage points below what the banks had negotiated. Furthermore, the offer would tie the banks' hands in future negotiations because they would have to relinquish their rights to negotiate with Poland on rescheduling outstanding debts.[17] Talk of default was in the air, however, as creditor banks rushed to restructure the commercial debt. By April 1982 Poland reached formal agreement with Western commercial banks on rescheduling. And by the close of 1983 Western governments had reopened negotiations on further rescheduling. By that time Poland had reduced imports from the West by 50 percent and the debt crisis appeared to be in remission.[18]

In negotiating new loans, however, Poland appeared to have the upper hand in exercising some leverage over creditors *within* the negotiations. Part of a 1984 rescheduling agreement with 500 creditor banks allowed Poland a grace period on interest payments on $200 million owed those banks. Usually banks only allow a grace period on the repayment of principal in rescheduling agreements. Between 1981 and 1984 Poland made no interest or principal payments on its official debt to Western governments.[19] The U.S., however, though largely constrained by Western European creditors, was granted one concession: in July 1984, in return for the release of all political prisoners, the United States withdrew its objection to IMF membership for Poland.

The Polish crisis, however, had a ripple effect throughout Eastern Europe. Deposit withdrawals and the absence of new credit led Romania to declare a moratorium on the repayment of its foreign debt in early 1982. Nine western banks put together a restructuring package, which deferred for three years 80 percent of the Romanian debt due in 1981. These nine banks negotiated without a mandate from the other 240 to 320 banks involved and offered the agreement as a fait accompli to other Romanian creditors. This was a risky decision. Because of cross-default clauses in syndication agreements, any creditor bank could have broken ranks and declared Romania in default, thus forcing other banks to do the same. Meager Romanian assets in the West, however, reduced the banks' incentive to do so. The IMF stood ready to release previously frozen credits to Romania, which raised the confidence of private bankers. And, as I shall discuss below, the regime of Nicolae Ceausescu took draconian measures to reduce imports. Thus, the crisis was averted.

At the same time, Hungary was facing similar problems. Early in 1982 the Hungarian central bank was beset by a wave of withdrawals by foreign institutions. In the first quarter of that year, $1.1 billion was withdrawn from the country, resulting in a sudden liquidity crunch. Even the Soviet Union withdrew funds, probably to aid in its own efforts to support Poland. Hungary was considered a crucial link in the fragile financial situation at the time. Bankers feared that if there were runs on Hungarian banks, runs on other Eastern European banks would be unavoidable. Confidence was at an all-time low. Romania's problems were out in the open; the DDR and the Soviet Union were low on foreign exchange, and the Euromarkets had been closed to the East, as banks expressed their desire to curtail further loans to CMEA countries. Hungary had already drawn down its existing line of credit with the Bank for International Settlements (BIS), but the BIS decided to act as a lender of last resort, arranging credits from thirteen different European central banks. This action was further enhanced by a line of credit from the IMF.[20] Hungary's decision to join the IMF in 1982 raised the confidence of Western bankers, and in the first eleven months of 1983 Hungary raised $385 million in syndicated loans on the Euromarkets.

The successful resolution of these problems helped other Eastern European countries to weather the general debt crisis without much damage. Bulgaria did not experience a credit cutback from the West during that difficult period. Czechoslovakia's low foreign debt ($3.5 billion in 1982) and its relatively low debt-service ratio gave that country a good reputation as a borrower. The DDR's special relationship with the BRD made that country a fairly good credit risk as well.[21]

The only country that did not face a debt problem during this period was the Soviet Union. For decades, through 1988, the debt position of the USSR was unassailably strong. Debt and ratios of relative indebtedness were low and deposits at Western banks were maintained at very high levels. In addition, the Soviet Union had massive stocks of gold that could be used as a reserve asset. Furthermore, central authorities acted very conservatively with regard to international finance and avoided large increases in foreign debt. Therefore, commercial banks were more than willing to lend to the Soviet Union.

Debt Resolution and Social Revolution

By the mid-1980s all of the countries in the region had satisfied creditors that they would not be vulnerable to default. Central planners were able to drastically cut imports, thus recording large trade surpluses with OECD countries. Furthermore, by 1982 OECD governments had aligned official rates with market rates for these countries, thus removing the cost advantage of borrowing from official sources. Following the debt crisis of 1982, and the valiant efforts these countries had made to restore their own credit standing, they were again able to raise large sums in commercial markets. As table 6.5 shows, commercial bank claims on Eastern European countries rose about 30 percent between 1981 and 1988, and the commercial bank share in total debt declined only moderately.[22]

The attempts to use financial leverage on the part of the United States in Poland did not go unnoticed in the region; perceptions of *mutual vulnerability* were raised, and other Eastern European countries were especially keen to avoid *Western* economic leverage; thus, they not only turned to private markets but reduced their borrowing needs. This was possible because central planners had total authority over aggregate borrowing in foreign markets.

In efforts to reduce their debt, they cut imports from the West by 16 percent in 1982, and by a further 7 percent in the first half of 1983. Exports to the West also grew by 4 percent in the first six months of 1983, after three years of export decline. Between 1981 and 1983 CMEA countries as a whole cut their imports from the West by 36 percent. During that period Poland and Romania had cut their imports by 50 percent.

But the import cuts took their toll on these countries' populations. Ruling elites had plunged their economies into debt, in part, to purchase consumer goods and raise wages to stave off domestic unrest. The sudden reduction in imports combined with ever-decreasing rates of economic growth and accompanying decline in living standards further squeezed populations who could no longer be mobilized by ideological appeals.

Recovery from the debt crisis of 1982 revitalized the interest of private lenders in the region, and between 1984 and 1989 the share of commercial unguaranteed debt in the totals increased. In this period easier terms on unguaranteed loans from banks were available, and interest rates on officially guaranteed export credits were increasingly aligned with market rates, thus further reducing incentives to use official credits. The Soviet Union in particular saw a rapid growth in the outstanding volume of unguaranteed credit.

The revolutions of 1989 were partly a response to the deepening economic crisis and the power of the central authorities to impose domestic hardships in the interest of satisfying foreign creditors.[23] Romania provides the most extreme example. In 1981 Nicolae Ceausescu decreed that basic foods would be rationed domestically and exported to earn foreign exchange; shortly thereafter he adopted a draconian austerity program to accelerate repayment of foreign debt. Ceausescu justified domestic food shortages that followed the rationing program on the ground that eating less was good for the people's health. He argued that "so far as our nutrition is concerned, we are already consuming too much."[24] In winter, electricity was rationed, and state law decreed that inside temperatures could not exceed 45 degrees Fahrenheit. Imports were cut to a minimum, resulting in the rapid obsolescence of production machinery. By 1989 foreign debt, which topped $10 billion at the beginning of the 1980s, had been repaid in full; imports from OECD countries fell from $4 to $1.2 billion between 1980 and 1989. As the 1990s began, Romania was in many respects an underdeveloped country whose living standards were below those of many Third World nations.[25]

The Introduction of Markets in Former Communist Regimes: New Vulnerabilities

When the Soviet Union released its grip on Eastern Europe in 1989, newly elected democratic regimes rushed to restructure their economies to enter the world market, seeking investments and technology on new terms in the hope of digging their economies out of crisis.

By 1991 virtually all of the former Warsaw Pact countries had made the decision to transform their societies by introducing full-fledged market economies; they had either promised or actually begun to decentralize decision making, diversify ownership, and liberalize prices and foreign trade. Were Western vulnerabilities lessened or intensified? Did the kind and degree of vulnerability change with the change in the economic and political systems of former communist regimes?

As could easily be expected, in the aftermath of communist collapse throughout the region, economic growth deteriorated significantly, unemployment rates soared, inflation accelerated, and shortages of basic goods worsened. And as could have also been anticipated, debt levels rose significantly. In 1990 the aggregate outstanding debt of the region rose by $9 billion, following a $15 billion increase in 1989. The net debt of the region grew by over 13 percent in 1990 to reach an all-time high of $123 billion.[26]

As shown in tables 6.1–6.5, all of the economic indicators depicted a worsening condition of overall indebtedness throughout the former CMEA region as the 1990s opened. In 1989 OECD calculations showed the region as a whole with a debt-export ratio of 181, projected to be 211 in 1990. Poland's debt-export ratio was five times the average in those middle-income countries classified as severely indebted by the World Bank.[27] Net interest payments as a percentage of exports doubled between 1985 and 1990, from 11 to 21 percent. And the debt-service ratio rose from 32 to 39 percent between 1985 and 1990. At the end of 1990 Poland's debt-export ratio was five times the average of middle-income countries classified as severely indebted by the World Bank.[28]

This deep indebtedness threatened to stifle the very process of economic transformation that the West had hoped for in the region since the end of World War II. The debt squelched both foreign and domestic impulses for the successful introduction of markets into former centrally planned economies. Because the risk was too great that profits would be confiscated to pay interest on the debt or made worthless by a collapse of the exchange rate, once reserves were exhausted, foreign companies became increasingly wary of investing in heavily indebted countries. Domestically, authorities complained that the debt was stifling the incentive to save and pay taxes; people began to ask why they should work so hard now to pay back past debts of old communists.

Efforts on the part of fragile governments to reduce the debt became much more difficult than they had been for central authorities in state-socialist regimes. The centrally planned economies were generally considered creditworthy by the international financial community precisely because, under central control, adjustments in financing requirements took the form of clear and consistent import reductions, and these cuts could be carried out effectively. But under decentralized political and economic regimes, import cuts were no longer a viable strategy to reduce indebtedness; import cuts would have to be massive and therefore politically unacceptable to fledgling democratic governments.

Not only would these governments not be *willing* to undertake these measures, they would not have the *ability* to do so, because there had been a weakening of control over foreign exchange and foreign trade. In the Soviet Union, for example, many independent banks and enterprises began to import or borrow in the West without the authorization or even the knowledge of Gosbank or the Vneshekonombank (the Soviet foreign trade bank). Decentralization also meant that individual enterprises were permitted to retain some of their hard-currency earnings, so that the central authorities lost track of foreign exchange revenues. For example, Georg Krupp, the director of the Eastern European division of Deutsche Bank argued that the bank had to deal with more than 40,000 Soviet companies, as compared with 40 central foreign trade organizations under central planning.[29] Because of this loss of central control, short-term claims against the Soviet Union rose from 1989 to 1991, draining liquid assets.[30] Finally, decentralization was exacerbated by ethnic conflicts that threatened political and economic fragmentation and the fragile legitimacy of democratic regimes, of which Yugoslavia provides an extreme example. Before the civil war began in early 1991, Serbia triggered a financial crisis that threatened to undermine the domestic monetary system and curtail negotiations with creditors. The Serbian parliament made a secret decision to take a large (900 million pounds) loan from the Serbian national bank, *against* its lending rules. This was more than half the new money the central government planned to lend to all Yugoslav banks in 1991. The illegal action severely undermined Prime Minister Ante Markovic's tight monetary policies and triggered inflation throughout the country. Needless to say, new loans from international financial institutions for economic restructuring and foreign debt servicing were halted.[31]

As decentralization provided fertile ground for the emergence of new vulnerabilities for lenders, private loans to the region as a whole quickly dried up.[32] In 1990 the region's credit rating in publicized capital markets was rapidly downgraded and banks increasingly refused to accept new credits. Traditional bank-to-bank and trade lines were canceled or simply not renewed and interbank deposits were withdrawn. Furthermore, the USSR's current account deficit was dangerously large, and the downgraded creditworthiness of the largest debtor did not provide a good outlook for economic prospects in the region;[33] Bulgaria suspended interest and amortization payments on its debt; all of Eastern Europe's debt was being sold at a large discount in secondary markets; political leaders throughout the region were calling for debt relief as the withdrawal of private lenders began to aggravate liquidity problems.

Finally, political leaders in the new regimes were no longer afraid of borrowing too much for fear that Western powers would apply financial leverage to achieve political ends; indeed, they were actively seeking Western help in order to successfully introduce markets into their economies.

Therefore, as the last decade of the twentieth century began, the balance of payments of all of Eastern Europe and the constituent republics of the Soviet Union faced a "historic" weakening that threatened a new and prolonged debt crisis. Three causes contributed: broken trade relations in the former CMEA region; the shift in the region to hard-currency trade; and the attempt to reorient trade toward OECD countries.

In 1990 intra-CMEA trade represented between 40 and 80 percent of members' overall trade. Regional economic links had been deeply rooted, not only in trade relations, but also in employment and production structures. For example, 30 percent of the output of both Hungarian and Czech machinery and engineering products was targeted for use in other CMEA countries. Transportation networks, including oil and gas pipelines and railways were oriented toward intraregional trade. This trade moved largely under long-term contracts, providing a certainty of production runs and employment. As these countries moved to hard-currency trade and began to look westward for new trade links, enterprises throughout Eastern Europe became vulnerable to a disintegration of their traditional markets.

Most important for the Eastern European countries were changing trade relations with the Soviet Union. Already in the late 1980s the collapse of the Soviet economy had resulted in a decline in paid orders for Eastern European goods and deliveries of Soviet oil that hurt Eastern European economies. Hard-currency trade with the Soviet Union resulted in significant deterioration of the terms of trade for the smaller countries but a large surplus with these countries for the Soviet Union. And as suggested in chapter 5, Eastern European countries are still vulnerable to political leverage resulting from continued economic dependence on the USSR. The new dollar-based system of trade with Russia, the sudden rise in the price of oil, the shortfall it was expected to produce, and the loss of established markets meant that balance-of-payments problems would dominate the foreign economic policy agenda of these countries in the 1990s.

Because the initial role of private finance in the region was not large and prospects for large private capital flows into the region were dim, the OECD expected that large increases in official financing would be necessary to ease balance-of-payments problems. But there were many differences within the broad range of capital flows potentially available from official sources. Official export credit agencies and officially guaranteed credits from banks in OECD countries had been important sources of capital, but as the 1990s began they granted credits on terms similar to those prevailing in private markets. Although these credits were not withdrawn, they were limited for the same reasons private capital flows were limited and could not provide the liquidity to finance trade deficits. The OECD estimated that Poland, Hungary, and Czechoslovakia (now two separate nations) would be able to keep aggregate borrowing needs under control and obtain significant flows from export credit agencies and international financial institutions. Any incremental needs could probably be met from bilateral and multilateral official flows. But Bulgaria, Romania, and the former USSR would probably not be able to control borrowing requirements, and a foreign financing gap was expected to emerge.[34]

Ironically, it is the very introduction of markets that made commercial lenders nervous and fear that they were more vulnerable with regard to "transition economies" than they had been under the old regimes. What were these new vulnerabilities? What can the financial aspect of economic vulnerability tell us about the sources of economic vulnerability in international relations as a whole? Another look at efforts to resolve Poland's new debt problems after communism provides some answers.

Poland: From Near Default to Unprecedented Forgiveness

Poland's debt burden in 1991 was staggering. As discussed earlier, Poland had completely stopped servicing its official debt in 1981 while continuing to service its commercial bank debts. The result was that unpaid interest on the official debt mounted, eventually dwarfing the commercial debt burden. By 1991 three-quarters of Poland's $45 billion hard-currency debt was owed to foreign governments. To make matters worse, Poland's economy shrank by 12 percent in 1990 under the impact of austerity measures aimed at achieving a free-market system. Industrial production plunged 23 percent and real wages fell 28 percent.[35]

As 1991 began the Polish government felt that it had no choice but to enter serious negotiations with Western creditors over debt reduction. Creditor governments opened with the suggestion that the debt be cut 30 to 40 percent; Polish negotiators countered with a request to cut the debt by 80 percent. The United States and Great Britain supported drastic cuts in the Polish debt, while Japan and Germany were against a massive writeoff. Echoing arguments made before the imposition of martial law in 1981, the Bush administration suggested that Poland's debt burden would seriously jeopardize the economic and political reform effort, and those efforts must not be allowed to fail, especially in view of the danger of economic and political instability spreading from the crumbling Soviet Union.

Europeans countered that too much debt forgiveness would set a precedent and have a snowball effect, leading other indebted nations to demand deep cuts.[36] Indeed, Mihaly Kupa, the Hungarian finance minister, claimed that the West's decision to reduce Poland's foreign debt was aggravating social tensions in Hungary and increasing domestic pressure for debt restructuring.[37]

Germany, as Poland's largest creditor, began negotiations by opposing deep cuts in Poland's debt. Japan opposed any debt forgiveness at all, insisting instead on the provision of new loans on concessional terms. Congressional leaders in the United States countered that Germany's economy had benefited greatly in the 1950s from large writeoffs of its debt to the United States; Poland should have the same opportunity. Partial forgiveness, they claimed, would only help with temporary balance-of-payments difficulties but would not be enough to stimulate foreign investment and would still mean a net capital flow from Poland for ten years to come.

Throughout the negotiations, Germany began to move toward the U.S. position; after all, it had received no payments on outstanding loans from Poland since 1984, so a writeoff—even a large one—could have had a positive effect on German finances if it led to regular repayments on the reduced debt.[38]

In the end, an agreement was reached to write off half of Poland's official debt; this was the most generous debt relief ever given to a debtor country by the Paris Club.[39] Nonetheless, the 50 percent writeoff was not without conditions: Poland agreed to comply with a three-year economic program devised by the IMF that would put half of the economy in private hands by 1993.[40] For its part, the United States canceled 70 percent of Poland's debt in the hope of encouraging other Western governments to go beyond the 50 percent reduction. The move was largely symbolic, since Poland owed the U.S. only about 10 percent of the total official debt. And although France followed with deeper reductions, Japan was apparently disgruntled with the decision, calling it politically motivated; the Japanese government hesitated to put through a $500 million loan to Poland that was under negotiation.[41]

Ironically, this "new" Polish debt crisis demonstrated again how U.S. foreign policy options had been constrained. In the earlier crisis, the U.S. had attempted to apply negative sanctions on Poland in order to "punish" the regime for the imposition of martial law. The Reagan administration was unable to pursue that policy because it met resistance from other creditors who had too much to lose with a declaration of default. In 1991 the U.S. wanted unprecedented debt forgiveness so that its aim of aiding a "successful" Polish transition to democracy and the market could be achieved. Again it had to compromise because of the resistance of other creditors, who perceived unacceptable losses that would result and who feared that Polish debt forgiveness would set a precedent, creating a "domino effect."

Such a "domino effect," however, seemed to be attenuated by cooperation among lenders to hold the line on debt forgiveness with Poland. As discussed earlier, Bulgaria had suspended payments of principal on its foreign debt in April 1990 and suspended interest payments in June of that year. Western banks accepted that Bulgaria was not in a position to service the debt and agreed among themselves to grant a ninety-day payment freeze that was rolled over several times. By April 1991 it looked as if many creditors would bow to pressure from Bulgaria; they argued that they would certainly lose money lent to Bulgaria if they pressed for early payment, because the pressure would lead to the failure of the reform effort. Failure of reform would *ensure* that the debt would never be repaid. Following Poland's example, Bulgaria requested debt reduction rather than long-term payment deferral, but creditors united to reject the request, arguing that Poland was a special case because most of its debt had been owed to governments rather than private lenders, and Bulgaria's debt was largely commercial.[42]

Conclusion

What do these events tell us about financial instability and debtor leverage as a source of economic vulnerability in international relations? Both during the Cold War and in its aftermath the East threatened insolvency. In both cases, threats of insolvency raised vulnerability fears because they took place in the context of a rapid growth of unregulated and largely unguaranteed commercial lending, and an interlocking banking system, which deterred the declaration of default but gave debtors leverage in rescheduling and restructuring negotiations. In both cases, overall U.S. foreign policy goals were vulnerable to the constraints that financial interdependence created.

Clearly the source of vulnerability changed as Eastern Europe and the Soviet Union moved from being considered adversary nations to the status of nations "in transition," suffering from acute economic crisis. Under central planning, central authorities could have orchestrated an effective debtor-leverage campaign; they could have intentionally manipulated financial instability to obstruct U.S. political goals. In Barry Buzan's terms, vulnerabilities were present but threats were not. Although they did not use debtor leverage to these ends, Eastern European governments did begin to borrow in the Eurocurrency markets in order to escape the conditionality of official financing. On the other hand, the resolution of the 1982 debt crisis demonstrated that central planners could attenuate financial instability by authoritatively slashing imports and bringing payments into balance. Thus, under central planning, the vulnerability of potential insolvency was attenuated, despite heightened fears of these regimes' ability to successfully pursue debtor leverage.

But the introduction of markets in fragile democracies has reversed the situation. Although the 1990s will bring higher levels of official finance to the region, meaning governmental control and conditionality to reduce debtor leverage, it also threatens new sources of financial instability. As the late Soviet and post-Soviet cases demonstrate, decentralization means that the authority to reduce balance-of-payments deficits is weakened, while balance-of-payments difficulties are exacerbated by attempts to reorient trade toward the West. Decentralization is further threatened by ethnic conflicts that threaten fragmentation. Finally, the Polish case shows that high levels of debt owed to diverse creditors can obstruct foreign policy goals intended to foster reform: German and Japanese creditors were reluctant to ease the reform process through debt forgiveness and the compromise finally reached did not fully meet U.S. foreign policy goals.

The history of East-West financial relations in the 1980s and the events of the early 1990s suggest that vulnerability in this area is high and mutual. Nonetheless, there are three factors that mitigate vulnerability for creditors. First, there is a renewed trend toward more official and less private lending; this means that lending will be regulated and largely guaranteed. It is unclear, however, whether fragile governments will be able to implement conditionality requirements without undermining their own legitimacy.

Second, creditors have been successful in reaching agreement among themselves about the terms of debt negotiations, and have presented debtors with a united front, undermining their ability to exert leverage in negotiations. Cooperation among creditors, however, does not solve the larger problem of the real threat of insolvency. As the Polish episode illustrates, debt forgiveness, the third way to attenuate the vulnerability problem, may be the only way to address this larger problem of mutual vulnerability.

7

Interdependence, Vulnerability, and the Consolidation of Market Control

This book is about how international economic interdependence affects national security. More precisely, it is about how the forces of global economic interdependence heighten perceptions of the state's vulnerability to external pressures in its efforts to provide for national security. The historical account of East-West trade and finance suggests that unexamined U.S. vulnerability claims about how these forces affect the state's ability to provide security have led to unnecessary political conflict among nations and unnecessary expansion of state power in domestic society. I have therefore specified and tested those claims, and I contend that, to the extent to which market control was consolidated by Western states, multilateral institutions, and private actors whose strategies coincided with the state's security requirements, Western vulnerability was in fact reduced and security enhanced.

In this concluding chapter I assess the strength of those arguments. To what extent did vulnerabilities lurk in East-West economic relations during the Cold-War era? Which efforts to reduce perceived vulnerabilities were unnecessary and which efforts were appropriate and successful? What factors contributed to success? What lessons can we draw from Cold-War-era trade to guide the formulation and implementation of future economic policies toward the former Soviet Union, Eastern Europe, new adversaries, and trade competitors?

I will provide an interpretation of the evidence presented here in order to more clearly specify the concept of economic vulnerability in international relations. I begin by reviewing arguments about the sources of vulnerability and vulnerability reduction in an environment of international economic interdependence. I then assess the evidence for those arguments drawn from the three cases of technology transfer, energy trade, and finance. Finally, I suggest lessons drawn from this assessment for future trade with both former adversaries and new rivals.

International Interdependence and National Vulnerability

The connection between international economic interdependence and national security has not been carefully explored in the international relations literature.[1] Little attention has been paid to security issues in studies of international interdependence, despite the fact that its growth has meant the nation-state's increasing vulnerability to external forces, a phenomenon commonly thought to have security implications. At first glance this is surprising, because vulnerabilities arising from growing economic transactions and linkages have resulted from the growing allocation of goods and services by international market forces. This has led to the state's increasing *dependence* on goods produced in other states, implying vulnerability to a disruption in the flow of these goods. As a consequence, these transactions and linkages have led to a *loss of autonomy* in economic decision making, and they have meant increasing *entanglements* that constrained foreign-policy choices. But the literature has not suggested hypotheses specifying the kinds of dependence, loss of autonomy, or entanglements that would directly threaten the state's ability to provide for national security.

This is not surprising: security studies have been concerned primarily with the phenomenon of war and with the threat, use, and control of military force.[2] The responsibility to society for countering military threats to national security has been lodged in the *state*; therefore, security studies have generally taken the "state" and its ability to ward off military threats and defend the nation in time of war as the central focus of analysis. International interdependence, though threatening the state's autonomy in other spheres, has not historically interfered with this task; until recently, the capabilities involved in the development and maintenance of military strength have not been subject to market allocation.

Indeed, by the end of the nineteenth century the nation-state had consolidated its monopoly on the use of force and its near-complete control over the supply of resources and territory used to enhance military power.[3] States without the internal capabilities to marshal resources for their military force joined together in alliances with others to enhance their security. They did *not* seek security through reliance on the market. Indeed, as Barry Buzan points out, markets are a constant source of *insecurity*; they threaten inefficient actors with extinction.[4] It is no wonder that modern states would not want to leave the vital function of securing their territory from military threats to the vagaries of the marketplace. So the market forces that gave rise to the vulnerabilities of interdependence and chipped away at the state's autonomy and capacity in international trade, investment, and finance did not appear to affect the state's capabilities to pursue its security interests.

At the beginning of the 1990s, however, analysts began to notice market forces encroaching on the allocation of resources with military significance.[5] An inability to control global markets for resources necessary for security leads to vulnerabilities of dependence. Theodore Moran argues that if the sources of supply to the defense industrial base are concentrated in too few hands, one state's security becomes dependent on others. As the state becomes increasingly dependent upon resources outside its borders, its ability to act autonomously is threatened and its capacity to channel resources to its military through authoritative allocation is diminished.[6] Furthermore, states in intense competition with one another will seek to manipulate markets to control the resources of others.[7]

For these reasons, even powerful states measure their economic vulnerabilities by assessing their own control over markets for strategic goods, their dependence on strategic resources located in the territory of other states, the ability and willingness of those states to control those resources, and the effects of their economic entanglements with others on their own power to control outcomes in such a way as to maintain their capabilities and reduce dependencies.[8] The central question, then, is not whether the forces of international economic interdependence decrease national security by shifting the allocation of military resources to the market, but whether states can consolidate their market control in ways that reduce others' power and market control and reduce their own dependence in order to enhance their security.

Indeed, for markets to operate at all, strong states are required. Janice Thomson and Stephen Krasner argue that the very basis for growing international interdependence was the consolidation of state power in the international system.[9] This is because states whose economies became interdependent are able to establish stable property rights; in fact, states are the only actors capable of doing so. Stable property rights established and maintained by state power are essential for the growth of international interdependence because "without secure property rights, market activities would be constrained because of uncertainty about the possessor's right to sell the commodity and the threat to achieve transfers through force and coercion rather than voluntary exchange." Those states whose economies have become competitive, interdependent, and strong have established property rights on the basis of market-rational economic behavior. The new vulnerabilities for the West originating in the old Soviet Union discussed throughout this book are largely a function of fragile states' inability to establish and control market processes.

Although states require that their trading partners be strong enough to consolidate sovereignty over property rights to stabilize markets, they cannot be *too* strong; in a competitive international economy where production is increasingly globalized, their trading partners are tempted to control and manipulate the markets that provide the goods for their security. Thus, vulnerability reduction is a function of enough market control in the right places to ensure security for the potentially vulnerable state.

The consolidation of market control for vulnerability reduction involves both the stabilization of property rights that ensure efficient allocation of resources and the ability to seize control of markets or prevent the control of markets by those who would jeopardize security. Indeed, under conditions of interdependence, too much market control by one's adversaries and trade competitors, and not enough market control by one's trading partners, provides the foundation for economic vulnerability in international relations. The consolidation of market control in the interests of securing the potentially vulnerable state is the key to vulnerability reduction.

The Consolidation of Market Control

This consolidation of market control can be achieved in five ways. First, a dominant state can prevent the development of markets that would make it vulnerable. This means the enactment of laws and regulations restricting investment, trade, and finance to prevent technology exports, curtail the import of strategic resources like energy, and prevent the growth of financial markets involving entanglements that could lead to security risks.

There are, however, limits to one state's ability to restrict the growth of markets in a liberal international economic environment. If one state restricts its own participation in a market, there are others that will try to seize the market. Therefore, the second way to consolidate market control is to join with others in international regimes to restrict the growth of markets that would jeopardize security. Although one state can coerce others to go along with its preferred market-restriction policies, this is less effective than consensus among the actors on the kind and scope of market restriction needed to reduce vulnerability. As we have seen, coercion and the potential resistance it can trigger often lead to disputes among potentially vulnerable states and thereby reduce the effectiveness of the restrictive regime. Agreement on vulnerability is the most stable foundation for multilateral efforts to coordinate vulnerability reduction.

Third, particularly with regard to technology diffusion in a liberal market environment, the strategies of private corporations to consolidate market control are a source of vulnerability reduction for commercial high-technology exporters. These strategies are designed to withhold key technologies and snare the importer in a relationship of dependence.

Fourth, vulnerability reduction is a function of sacrifice on the part of corporations and citizens of potentially vulnerable states. In terms of resource dependence, this may mean conservation of resources to reduce demand; in finance, it may mean debt forgiveness on the part of lenders so that debtors can gain more control over their economies and reduce financial instability.

This last point leads to the fifth means of vulnerability reduction. I have argued here that economic vulnerability is reduced when trading partners are able to stabilize their economies on the basis of market-rational behavior. In the post-Soviet East-West trade environment, as well as in North-South economic relations, Western states can promote stabilization through aid and assistance policies.

We can now evaluate the evidence for these arguments. To what extent was Western security vulnerable to the forces of international interdependence in its Cold War East-West trade? Who gained and who lost market control in each of the three areas examined here?

Evaluating the Evidence

Vulnerability and Western Market Control

In chapter 3 I examined vulnerabilities in the transfer of commercial high technology from the West to the Soviet Union. Economic nationalists in the U.S. policy debate warned of grave vulnerabilities for the West resulting from these transfers. Western states would lose control of high-technology markets to private actors and other exporters, who would in turn sell technology to those who would use it to indirectly enhance their military power. Commercial high-technology importers would then be able to close the so-called technology gap between themselves and the exporters, increasing the exporter's vulnerability. Economic nationalists advocated the expansion of technology-export restrictions—the first means of vulnerability reduction discussed here—in order to prevent these vulnerability effects.

I assessed the evidence for this argument at two levels. I first attempted to look at the effects of Western technology on Soviet economic performance. This was admittedly a difficult task, because of methodological problems encountered in separating the effects of technology in general and Western technology in particular from all the other factors that affect a nation's economic performance. Although evidence available during the Cold War was only suggestive of the minimal impact of Western technology, Soviet economic performance disintegrated so dramatically throughout the 1980s, that by the Cold War's end it became clear that Western technology did little to contribute to Soviet economic strength. The analysis suggests that for vulnerability effects to be present, imported commercial high technologies would have to be diffused throughout the relevant sector and the economy as a whole. Technology diffusion, in turn, was a function of strong linkages throughout the economy. In the Soviet economy, those important linkages simply did not exist.

The analysis then turned from an examination of the impact of Western technology on the Soviet economy to an assessment of the kinds of technology that the Soviet Union was actually importing. The justification for this focus was that even if Western technology had been efficiently used in the Soviet economy, its vulnerability effects would have been minimal if the technologies imported had simply been run-of-the-mill. Because the "Bucy Report" argued that joint ventures and other forms of industrial cooperation would dramatically ease Soviet import of critical Western commercial technologies, I examined those joint ventures and the technology-transfer strategies of Western corporations involved to determine what kind of technologies were finding their way into the Soviet economy.

What the assessment at this second level of analysis revealed was that rather than permitting the Soviets to acquire state-of-the-art production technology, joint-venture arrangements, and Western corporate strategy worked to ensure Soviet *dependence* on standardized Western production techniques. Most joint-venture agreements were in extractive industries, commodity production, services, and the marketing of Western imports. Joint ventures in manufacturing industries were largely confined to assembly operations, adding little value to the goods produced and intended for the Soviet market rather than for export. Component parts for Soviet plants were sourced in the West, inhibiting the creation of linkages between the joint venture and the rest of the economy. Corporate officials believed that transfer of obsolete technology through these ventures was sufficient to capture domestic market share. Contractual provisions ensured that the most advanced Western technologies were withheld from the Soviet economy. The promise of technology transfer was used as a "hook" in order to get a foot into the Soviet market, and "core" technologies were rarely included in joint venture agreements.

With regard to the vulnerabilities associated with the transfer of commercial technology, then, the third means of consolidating market control seemed to be dominant: the strategies of multinational corporations engaged in joint ventures in the Soviet Union actually inhibited the transfer of those commercial high technologies that could have indirectly contributed to Soviet military power. The vulnerability effects, in this case, although minimal, were grossly exaggerated in the policy debate: Reagan administration officials, in particular, confused Soviet technology-acquisition efforts with results in the economy, ignored diffusion problems, and misread the objectives and strategies of the corporations selling technology to the Soviet Union. Based on unexamined vulnerability claims, they therefore expanded export control regulations that ultimately proved to be irrelevant.

In chapter 4 I was also compelled to assess vulnerability at two levels. The argument for exporter vulnerability claims that not only can trading partners import technology to enhance industrial development, but they can acquire military goods that diminish the exporter's relative defense capabilities in commercial markets. Market allocations of military resources has grown, because military power increasingly relies on commercial inputs. There are two related reasons for this. First, modern weaponry is developed as a "system" that includes command, control, and communications components, as well as logistics and support services developed in the commercial sector. This means that commercial firms that respond primarily to market signals produce goods necessary to the maintenance of military strength.

Second, the postwar period has witnessed the growth of weapons systems developed in commercial environments previously considered off-limits to military activity. The capabilities for land, sea, air, and space warfare have grown tremendously, and the range and targeting capabilities of weaponry have been perfected. This means that commercial and military environments have come to overlap in many more ways than were previously possible.

This overlap has meant that the resources in these environments have come to have a "dual" use. Satellites survey the globe to detect weather patterns in order to predict crop performance; the same technology can be used to verify whether states are adhering to arms control agreements. The microchip fragments that were identical to bomb-trigger components discovered in the wreckage of Pan Am flight 103 in Lockerbee, Scotland can be found in wristwatches, computers, and VCRs.[10] Electronic components developed for automobiles have been adapted for use in tanks. Dual use means that the same technologies needed for weapons systems are also traded in commercial markets.

In the public literature, however, there is very little evidence that this dual-use technology did or did not find its way into the Soviet military sector, and little is known in the West about the direct impact of Western technology on Soviet military capability. An analysis of any gap between the development of U.S. and Soviet military systems tells us little about that impact for the reasons discussed above, except to show that the gap has always been large in favor of the West, despite claims of increasing sales of dual-use technologies; if Western technology did find its way into the Soviet military sector, it did little or nothing to narrow the gap. What the discussion suggests is that exaggerated vulnerability claims were not based on good evidence—at the very least, that evidence was not made public; but the evidence is not strong enough to show that vulnerability was low.

Therefore, by analyzing the strengths and weaknesses of the COCOM embargo regime, I attempted to assess whether technologies with military significance were actually entering the Soviet Union. The examination of struggles within COCOM and a closer look at Toshiba Corporation's illegal sale of submarine-quieting technology to the Soviet Union suggests two conclusions: disagreement between Europe and the United States over the scope of the embargo regime weakened it and opened the way for private firms to violate COCOM rules, increasing the number of illegal technology transfers. Nonetheless, COCOM was largely effective, according to official sources, in preventing the transfer to the Soviet Union of technologies with military significance.

These findings present a paradox: if COCOM was weakened by dissent, how could it have been judged effective? The answer lies in the agreements that actually existed within COCOM: a select number of goods were not in dispute and were carefully controlled by member states, goods that would have most likely made a difference to Soviet military power. The consensus that did exist among COCOM members provided a basis for effective multilateral market control.

There are two general conclusions to be drawn from the evidence on the vulnerability effects of technology transfer presented in chapters 3 and 4. First, if technology-exporting states wish to jointly restrict technology exports and effectively prevent illegal transfers, an agreement on the scope and kind of vulnerability can enhance multilateral consolidation of control over technology exports—particularly control over illegal transfers. The consensual agreement that existed to control a select set of critical items *did* indeed contribute to a consolidation of joint market control—the second means of vulnerability reduction. Coercive efforts on the part of the United States toward its allies were less helpful and only led to disputes that weakened the legitimacy of the regime and increased the odds of illegal transfers. Despite that weakening, the consensus on restricted goods that did exist prevented vulnerability.

Given the lack of evidence *for* vulnerability, Reagan administration policies in the 1980s were irresponsible and unnecessary. Part of the strategy to gain increased executive authority to reduce vulnerability in economic relations with Warsaw Pact countries was to exaggerate vulnerability claims for the purpose of expanding the scope of the state in domestic society in order, allegedly, to protect national security.

The consolidation of market control took the form of broadened unilateral export controls that impinged on basic constitutional freedoms in the United States, leading to the increased militarization of civil society. Expanded export controls restricted attendance at scientific conferences where even unclassified material was presented, and the Department of Defense was required to review unclassified scientific research before publication.[11]

Furthermore, the exaggeration of these claims permitted the expansion of state power through overly restrictive export controls that may have actually harmed national security in an era in which the U.S. defense industrial base has become increasingly globalized. As I suggest in chapter 1, export controls were consistently given priority over measures with the potential to increase U.S. international competitiveness.[12] A faulty definition of vulnerability can harm real efforts to protect national security.

In chapter 5 I assessed the arguments for resource dependence by examining Western Europe's (and to a lesser extent Eastern Europe's) natural-gas trade with the Soviet Union. The argument for resource dependence claims that an importer's vulnerability to an exporter's influence over its political choices or over its own capabilities varies with the intensity of its need for imports and with the degree of the exporter's control over the needed good.

Taking the Urengoi pipeline crisis of 1982 as its starting point, the evidence shows that the United States did *not* have a strong case for arguing that Western Europe was vulnerable before that crisis, according to the criteria of the argument for resource dependence. U.S. vulnerability fears triggered by the pipeline construction plans were based on beliefs that there were few alternatives to Soviet imports and little flexibility to switch suppliers. But the evidence suggests that both domestic and foreign alternative sources of supply *did* indeed exist, and that contingency plans in place before the crisis erupted—plans known to U.S. officials—increased flexibility and decreased vulnerability. Western European states had plans, or had already implemented plans, to diversify foreign suppliers, expand the capabilities of domestic suppliers, add fuel-switching capabilities, and expand stockpile capacity. In all of these measures, states governed and regulated markets in order to reduce vulnerabilities, thereby consolidating market control.

Furthermore, it was clear before the pipeline crisis that there were few channels of domestic political influence created by natural-gas imports from the Soviet Union and that its ability to exercise political influence as a result of gas trade was minimal. Governments were therefore capable of imposing sacrifices on their populations if necessary. The 1983 IEA agreement provided an additional brake on resource dependence based on multilateral consensus, but was not in itself the key to vulnerability reduction.

This case shows dramatically how coercive efforts to gain compliance for the consolidation of market control are ineffective and that agreement on the kind and scope of vulnerability faced by strategic resource importers can resolve disputes and strengthen multilateral market control.

If vulnerability is measured by the intensity of "entanglements" that reduce the ability to control outcomes, the examination in chapter 6 of Western financial relations with Eastern Europe and the former Soviet Union provides evidence about vulnerability effects that is less straightforward than the other two cases. The argument for the vulnerabilities in debtor leverage and financial instability rests on both the instability and uncertainty of the international financial system and on the potential for debtors to exploit that uncertainty for their own bargaining advantage. Large debts, the rise in commercial lending, and the global overexposure of an interlocking banking system all exacerbate the vulnerability of lenders. To the extent that vulnerability is mutual and debtors are willing to play "chicken" and make credible threats, the vulnerability of lenders to bargaining pressure is increased even further. To the extent that the debt burden is so great that debtors are faced with negative growth rates and net capital outflows, the threat of default and the vulnerability of lenders is even higher.

During the Cold War, state-socialist regimes threatened insolvency in their financial relations with the West. Ironically, centralized state control over financial relations represented both a source of threat and a promise of stability. On the one hand, centralized governments under Moscow's control were capable of initiating a campaign of unified debtor leverage, placing Western banks in a precarious financial situation and potentially obstructing U.S. political goals. The East's vulnerability to the curtailment of Western finance, however, prevented that threat from materializing. On the other hand, centralized governments were able to reduce the threat of insolvency because they had the power and authority to bring payments into balance.

This evidence suggests that while claims of Western vulnerability were exaggerated in the case of commercial technology exports and Western European dependence on Soviet natural gas, *mutual* vulnerability was high in East-West trade finance in the early 1980s. Both states and private actors lost some control over markets during this period; ironically, it was the ability of centralized governments in Eastern Europe to gain control by reaching credible agreements with Western banks that reduced the West's vulnerability.

The evidence, then, is not uniform across the three cases. For both technology and natural-gas trade, interdependence appeared to be asymmetrical in favor of the West, conferring more power on the West than on the Soviet Union. Asymmetrical interdependence provided resources for market control based on private corporate strategies and multilateral consensus. In finance, however, interdependence was more symmetrical, and therefore a reduction in Western vulnerability was dependent on Eastern European governments' ability to gain control over their own economies to reduce the threat of default.

Overall, then, given the multiple means for market control available in the West, Western economic vulnerability in East-West relations was low during the Cold War. The explanation does not lie in the low levels of interdependence; aggregate levels of investment do not measure the importance of specific technology transfers. Western European natural-gas trade with the Soviet Union was significant, and Western financial commitments in Eastern Europe and the Soviet Union were a cause of great concern for banks and governments alike. Indeed, the explanation for relatively low Western vulnerability lies in the consolidation of market control to take the necessary vulnerability reduction measures. The measures that proved to be most feasible were those based on solid agreement among all actors about the kind and extent of vulnerability.

Low Western vulnerability, however, meant high vulnerability for the Soviet Union. Indeed, as the Soviet Union and Eastern Europe entered into more interdependent relations with the West, they did so with little means by which to consolidate their own market control. The argument for low Western vulnerability in technology and energy trade and mutual vulnerability in finance contains additional evidence of high vulnerability for the Soviet Union and Eastern Europe during the Cold War.

Vulnerability and the Weakening Soviet State

Stalin refused to become part of the new postwar international economic order and attempted to steer the Soviet Union in the direction of economic autarky. But Soviet growth rates fell not only because of the distortions of central planning but also as a result of the inherent inefficiencies of autarky.

Over time, the Soviets found themselves on the sidelines in the race for economic prosperity as their technical expertise in commercial industry began to lag far behind the industrial capitalist nations. Weapons systems requiring dual-use technologies meant that military strength increasingly rested on civilian technologies. And Soviet civilian technological innovation lagged further and further behind that of the West. The continuation of autarkic policies in an increasingly global network of resources pulled defense innovation further behind.

Illustrating the principle that trailing states attempt to imitate leading ones,[13] Soviet leaders beginning with Khrushchev initiated measures that would lead to a systematic but highly controlled opening to the international economy, while still preventing the creation of internal markets. Nonetheless, the technology gaps between the USSR and the West widened and multiplied.

The Soviet state responded to its increasing vulnerability with expanded efforts to acquire Western technology vital to military industries. As argued in chapter 4, although the Reagan administration mistook both legal and illegal technology-acquisition efforts in the late 1970s and early 1980s for positive results in the Soviet defense sector, the acquisition efforts were real. Nonetheless, they failed to achieve their objective; acquisitions did nothing to narrow the high-technology gap between the Soviet Union and the West. In fact, the gap continued to grow.

Only when Gorbachev came to power did the Soviet regime open the floodgates to the international economy. Because internal economic rigidities persisted, Western technology was purchased as a substitute for economic restructuring; if Soviet industries were to compete in the world market, innovative technology would have to be imported. Soviet planners knew that if they tried to compete in the international economy with sales of oil, timber, furs, and other commodities, they would never be as competitive as those states that produced computers, advanced components, and new materials.

But the establishment of market ties with the West failed to strengthen the economy and the security of the Soviet state. Although the overriding reasons for such failure were internal, asymmetrical interdependence with the West meant that external markets were controlled by Western states and Western firms; as we saw above, Western security and corporate concerns shaped the way the Soviet Union was initially integrated into the international economy. That integration was characterized by both dependence and peripheralization.

Furthermore, hard currency was required for technology purchases from the West, and hard currency could be earned only through increased exports. As described in chapter 5, however, export earnings were subject to the vagaries of commodity markets, and when they could not cover imports, technology had to be purchased with Western credits.

Growing internal economic weakness meant that the Soviet Union and the rest of the Warsaw Pact was eventually plunged into debt to purchase consumer goods and raise wages to stave off domestic unrest. Chapter 6 tells the story of how Eastern European and later Soviet debt to the West reached dangerously high levels, only to be reduced by drastic cuts in Western imports and massive rescheduling. Subsequent decreases in economic growth rates and decline in living standards squeezed populations who could no longer be mobilized by ideological appeals. The fate of the Soviet state in the international economy was moving down the precarious path traveled by many Third World countries: a weak state saddled with mounting debt and unfavorable terms of trade. The income gap between the Soviet Union and the West was growing, further undermining the Soviet state's internal legitimacy.

In sum, Soviet economic vulnerability in international relations is the story of how the state first lost out on the capabilities acquired through the international diffusion of technology, and of how it subsequently became dependent on markets controlled by the West as its own defense industrial base became subject to the forces of globalization. Finally, it became the story of a state's collapse in the face of its inability to stabilize market forces under conditions of economic weakness.

Explanations for Exaggerations of the Threat

The question remains: given low vulnerability for the West in East-West trade and high vulnerability for the Soviet Union, *why* did the Reagan administration exaggerate economic vulnerability claims? Answers to this question, of course, are beyond the scope of this study; nonetheless, because conclusions are not the place to be overly cautious, it is worthwhile to speculate briefly on this issue.

There is a small and controversial literature on the Reagan administration's exaggeration of the Soviet military threat, revealing that there is still dispute over whether the threat was exaggerated, and it is clearly a topic in the debate on "how the Cold War was won." Nonetheless, despite its controversial nature, hypotheses drawn from this literature might be useful in illuminating the exaggeration of the West's economic vulnerability in East-West trade as well.

The literature can be divided into four types of explanations. Two of these focus on the peculiarities of the Reagan administration: the politics of coalition building and maintenance and Reagan's hidden agenda to reconceptualize security policy. Two alternative explanations look to longer-term processes in American foreign policy: misperception based on an ideology of containment and bureaucratic self-interest. These latter arguments share the belief that the Reagan administration was far from unique in exaggerating the Soviet threat; for ideological and bureaucratic reasons, external threats are often exaggerated, and throughout the Cold War the Soviet threat was no exception.[14] What follows is a brief summary of each of these schools of thought and an assessment of their utility in explaining exaggerations of economic vulnerability.

Coalition Politics

Gail Lapidus and Alexander Dallin suggest that the Republican landslide election of 1980 was based on a historic realignment of electoral forces, some of which had hitherto been in the Democratic camp and some of which had been politically inactive.[15] The interests of these groups were widely divergent, ranging from the Moral Majority to oldline Republicans to neoconservatives. The only common issue that held this coalition together was fear of the Soviet military threat. During the presidential campaign of 1980 Reagan attacked Carter for being "soft" on communism; the hostage crisis played into his hands, and indeed, the American public felt more vulnerable than it had for years, despite the fact that the Carter administration had moved toward a much more aggressive nuclear policy. To bolster its own political support, then, the Reagan administration needed to exaggerate the Soviet threat so that it could maintain the coalition after the election when criticism of past policies had to give way to a new program.

The Hidden Agenda

A second explanation says that the exaggeration of the threat was not simply a *response* to the need for arguments that would bolster political support, but rather it was central to the internal goals of the administration itself and its desire to build up U.S. military strength. Exaggeration of the Soviet threat was necessary in order to overcome potential resistance from Congress for massive increases in defense spending.[16] This explanation rests on the view that Reagan administration officials were part of the "cult of the offensive," who believed that the United States could be made invulnerable to a Soviet nuclear attack through pursuit of a counterforce nuclear strategy. All "cults of the offensive" exaggerate the enemy's capabilities and underestimate one's own domestic forces.[17] This view violated the stated policy of containment and therefore had to be hidden.

Stephen van Evera and Barry Posen argue that American military capability was adequate to meet the goals of containment, but Reagan wished to reconceptualize that policy, adding offensive nuclear capabilities, new forces for Third World intervention, and the resources to fight a prolonged conventional war. Because a reconceptualization of policy was perceived to be too controversial, and budget increases for new missions were likely to be stalled in Congress, the administration strategy was to portray present capabilities as inadequate to meet the Soviet threat, all within the strategy of containment. Thus, an exaggeration of that threat was necessary to obtain the increases needed for the new missions without an argument that containment was no longer a valid security policy.[18]

Misperceptions based on Containment Ideology

There are those who argue, however, that the policy of containment itself and the way it was interpreted in different periods throughout the Cold War necessarily led to the exaggeration of vulnerability claims. Containment, in the hands of the "essentialists" described in chapter 1, held that the USSR was inherently evil without prospects for change. It further claimed that the Soviet Union was aggressively expansionist, and would take over the world if not stopped. Coexistence with the Soviet Union was therefore not possible.[19] This view was embodied in the Reagan administration's characterization of the Soviet Union as the "evil empire."

Information filtered through these ideological lenses could easily lead to a misperception of the Soviet threat. All Soviet behavior could be interpreted to fit the "essentialist" view. For example, arms control agreements were seen as a farce that the Soviets would use to stall for time while they continued to rearm in secret. When those holding this view attained positions of political power, they promoted an aggressive, anti-Soviet policy and knowingly exaggerated the Soviet threat in order to justify raising defense budgets and rallying the American public to the cause of global interventionism.[20] Chapter 1 recounts how even when the Cold War and the Soviet Union were on the verge of disappearing, skeptics believed that Soviet moves toward arms reduction and opening to the West were nothing more than ploys to enhance state power.

Bureaucratic Self-Interest

The basic premise of this explanation is that bureaucracies, once instituted, take on a life of their own and implement only those policies that will benefit them. Policy and administration cannot be separated, and central foreign and defense bureaucracies benefit from either the exaggeration or the understating of the enemy's threat, depending on the current policy environment.

John Prados argues that throughout the Cold War, the CIA and military intelligence agencies vacillated in their estimation of the Soviet threat.[21] In the 1960s and 1970s, for example, the CIA underestimated the pace of the Russian ICBM and SLBM buildup, as well as the Soviet defense budget and missile accuracy rates. But it also *overestimated* Soviet bomber forces, and therefore the bomber and missile "gaps." Prados suggests that erroneous estimates resulted from attempts to please political superiors who held varying views of the Soviet Union, organizational stakes in certain estimates, and the demand for constant information and analysis, combined with extreme displeasure at "wrong answers," which resulted in vague and tentative estimates.

Stephen van Evera argues that a paradox exists for organizations in a competitive environment; on the one hand, without constant evaluation of the external environment, the organization will founder; on the other hand, truly objective evaluation will necessarily threaten the jobs and status of incumbent members of the organization. They will actively suppress new data and engage in self-serving propaganda. Van Evera goes so far as to argue that myth-making to serve the bureaucratic-political agenda "becomes the one essential art of government more important than statesmanship or farsightedness or even effective administration."[22]

Which of these explanations provides the most utility in helping us understand the exaggeration of economic vulnerability in East-West relations? Certainly there are traces of evidence to support each of the four arguments, and none stands out as a dominant explanation. For example, as we have seen throughout the period of the Soviet Union's existence, essentialists, skeptics, and economic nationalists have drawn on an extreme interpretation of containment to bolster their belief in economic vulnerability, and they have interpreted Soviet behavior through these ideological lenses, even if it meant distorting information to fit the belief.[23] Essentialists in the Reagan administration were no exception.

But in one illustration we saw how the Reagan administration responded to a domestic coalition claiming economic vulnerability as the reason to declare Poland in default. Recall that with Poland's declaration of martial law in 1981, a coalition of right-wing groups, headed by the Conservative Caucus and supported by Caspar Weinberger from within the administration, pressured for a declaration of Poland's default, arguing that the West's financial relations with the East were strengthening the economies of the Warsaw Pact. They claimed that a declaration of default would have severed those relations and weakened the enemy. Although Western European pressures on the U.S. to eschew a default declaration won out in the end, it was clear that domestic political pressures on the administration to exaggerate vulnerability claims were evident.

Explanations for the exaggeration of economic vulnerability based on bureaucratic self-interest are more problematic but worth exploring in future research. In chapter 3 we saw that the CIA consistently underestimated Soviet economic power, and chapter 4 shows that while the Department of Defense was publishing reports that warned of extreme vulnerability resulting from technology trade, other government agencies were publishing reports that supported an argument for low vulnerability. In any event, government agencies, though they may have espoused the rhetoric of vulnerability, did not always "cook" the data to support it. In many cases, they just did not provide the evidence, and in others the information offered simply did not provide evidence to support vulnerability claims. For example, vast amounts of data were collected to support claims of Soviet acquisition of Western technology; those claims were confused with arguments that the acquired technology actually enhanced Soviet economic and military power. Overwhelming evidence supported the wrong argument and permitted vulnerability claims to be exaggerated. The question remains, however, why did some agencies stress vulnerability claims while other agencies—

often those in the economic nationalist camp—underplay vulnerability?

Evidence presented in chapter 4 provides some clues that might support the "hidden agenda" explanation. The dual-use technologies of greatest concern to the Reagan administration were those developed in the United States that could provide perceived offensive capability; technologies that made targeting more accurate, and technologies necessary to the Strategic Defense Initiative, as well as the military application of biological innovations and genetic engineering. The Reagan administration, in developing these technologies, seemed to be actively engaged in altering the technological foundation of strategic doctrine. And the administration may have exaggerated the threat of Soviet acquisition of these technologies in order to bolster domestic support for developing them to actually counter the threat.

A fifth argument, focused on alliance politics, can also partly explain the exaggeration of Western economic vulnerability in East-West trade. In each of the three areas under consideration here, the United States government quarreled with its allies over whether and how markets should be restricted to prevent vulnerability in East-West trade. As we have seen, U.S. coercion of its allies was ineffective and counterproductive in all three cases. In the absence of an ability to coerce its allies into tight restriction of markets, the U.S. attempted to persuade them to go along with its preferences by raising fears of trade vulnerability. Part of that persuasion effort was to exaggerate vulnerability claims in order to extract compliance without coercion. But the evidence shows that exaggerated and unfounded vulnerability arguments fell on deaf ears.

Clearly, exaggerated claims of economic vulnerability in international relations were not unique to the Reagan administration. When all is said and done, however, none of the explanations alone is wholly satisfying. What is essential, however, is that future vulnerability claims be warranted by sound evidence in order to elicit multilateral agreement and aid in the construction of sound policy. Indeed, fears of economic vulnerability in international relations did not die with the Soviet Union, and they have already emerged in new, post-Cold War guises.

Implications for the Future

New Vulnerabilities in Old Places

With the death of the Soviet state and the birth of fragile new governments in the region, Western nations face a new set of vulnerabilities in their investment, trade, and finance relations with postcommunist countries. As argued in chapter 2, it is the former adversary's *loss of market control* and inability to establish stable property rights on the basis of market-rational behavior that is the chief source of vulnerability in all three areas. No longer is the state perceived to be too strong; it is too weak.

In investment and energy trade, the post-Soviet economic environment of the region is characterized by the demise of political control over the economy and a rise in anarchic economic behavior. The hallmark of centrally planned economies with controlled prices, assured employment, subsidies, and trade autarky was stability; ensuring the simultaneous introduction of markets and macroeconomic stability was simply not possible for a state weakened by sustained economic crisis. The Soviet state lost control of the economy, and in the process lost the legitimacy to govern it.

As a consequence, although the state relinquished its control over stable central planning, it did not have the power to establish stable markets. Massive confusion and economic stalemate ensued. Even before the death of the Soviet state, the economy reverted to what State Planning Committee Chairman Yuri Maslyukov called "chaotic barter operations, republican customs barriers to trade, theft, and speculation."[24] Gorbachev admitted that "mechanisms of sound competition failed to work. Direct ties are of a premarket, natural character. Commodity and money relations are not developing."[25] People simply stopped paying taxes; as if to foreshadow the events of August 1991, in November 1990 Gorbachev gave a speech to the Supreme Soviet proposing an eight-point program to "reform and strengthen without delay the structure of state power." Clearly, he saw that the state was crumbling.

In chapter 4, for example, we caught a glimpse of some of the economic consequences: uncertainty over control of economic forces and the disintegration of the Soviet state began to force thousands of Soviet scientists trained in building nuclear and chemical weapons to sell their expertise to states like North Korea or Iraq, thus increasing the "threat" from those areas to the West.[26]

Similarly, in chapter 5 I discussed how the "threat" of a powerful Soviet Union cutting off energy supplies to the West in order to harm Western economies or manipulate Western politics had also virtually disappeared. But the West was still vulnerable to energy supply cutoffs, no matter what the intention. In late 1991, for example, the Russian republic announced a ban on oil exports. Ninety percent of all "Soviet" oil is produced in Russia, and the former Soviet Union was the biggest world oil producer. The reasons for the cutoff were clearly *not* tied to the "threats" the West perceived throughout the Cold War period, but reflected declining production capability and was part of an internal struggle within Russia between the state and private actors over the control of exports.[27] The ban illustrates the West's new potential vulnerability to a supply cutoff despite the disappearance of the Cold War threat. Threats change; vulnerabilities remain.

Finally, the disintegration of state control in former communist regimes over external markets creates new vulnerabilities for Western nations in their financial relations. The threat of insolvency looms again, yet this time it is more serious. State authority to reduce imports to bring payments into balance has been greatly diminished; central control over banking has been weakened. Western creditors are now more vulnerable than ever.

Nonetheless, Western nations in concert have consolidated their power in this area to reduce their vulnerability, countering their vulnerability to debtor insolvency by moving away from private to official lending; Western states are now the chief lenders to the East, meaning that lending will be regulated and guaranteed. They have also cooperated among themselves to present a unified front to borrowers, reducing their vulnerability to the threat of debtor leverage.

Yet the "entanglements" of finance constrain other Western policy choices. The Polish debt negotiations of 1991 demonstrated the diminished capability of the United States to control outcomes in this area. Arguments for deep reductions in Poland's official debt were countered by other arguments that extensive debt forgiveness for Poland would set an unacceptable precedent—and other Eastern European countries would clamor for forgiveness as well. Although Poland did receive a substantial debt reduction, it was not as large as the U.S. believed was needed to ensure the success of the liberalization project.

What the evidence across the three cases suggests is that if the West is to reduce new vulnerabilities in old places, it must aid its former rivals in gaining market control based on market-rational behavior. This will not be easy, because entrenched political forces that benefit from anarchy in the system have fought against the introduction of market reforms. It is beyond the scope of this study to examine specific policies the West can pursue to promote markets and democracy;[28] nonetheless, the analysis here points to clear Western interests in bolstering the state power and market behavior of former adversaries.

With regard to the future of export controls in the region, to the extent that the former Soviet Union retains its nonadversary status, the West can jointly move away from market control through technology denial to a policy of presumed export approval in order to facilitate the diffusion of "technologies of democracy." Such a policy, based on the verification of end use, should not be difficult, given the new transparency of the former Soviet economies and political systems.[29]

Finally, Western nations should expand their own markets for the purchase of missiles, rocket engines, satellites, space reactors, spacecraft, and other aerospace technology from the former Soviet Union, in order to prevent former Soviet scientists from selling their knowledge to potential military rivals in the Third World. Blocking the purchase of these items in order to force the decline of the Russian space and military industry would be ultimately counterproductive.[30]

Old Vulnerabilities in New Places

With the end of the Cold War, the United States turned toward the Third World as a new source of threat to its interests. Efforts to prevent the proliferation of weapons of mass destruction and dual-use technologies to new potential adversaries were at the top of the foreign policy agenda.

The new—and largely unilateral—policy initiatives were grounded in revelations about the effects of technology trade with Iraq before the Gulf War and recognition of the lack of multilateral controls on proliferation. Western firms legally sold Iraq machinery that could be used in the production of nuclear weapons—indeed, the U.S. Commerce Department itself approved 771 licenses to export $2 billion worth of computers, chemicals, and communications equipment to Iraq between 1985 and 1990.[31] Furthermore, throughout this period, Iraq had pursued the production of nuclear weapons but had been in good standing with the International Atomic Energy Agency (IAEA) because it had masked its weapons program with civilian projects.

American policy initiatives also come in the wake of arguments that the international nuclear nonproliferation regime had decayed. At the 1990 Non-Proliferation Treaty (NPT) review conference, Third World countries stated that they would not extend the treaty after 1995 unless the nuclear powers agreed to a comprehensive ban on nuclear testing. Indeed, beginning in the mid-1960s, non-NPT members Israel, India, Pakistan, and South Africa all attained nuclear weapons capabilities; Iran, Libya, North Korea, and Taiwan were all signatories but were actively pursuing nuclear weapons capabilities. In addition, countries that did not have active nuclear weapons programs, such as Belgium, Germany, Japan, and Switzerland, were all stockpiling large quantities of plutonium and weapons-grade uranium. Both Germany and Japan had active civilian nuclear programs. In addition to this potential proliferation, news leaks reported six ex-Soviet nuclear warheads missing from Kazakhstan and Ukraine.[32]

Furthermore, because COCOM was not organized to restrict technology transfers to noncommunist countries, and because no regime existed to do so, technologies useful in the construction of nuclear, chemical, and biological weapons were legally available to many "dangerous" countries. A revamping of COCOM, or a new regime, is necessary, because as the case of Germany's transfer of weapons technology to Libya illustrates, traditional export controls will not be effective as there is little uniformity in exporters' policies.

As new regimes are constructed and old ones revamped, decision makers can learn from the conflictual Cold War history of the East-West trade. Without adequate vulnerability assessments, nonproliferation policy runs high risks of preventive war to destroy alleged weapons before they are developed. Without vulnerability assessments, vulnerability claims are likely to be exaggerated; the potential adversary's power will be portrayed as much greater than it actually is in order to garner support for policies of vulnerability reduction. New regimes must incorporate strict guidelines for vulnerability assessment that will produce evaluations upon which consensus can be reached.

The arguments and assessments of Cold War vulnerability can provide lessons for the future. Those lessons of caution, consensus based on sound evidence, and limited but cooperative market control are consistent with arguments made by the National Academy of Sciences in 1991 that "proliferation controls must be focused only on narrowly proscribed military activities or items that are required directly for weapons systems and must include, to the extent practicable, verifiable end use assurances. Lacking such specificity, efforts to control exports of proliferation-related technologies create a risk similar to that encountered in the case of COCOM controls on dual-use technology—namely, imposing significant economic costs that may be disproportionate to their effectiveness."[33]

The body of the Cold War is still warm, yet it is now time to write the obituary and learn its lessons. Exaggerated claims about Soviet power characterized American foreign policy throughout the Cold War.

Though the Soviet Union was not without its strengths during this era, the evidence presented throughout this book and elsewhere suggests it was in a weaker position overall. Nuclear deterrence meant that the central question was not which state could gain superiority over the other with regard to weapons of mass destruction, but rather which side could achieve the capability of destroying the other's nuclear capability. In the U.S.-Soviet relationship, mutual vulnerability characterized the strategic relationship, making most force comparisons irrelevant.

Nevertheless, the rhetoric of U.S. Cold War foreign policy was filled with dire warnings of vulnerability that are likely to emerge again with new rivals. The "bomber gap" of the mid-1950s, the "missile gap" of the late 1950s, the "ABM gap" of the 1960s, the strategic and tactical gap and the "window of vulnerability" of the early 1980s all proved to be illusory.[34] This study has argued that warnings about the closing of the technology gap with the Soviet Union were largely illusory as well.

If the state needs to expand its power to protect national security, it should, at the very least, carefully assess threats and vulnerabilities in order to judiciously determine its security requirements. And in an era of globalized production and exchange, economic vulnerability reduction must necessarily be a cooperative task that can only be accomplished through agreement on the security implications of economic relationships.

Notes

1. The Unresolved Question

1. See Henry R. Nau, "Conclusion: Export Controls in a Changing Strategic Context," in Gary K. Bertsch and Steven Elliott-Gower, eds., *Export Controls in Transition* (Durham, N.C.: Duke University Press, 1992), p. 317.

2. In the public-policy literature, this argument has been made forcefully by Aaron Wildavsky in *Speaking Truth to Power* (Boston: Little, Brown, 1979), and "The Self-Evaluating Organization," *Public Administration Review* 32(5) (September/October 1972):509–520. See also Horst W. J. Rittel and Melven Webber, "Dilemmas in a General Theory of Planning," *Policy Sciences* 4 (1973):155–169, for an excellent discussion of the difficulties of separating out those policy problems that can be solved by examining the "evidence" on both sides of the debate ("tame" problems) and those that are too politically explosive and controversial to be resolved through an assessment of the evidence ("wicked" problems). Export control problems are "wicked" in the sense that, for example, even if vulnerability were minimal, there might be diplomatic or domestic political reasons *not* to trade with a potential adversary. The problem has been that vulnerability rhetoric has often been used in the service of other goals without an acknowledgment that this is the case. For case studies that illustrate this point, see Beverly Crawford and Stefanie Lenway, "Decision Modes and Regime Change: Western Collaboration on East-West Trade" *World Politics* 37(3) (April 1985):375–402; Beverly Crawford, "Western Control of East-West Trade Finance: The Role of U.S. Power and the International Regime," in Gary K. Bertsch, ed., *Controlling East-West Trade and Technology Transfer: Power, Politics, and Policies* (Durham, N.C.: Duke University Press, 1988), pp. 280–312; and Beverly Crawford, "Changing Export Controls in an Interdependent World: Lessons from the Toshiba Case for the 1990s," in Bertsch and Elliott-Gower, eds., *Export Controls in Transition*, pp. 249–290.

3. For an excellent discussion that makes this point, see Stephen van Evera, "Why States Believe Foolish Ideas: Non-Self-Evaluation by Government and Society," paper presented at the annual meeting of the American Political Science Association, September 1988.

4. In Hungary, for example, rapid privatization before enterprise values were established led to transactions that favored former managers. These included Hungarhotels, Tungsram, Ibusz, Apisz, and the Hungarian Steel Goods Factory. See David M. Kemne, *Economic Transition in Eastern Europe and the Soviet Union: Issues and Strategies* (New York: Institute for East-West Security Studies, 1991).

5. See Stephen Krasner, *Structural Conflict* (Berkeley: University of California Press, 1985).

6. Barry Burzan, *People, States, and Fear*, 2d ed. (Boulder, Colo.: Lynne Reiner, 1991), pp. 112–116.

7. See Kenneth N. Waltz, *Theory of International Politics* (Reading, Mass.: Addison-Wesley, 1979), chap. 7.

8. Ibid., pp. 124–131.

9. Marie-Helene Labbe, "Controlling East-West Trade in France," in Bertsch, ed., *Controlling East-West Trade*, p. 200; Hans-Dieter Jacobsen, "East-West Trade and Export Controls: The West German Perspective," in Bertsch, ed., *Controlling East-West Trade*, p. 165; Gary K. Bertsch and Steven Elliott, "Controlling East-West Trade in Britain: Power, Politics, and Policy," in Bertsch, ed., *Controlling East-West Trade*, p. 218.

10. Michael Kreil, "West Germany: The Dynamics of Expansion," in Peter J. Katzenstein, ed., *Between Power and Plenty* (Madison: University of Wisconsin Press, 1978), pp. 201–208.

11. Unlike the BRD, however, the relationship is not a formal one, but informal; the Department of Trade and Industry simply seeks the views on policy and on specific cases of a number of large corporations and trade associations on a regular basis. See Bertsch and Elliott, "Controlling East-West Trade in Britain," p. 220.

12. On the political struggle between Congress and the executive, see William J. Long, *U.S. Export Control Policy: Executive Autonomy vs. Congressional Reform* (New York: Columbia University Press, 1989).

13. For the full story leading to this outcome, see Michael Mastanduno, "Trade as a Strategic Weapon: American and Alliance Export Control Policy in the Early Postwar Period," *International Organization* 42(1) (Winter 1988):138.

14. See, for example, Michael Mastanduno, *Economic Containment: The Western Politics of East-West Trade* (Ithaca: Cornell University Press, 1992); Bruce Jentleson, *Pipeline Politics: The Complex Political Economy of East-West Energy Trade* (Ithaca: Cornell University Press, 1986); Long, *U.S. Export Control Policy*; Bertsch, ed., *Controlling East-West Trade*; and Bertsch and Elliott-Gower, eds., *Export Controls in Transition*.

15. See Michael Mastanduno, "Strategies of Economic Containment: United

States Trade Relations with the Soviet Union," *World Politics* 37 (July 1985):503–531.

16. George F. Kennan, *Memoirs 1925–1950* (New York: Pantheon, 1967), p. 268.

17. "United States Objectives and Proposals for National Security," Report to the National Security Council, April 14, 1950 (NSC 68), p. 28.

18. For an excellent history of the origins of this policy, see Robert A. Pollard, *Economic Security and the Origins of the Cold War, 1945–1950* (New York: Columbia University Press, 1985).

19. Export Control Act of 1949, section 1b. The full text of the law is reprinted in Gunnar Adler-Karlsson, *Western Economic Warfare* (Stockholm: Almqvist and Wiksell, 1968), pp. 217–219.

20. For a full discussion of Western European views on East-West trade during the early Cold War period, see Beverly Crawford, "The Roots of European Autonomy in East-West Trade," in Beverly Crawford and Peter W. Schulze, eds., *The New Europe Asserts Itself: A Changing Role in International Relations* (Berkeley: Institute of International Studies, 1990), pp. 251–279. See also Jentleson, *Pipeline Politics*.

21. An early statement of this view is spelled out in a study conducted by the Economic Commission for Europe, which stated that the flow of goods in Europe should be allowed to take its "natural" course. ECE Ad Hoc Committee on Industrial Development and Trade, United Nations, ECOSOC, E/ECE/10/2, August 14, 1948.

22. For a more extensive discussion of conflicting U.S. and European views of the Soviet Union, see Miles Kahler, "The United States and Western Europe: The DIplomatic Consequences of Mr. Reagan," in Kenneth A. Oye, Robert J. Lieber, and Donald Rothchild, eds., *Eagle Resurgent? The Reagan Era in American Foreign Policy* (Boston: Little, Brown, 1987), pp. 304–306.

23. During 1945–46 this was also the prevailing view in American official circles, but by mid-1947, the goal of trade denial took the dominant position. See Pollard, *Economic Security*, p. 162.

24. For the British expression of this view, see Elisabeth Barker, *The British Between the Superpowers, 1945–1950* (Toronto: University of Toronto Press, 1983), pp. 209–213.

25. For example, Norway tried to protect its export of aluminum and ships; Denmark tried to protect tankers; England wanted to exempt rubber from the embargo; and West Germany attempted to exempt Ruhr products. See Sinclair Weeks, "The U.S. Stake in World Trade," *Department of State Bulletin* 862, 1955.

26. Pollard reports that a group of twenty "revisionist" senators organized by Republican whip Kenneth Wherry hoped either to cripple the ERP with amendments or at least to cut the funds for the plan by one-third because they were not willing to tolerate Western European trade with the East and because they did not want the extensive tariff reductions that the State Department regarded as crucial to multilateral commerce. See Pollard, *Economic Security*, p. 149.

27. The NSC's "R" procedure for export controls mostly restrained trade in military-related materials, such as those that the Atomic Energy Commission identified as essential to the production of atomic weapons. Yet by declaring all of Europe as a recovery zone to which the export controls applied, the "R" procedure theoretically achieved "total control of shipments to Eastern Europe without apparent discrimination." Ibid., p. 162.

28. Quoted in ibid., p. 236.

29. Acheson, in particular, feared that if Western European governments were forced to choose between U.S. aid and trade with the East, they would choose the latter. See Michael Mastanduno, "Trade as a Strategic Weapon," p. 135.

30. Dean Acheson, *Present at the Creation: My Years in the State Department* (New York: W. W. Norton, 1969), p. 634.

31. The central set of beliefs guiding this argument were that domination of Eastern Europe strengthened the Soviet Union and that the Soviet and satellite governments wanted to increase trade with the West so as to get the equipment, machinery, and raw materials needed to maintain that strength. Therefore, the West should not merely deny strategic goods, but should refuse to supply any capital goods or technical equipment to the bloc so as not to build up the war potential of the Soviet adversary. *Telegrams* from Kelly to Bevin, July 14, 1949 and October 5, 1949 in Foreign Office Files 371/77619, Public Record Office, London, cited in Barker, *The British Between the Superpowers*, p. 210.

32. Letter to Kelly, December 2, 1949, Foreign Office Files 371/77619, Public Record Office, London, cited in Barker, *The British Between the Superpowers*.

33. *Board of Trade Journal* (February 12, 1949):304.

34. Adler-Karlsson, *Western Economic Warfare*, p. 43.

35. Ibid., p. 38.

36. Barker, *The British Between the Superpowers*, p. 211.

37. *Board of Trade Journal* (August 18, 1951):337–338.

38. Adler-Karlsson, *Western Economic Warfare*, p. 38.

39. Mastanduno, "Trade as a Strategic Weapon," p. 138.

40. Konrad Adenauer, *Erinnerungen 1945–1953* (Stuttgart: Deutsche Verlags-Anstalt, 1965), p. 576. Dulles mentioned in particular current German shipments of rolling-mill parts to Hungary, an item not on the COCOM embargo list.

41. Adler-Karlsson, *Western Economic Warfare*, p. 17; emphasis added.

42. In 1950 total Western European trade with the East bloc totaled $1.466 billion, which was actually down 18 percent from 1949; by 1951, at the height of the Korean War, it totaled $1.756 billion. In 1953 the total was $1.698 billion, and by 1954 it had climbed to $2.013 billion. French exports to the Soviet bloc grew steadily during those years; British exports, however, declined 37 percent between 1950 and 1951 and remained level until 1954. West German exports declined 15 percent between 1950 and 1952 but grew 6 percent between 1952

and 1953. The West German decline can be explained by the fact that by 1951, Germany was not in control of its own export policy. A "Tripartite Export Controls Committee" and a "Tripartite Customs Group" made up of England, France, and the United States supervised West German trade with the East. In 1952, however, the Bundestag adopted a resolution demanding a normalization of trade with the communist nations. Adler-Karlsson, *Western Economic Warfare*, pp. 71–72.

43. Bruce W. Jentleson, "The Western Alliance and East-West Energy Trade," in Bertsch, ed., *Controlling East-West Trade*, p. 325.

44. For an excellent discussion of U.S. arguments to restrict East-West trade finance in the 1950s and 1960s, see Samuel Pisar, *Coexistence and Commerce* (New York: McGraw-Hill, 1970), pp. 107–114.

45. For the story of how this conflict between the United States and its allies was played out, see Crawford, "Western Control of East-West Trade Finance," pp. 280–312.

46. Detente strategies were diverse and often reflected conflicting perceptions among decision makers. Strategies emphasizing the importance of economic interdependence in mitigating conflict appeared most consistently in the Soviet literature. See, for example, Leonid Brezhnev, *Peace, Detente, and Soviet-American Relations: A Collection of Public Statements* (London: Harcourt, Brace, Jovanovich, 1979). For diverse U.S. views, see "Basic Principles of Relations Between the United States of America and the Union of Soviet Socialist Republics," *Department of State Bulletin* (June 26, 1972):898–899; Henry Kissinger, "Detente with the Soviet Union: The Reality of Competition and the Imperative of Cooperation," *Department of State Bulletin* (October 14, 1974):505–519; Zbigniew Brzezinski, "The Competitive Relationship," in Charles Gati, ed., *Caging the Bear* (Indianapolis: Bobbs-Merrill, 1974), pp. 157–199; and Kenneth Jowitt, *Images of Detente and the Soviet Political Order* (Berkeley: University of California Institute of International Studies, 1977).

47. Eugene Zaleski and Helgard Weinart, *Technology Transfer Between East and West* (Paris: OECD, SPT [77], 16, 1st revision, 1980), p. 137.

48. Kissinger, "Detente with the Soviet Union," p. 508.

49. See Warner R. Schilling, "U.S. Strategic Nuclear Concepts in the 1970s," in Stephen E. Miller, ed., *Strategy and Nuclear Deterrence* (Princeton: Princeton University Press, 1984), p. 184.

50. A comprehensive review of the evolution of U.S. export control legislation through the 1970s and the early 1980s can be found in U.S. Congress, Office of Technology Assessment, *Technology and East-West Trade* (Washington, D.C.: U.S. Government Printing Office, 1983). See also Mastanduno, *Economic Containment*, chap. 3.

51. Quoted in *The Economist* (May 22, 1982):69.

52. "New Directions in U.S. Trade Policy," speech before the International Trade Committee, National Association of Manufacturers, January 13, 1982, p. 10.

53. Stephen Krasner, "Structural Causes and Regime Consequences: Regimes as Intervening Variables," in Stephen Krasner, ed., *International Regimes* (Ithaca: Cornell University Press, 1983), pp. 1–21.

54. For this behavioral approach to regime norms, see Robert Axelrod, "An Evolutionary Approach to Norms," *American Political Science Review* 80(4) (December 1986):1097.

55. Joseph Fitchett, "It's 16 to 1 Against U.S. on the Eve of Paris COCOM Meeting," *International Herald Tribune* (October 25, 1989):7.

56. James M. Markham, "For West Europeans, Another Missile Debate," *New York Times* (January 25, 1989):A4. By January 1990, the Soviets had reached an agreement with the new Hungarian government to withdraw all troops stationed in Hungary since 1956. See John J. Fialka, "Warsaw Pact's Military Strength is Seen Changed," *Wall Street Journal* (January 24, 1990):A10.

57. Thomas L. Friedman, "U.S. Says Soviets Apparently Cut Arms Spending," *New York Times* (November 14, 1989):A9.

58. At a CMEA meeting held in Sophia, January 9–10, 1990, members decided to name a special commission to draft a plan for revamping the arrangement to make it compatible with free-market principles. See Tim Carrington, "East Bloc to Transform Comecon, Retain Economic Ties to Moscow," *Wall Street Journal* (January 10, 1990):A10. The unit of account for CMEA transactions was called a "transferable ruble." Soviet buyers paid transferable rubles for the merchandise they acquired from Eastern Europe, and the Eastern Europeans then used these units to buy energy supplies and other raw materials from the Soviet Union. The Soviet Union provided an assured market for Eastern European products as well as an assured supply of energy to Eastern Europe. Although it would clearly benefit the Soviet Union, the shift would prove to be difficult for a number of reasons. CMEA countries are short of hard currency and prefer to spend it on imports from the West, rather than on imports from each other. The Soviet Union, however, under world market prices, would pay less for most imports from Eastern Europe, while, at current prices, still receiving market price for its oil exports. Indeed, under the new system, Moscow's net hard currency earnings would increase.

59. For an excellent example of this position, see Jerry Hough, *Opening the Soviet Economy* (Washington, D.C.: Brookings Institution, 1988).

60. See U.S. Department of Defense, *Soviet Military Power: An Assessment of the Threat, 1988* (Washington, D.C.: U.S. Government Printing Office, 1988), p. 32.

61. For representative arguments, see Frederick Bonnart, "NATO Needs to Get Its Message Across," *Wall Street Journal* (August 15, 1988):17; Frank C. Carlucci, "No Time to Change U.S. Defense Policy," *New York Times* (January 27, 1989):A16; Stephen M. Walt, "Our Forces' Restructuring: Thinner, But Still Fit to Fight," *Los Angeles Times* (November 28, 1989):B7; Judy Shelton, *The Coming Soviet Crash: Gorbachev's Desperate Pursuit of Credit in Western Financial Markets* (New York: Free Press, 1989); and DOD, *Soviet Military Power 1988*, p. 35. For an

excellent statement of the "skeptics' " view, see "Z," "To the Stalin Mausoleum," *Daedalus* 119(1) (Winter 1990):338.

62. U.S. Central Intelligence Agency and Defense Intelligence Agency, "Gorbachev's Modernization Program: A Status Report," a paper presented to the Subcommittee on National Security Economics of the Joint Economic Committee, Congress of the United States, March 19, 1987, p. 5.

63. U.S. Department of Defense, *Soviet Military Power: Prospects for Change, 1989* (Washington, D.C.: U.S. Government Printing Office), p. 135.

64. A good summary and statement of these views can be found in Sumner Benson, "The Security Perspective on Export Control Policy in the 1990s," in Bertsch and Elliott-Gower, eds., *Export Controls in Transition*, pp. 9–36.

65. Fitchett, "It's 16 to 1 Against U.S.," p. 7.

66. *Foreign Broadcast Information Service* (hereafter cited as *FBIS*), EAS 89–169, "COCOM Talks with U.S. Fail to Reach Accord" (from *Korean Times* [January 9, 1989]) (September 1, 1989):27. COCOM's eventual promise to relax controls, however, made it easier for South Korea to comply. Effective July 1, 1990, Korea introduced an export control system that restircted the export of those strategic items to communist countries that were on the COCOM list. *FBIS*, EAS 90–116, "System to Control Exports to Communist Nations" (from *Korean Times* [June 13, 1990]:3) (June 15, 1990):30.

67. In 1985 the President's Commission on Industrial Competitiveness issued a report warning that America's share of the world market had declined in seven out of ten "sunrise industries." See Stephen Cohen, David Teece, Laura D'Andrea Tyson, and John Zysman, *Competitiveness. Vol. III, Global Competition: The New Reality. The Report of the President's Commission on Industrial Competitiveness* (Washington, D.C.: U.S. Government Printing Office, 1985). See also U.S. Department of Defense, *Bolstering Defense Industrial Competitiveness: Preserving Our Heritage, Securing Our Future*, Report to the Secretary of Defense by the Undersecretary of Defense (Acquisition), July 1988; Defense Science Board, *The Defense Industrial and Technology Base*, Final Report of the Defense Science Board 1988 Summer Study, October 1988.

68. A comparative rating of semiconductor suppliers computed by the Department of Defense indicated a dramatic drop in the rank of U.S. semiconductor firms between 1985 and 1987. Motorola dropped in rank from second to fourth, Intel from eighth to tenth, and Texas Instruments from third to fifth. Among the ten leading chip producers, six were Japanese, three were American firms, and one was an American joint venture involving a European firm. See Defense Science Board Task Force, *Defense Semiconductor Dependency* (Washington, D.C.: Office of the Undersecretary of Defense for Acquisition, 1987), p. 51.

69. U.S. Department of Defense, *Critical Technologies Plan for the Committee on Armed Services, United States Congress* (Washington, D.C.: U.S. Government Printing Office, May 5, 1989).

70. These fears were somewhat assuaged by the announcement made by

Cray Computer Corporation that it was developing a new supercomputer that uses gallium arsenide chips. See John Markoff, "Computer Star's New Advance," *New York Times* (February 17, 1990):19.

71. Akio Morita and Shintaro Ishihara, *The Japan That Can Say "No": The New U.S.-Japan Relations Card* (Washington, D.C.: U.S. Department of Defense [mimeo], 1989), pp. 3–4.

72. Quoted in John Eckhouse, "U.S. May Loosen High-Tech Export Rules," *San Francisco Chronicle* (January 20, 1990):B1.

73. William J. Broad, "Industries Fight Ban on Using Soviet Rockets," *New York Times* (December 13, 1987):1, and Broad, "American Company and Soviet Agree on Space Venture," *New York Times* (February 21, 1988):1. In October 1990, Senate and House conferees agreed to ban the launching of U.S. satellites from Chinese vehicles unless the U.S. trade representative could certify that China was observing a bilateral fair-pricing agreement. See Eduardo Lachica, "Conferees Toughen Rules for U.S. to Restrict Exports," *Wall Street Journal* (October 22, 1990):A16.

74. On the issues surrounding the proposed Fairchild-Fujitsu merger, see "Fujitsu to Acquire 80% of Fairchild," *Electronic News* (October 27, 1986):1; "Integrated Circuit Technology Transfer Concerns U.S. Officials," *Aviation Week and Space Technology* (November 10, 1986):31; David E. Sanger, "Japanese Purchase of Chip Maker Canceled After Objections in U.S.," *New York Times* (March 17, 1987):1; and John W. Wilson, "What the Fairchild Fiasco Signals for Trade Policy," *Business Week* (March 30, 1987):28.

75. Secretary of State James Baker, "The Challenge of Change in U.S.-Soviet Relations," address to the Center for Strategic and International Studies, Washington, D.C., May 4, 1989; *Current Policy* no. 1170 (Washington, D.C.: Department of State, Bureau of Public Affairs, May 1989), p. 2.

76. Quoted in Thomas L. Friedman, "U.S. Voicing Fears of Effect on West from Gorbachev," *New York Times* (September 16, 1989):1.

77. Fitchett, "It's 16 to 1 Against U.S.," p. 7.

78. This view was expressed repeatedly by Western European officials and corporate executives in interviews conducted in August 1990. See also Advisory Committee for Trade Policy and Negotiations, *Europe 1992* (Washington, D.C.: Advisory Committee for Trade Policy and Negotiations, November 29, 1989). The report warned that the Bush administration must give the highest priority to reforming export controls or risk being shut out of European markets. Because Europeans saw American export control policy as misguided, they threatened to buy fewer American products that embodied high technology and to exclude American companies from cooperative research projects in high technology. For a good example of American industry's position on this issue, see "Chip Makers Tell DoD: Let Us Sell Rad-Hard Chips Overseas," *Electronic Business* (July 1, 1989):18.

79. Excerpts from Baker's speech are reprinted in *New York Times* (October 17, 1989):A8. Following Baker's lead, the Pentagon conceded to relax control on the least powerful mainframe computers to the Soviet Union and Eastern

Europe, leaving all responsibility to the Commerce Department. See Michael Wines, "U.S. Easing on Exports of Computers," *New York Times* (March 31, 1990):17.

80. In 1985, COCOM rules were revised to permit many items requiring COCOM review to the Soviet Union and Eastern Europe to be approved for China as "administrative exceptions." In other words, COCOM members could transfer much sensitive technology to China at their discretion. See William A. Root, "An Appraisal of Objectives and Needed Reforms," in Bertsch, ed., *Controlling East-West Trade*, p. 420.

81. Eduardo Lachica, "U.S. Seeks Cut in Trade Curbs for East Europe," *Wall Street Journal* (January 23, 1990):A15.

82. Quoted in Patrick E. Tylor, "Pentagon Paper Says Soviets Are Still a Threat in Third World," *San Francisco Chronicle* (February 13, 1990):A13.

83. A compromise was reached between the United States and Western Europeans on the countries targeted for decontrol. The U.S. had pressed for freer controls on items bound for Central and Eastern Europe and continued restrictions on the Soviet Union. It was finally formally agreed that all countries on COCOM's list of restricted nations would benefit from the new relaxation, even the Soviet Union. In fact, however, Poland, Hungary, and Czechoslovakia were given the same trade privileges accorded to China, but restrictions on the Soviet Union, Bulgaria, and Romania, although somewhat loosened, were tighter than for the former three.

84. On the agreement to relax controls on fiber-optic cables, see Keith Bradsher, "Pact Seeks Looser Curbs on Exports," *New York Times* (March 6, 1992):C1.

85. See, for example, Clyde H. Farnsworth, "U.S. Balks at Easing Export Curbs," *New York Times* (March 4, 1991):C3.

86. Philippe Marcheteau, personal communication, August 9, 1990.

87. See Anthony Ramirez, "Business is Losing Patience with the Cold War's Export Police," *New York Times* (January 26, 1993):18.

2. The Case for Economic Vulnerability in International Relations

1. Robert O. Keohane and Joseph S. Nye, *Power and Interdependence* (Glenview, Ill.: Scott, Foresman, 1989).

2. Vinod Aggarwal, *International Debt Threat* (Berkeley: Institute of International Studies, 1987), pp. 1–6.

3. Technology is generally defined as the state of knowledge relevant to production. High technology is defined as that technology that has a large percentage (over 5 percent) of a firm's investment in research and development. It is usually capital-intensive, while conventional technology is usually more labor-intensive. High technology requires a large element of complex patented or nonpatented proprietary know-how. It is highly technical and almost always accompanied by the delivery of substantial services and spare parts. Conventional technology can be embodied in a product that is often, but not necessarily, accompanied by maintenance and operations data. It is often available for

sale through engineering and construction firms, rather than the firm that originally developed the technology. Finally, high technology is characterized by rapid change; when it is sold at the beginning of the product cycle, it is strong, unique, and highly competitive. When it is sold at the end of the product cycle, it is weaker and begins to approach the conventional category.

4. The chemical weapons Iraq used against Iran and the Kurds were developed from equipment and chemicals provided by Germany. Indeed, during the 1980s, a group of West German companies helped Iraq construct two large missile and chemical-weapons development facilities, the cornerstone of Saddam Hussein's effort to build an indigenous military/industrial base. See Janne E. Nolan, "How to Stymie Iraq—For a While," *New York Times* (April 3, 1990):A15; Frederick Kempe, "Germans Had Big Role in Helping Iraq Arm, Internal Report Shows," *Wall Street Journal* (October 2, 1990):A1.

5. See John Zysman, "Redoubling the Bet: Power, Wealth, and Technology," Berkeley Roundtable on the International Economy Working Paper no. 38, University of California, Berkeley, October 1989.

6. Klaus Knorr, *Power and Wealth* (New York: Basic Books, 1973), p. 54. Robert Gilpin has argued that the introduction of these innovations altered the significance of the economic base of state power by decreasing the cost of weaponry, thus allowing less wealthy societies to gain military advantages. See *War and Change in International Politics* (Cambridge: Cambridge University Press, 1981), pp. 59–66. On the advantages of "stealth" technology, see David Buchan, "Western Security and Economic Strategy towards the East," *Adelphi Papers*, no. 192 (London: International Institute for Strategic Studies, 1984), p. 16.

7. See Gilpin, *War and Change in International Politics*, p. 63. One example comes from the sixteenth century when Japan had higher-quality firearms than the Europeans. The introduction of the firearm, however, began to undermine the power of the samurai class, and the Japanese nobility was able to ban this weapon for almost two hundred years. See Noel Perrin, *Giving Up the Gun: Japan's Reversion to the Sword, 1543–1879* (Boulder, Colo.: Shambhala Press, 1980).

8. National Science Foundation, *National Patterns of Science and Technology Resources, 1984*, NSF Report 84–11 (Washington, D.C.: National Science Foundation, 1985).

9. Harvey M. Sapolsky, "Science, Technology, and Military Policy," in Ina Spiegel-Roesing and Derek de Solla Price, eds., *Science, Technology, and Society* (London: Sage, 1977), p. 443.

10. Sanford Lakoff, "Scientists, Technologists, and Political Power," in Spiegel-Roesing and de Solla Price, eds., *Science, Technology, and Society*, p. 366.

11. The point is made by John Zysman and Stephen S. Cohen, *Manufacturing Matters* (New York: Basic Books, 1987).

12. Knorr, *Power and Wealth*, chap. 3; Paul Seabury, "Industrial Policy and National Defense," in Chalmers Johnson, ed., *The Industrial Policy Debate* (San Francisco: Institute for Contemporary Studies, 1984), p. 257.

13. John U. Nef, *War and Human Progress* (New York: W. W. Norton, 1963), pp. 176, 319.

14. J. Fred Bucy, "On Strategic Technology Transfer to the Soviet Union," *International Security* 1(4) (Spring 1977):27. See also Jay Stowsky, "Competing with the Pentagon," *World Policy Journal* 3(4) (Fall 1986).

15. Victor Basiuk, "Security Receeds," *Foreign Policy* 53 (Winter 1984–84):50.

16. The fact that commercial technology increasingly provides the foundation for advances in weaponry rather than the other way around has led critics to conclude that excessive funding for military R and D detracts from funding that might otherwise be available for commercial innovation, and thus reduces national security. John Zysman has written:

> Government funding of military applications shunts people away from civilian projects by helping military projects outbid civilian ones for talent. The result is that the price of engineering talent is pushed up for the civilian sector, and adequate talent is often still not available. This both raises costs and brings firms to undertake some development efforts offshore. A different problem is that small start-up firms that initially develop advanced technology for military applications with Department of Defense money are often not permitted to develop the technology for commercial markets. . . . The result is that military spin-off may delay rather than facilitate commercial application and can delay—not accelerate—the mastery and development of the technology.

See Zysman, "Redoubling the Bet," pp. 13–14.

17. The best discussion of this issue can be found in Jeffrey A. Hart, "Strategic Impacts of High Definition Television for U.S. Manufacturing," report to the National Center for Manufacturing Sciences, 1989. On HDTV as a dual-use technology, see Congressman Edward Markey, "Consumer Electronics, HDTV and the Competitiveness of the U.S. Economy," report submitted to the House Telecommunications and Finance Committee, February 1, 1989; Robert Cohen and Kenneth Konow, "Telecommunications Policy, High Definition Television, and U.S. Competitiveness," Washington, D.C., Economic Policy Institute, 1989; and Norm Alster, "TV's High-Stakes, High-Tech Battle," *Fortune* (October 24, 1988):161–170.

18. Kempe, "Germans Had Big Role," p. A18.

19. U.S. Central Intelligence Agency, *Soviet Acquisition of Western Technology* (Washington, D.C.: CIA, April 1982), p. 13.

20. Sapolsky, "Science, Technology, and Military Policy," p. 451.

21. On these dual-use technologies and the problems involved in attempts to assess their military significance, see Maurice J. Mountain, "Technology Exports and National Security," *Foreign Policy* 32 (Fall 1978):101; Ellen Frost and Angela E. Stent, "NATO's Troubles with East-West Trade," *International Security* 8(1) (Summer 1983):184; and William A. Root, "Trade Controls That Work," *Foreign Policy* 56 (Fall 1984):62.

22. Caspar Weinberger, *The Technology Transfer Control Program, A Report to the*

98th Congress (Washington, D.C.: U.S. Government Printing Office, February 1984), pp. 19–21.

23. On the concept of the technology gap, see John W. Kiser, "What Gap? Which Gap?" *Foreign Policy* 32 (Fall 1978):90–94; Bucy, "On Strategic Technology Transfer," p. 33; and George D. Holliday, "Survey of Sectoral Case Studies," in Organization for Economic Cooperation and Development, ed., *East-West Technology Transfer* (Paris: OECD, 1984), p. 76.

24. Albert O. Hirschman, *National Power and the Structure of Foreign Trade* (Berkeley: University of California Press, 1980), pp. 4–5.

25. A crucial requirement for the successful adoption of foreign technology and rapid economic development was the mobilization of underutilized resources by a strong state, which gave these two countries the "advantages of backwardness." See Alexander Gerschenkron, *Economic Backwardness in Historical Perspective* (Cambridge, Mass.: Harvard University Press, 1962).

26. From 1951 to 1984, the Japanese signed more than 42,000 contracts for technology purchases from abroad. See Nicholas D. Kristof, "Americans Picking Japanese Brains," *New York Times* (September 18, 1985):sec. 3, p. 1.

27. On linkage requirements for technology diffusion, see Michael G. Borrus, *Competing for Control: America's Stake in Microelectronics* (Cambridge, Mass.: Ballinger, 1988), pp. 36–40. See also Elhanan Helpman and Paul R. Drugman, *Market Structure and Foreign Trade: Increasing Returns, Imperfect Competition, and the International Economy* (Cambridge, Mass.: MIT Press, 1986).

28. The "product cycle theory" is usually employed to explain those incentives. Essentially, the theory identifies three stages in the life cycle of a product. In the *innovative* stage, the product is produced for the firm's own market. As the product is imitated by other firms and the domestic market is threatened, the innovator begins to export the good in order to expand its market share. This is called the *maturing* stage of the cycle. In the *standardized* stage, when the exports are threatened by overseas competitors, the innovator decides to produce the product abroad, where production costs are cheaper, and then sell it back to the home market to compete with more expensive versions of the product produced domestically. This theory was developed by Raymond Vernon in *Sovereignty at Bay* (New York: Basic Books, 1971), chap. 3.

29. On this point, see Robert Gilpin, *U.S. Power and the Multinational Corporation* (New York: Basic Books, 1975), pp. 164–167; and Jack Baranson, "Technology Exports Can Hurt Us," *Foreign Policy* 25 (Winter 1976–77):180–194.

30. *An Analysis of Export Control of U.S. Technology—A DoD Perspective: A Report of the Defense Science Board Task Force on Export of U.S. Technology* (Washington, D.C.: Office of the Director of Defense Research and Engineering, February 4, 1976).

31. The literature on global industrial cooperation is growing rapidly. See, for example, OECD, *Technical Cooperation Agreements Between Firms*, DSTI/SPR 86–20, Paris, 1986; Ken Ohmae, *Triad Power* (New York: Free Press, 1985); Harold Perlmutter and D. Heenan, "Cooperate to Compete Globally," *Harvard*

Business Review 86 (March-April 1986); J. Peter Killing, *Strategies for Joint Venture Success* (New York: Praeger, 1983); and C. P. Zeithaml and V. A. Zeithaml, "Environmental Management: Revising the Marketing Perspective," *Journal of Marketing* (Spring 1984). For a critical perspective, see Robert B. Reich and David Walters, "Joint Ventures with Japan Give Away Our Future," *Harvard Business Review* 86 (March-April 1986):78–86. As foreign firms attempt to jump protectionist barriers in the United States, industrial cooperation is increasingly common on U.S. soil. Between 1985 and 1987, more than 1,000 such agreements were negotiated between U.S. and European firms alone. See Daniel A. Sharp, "Combat Protection with Global Alliances," *Wall Street Journal* (June 1, 1987):29.

32. On the importance of training and person-to-person technology transfer, see William H. Gruber and Donald G. Marquis, eds., *Factors in the Transfer of Technology* (Cambridge, Mass.: MIT Press, 1969). See also Carl MacMillan, "East-West Industrial Cooperation," in U.S. Congress Joint Economic Committee, *East European Economics Post-Helsinki* (Washington, D.C.: U.S. Government Printing Office, 1977), pp. 1192–1193.

33. This argument is made by Jack Baranson, *International Transfer of Industrial Technology by U.S. Firms and Their Implication for the U.S. Economy* (Washington, D.C.: U.S. Department of Labor, International Labor Affairs Bureau, Office of Foreign Economic Research, September 1976).

34. U.S. Congress, House of Representatives, Committee on Appropriations, *Hearings: Department of Defense Appropriations for 1984, Part I,* 98th Cong., 2d sess., 1984, p. 273.

35. See Kempe, "Germans Had Big Role," p. A18.

36. For a good discussion of the costs and benefits of export-led growth and import substitution industrialization, see Bela Balassa, ed., *Development Strategies in Semi-Industrial Economies* (Baltimore: Johns Hopkins University Press, 1982).

37. Robert D. Putnam, "Diplomacy and Domestic Politics: The Logic of Two-Level Games," *International Organization* 42(3) (Summer 1988):427–460.

38. Stephen Haggard and Beth A. Simmons, "Theories of International Regimes," *International Organization* 41(3) (Summer 1987):515.

39. This argument is developed fully in Crawford and Lenway, "Decision Modes and International Regime Change," pp. 380–387. I must hasten to add here that defining the terms of the vulnerability debate will not automatically lead to the legitimizing consensus that makes regimes strong. Differing political and economic interests lurk behind differences over definition; states attach different utilities to different consequences of trade and export control, giving rise to simple conflicts of interest.

40. Johan Galtung, "On the Effects of International Economic Sanctions, with Examples from the Case of Rhodesia," *World Politics* 19 (April 1967):385.

41. Robert Stobaugh, "World Energy to the Year 2000," in Daniel Yergin and Martin Hillenbrand, eds., *Global Insecurity* (New York: Penguin, 1983), pp. 29–57.

42. Stephen D. Krasner, "Oil is the Exception," *Foreign Policy* 14 (Spring 1974):68–84.

43. On the difficulties involved in imposing collective trade restrictions, see Margaret Doxy, *Economic Sanctions and International Enforcement* (London: Oxford University Press, 1971); and M. S. Daoudi and M. S. Dajani, *Economic Sanctions: Ideals and Experience* (London: Routledge and Kegan Paul, 1983).

44. In that year the Soviet grain harvest had fallen 48 million tons (21 percent) short of production targets. As a result, the Soviet government made plans to import 35 million tons of grain over the next twelve months. See Robert Paarlberg, "Lessons from the Grain Embargo," *Foreign Affairs* 59(1) (Fall 1980):144.

45. "Proposed Trans-Siberian Natural Gas Pipeline," *Hearings Before the Committee on Banking, Housing, and Urban Affairs, United States Senate*, November 12, 1981 (Washington, D.C.: U.S. Government Printing Office, 1982), p. 116.

46. For a careful analysis of this case, see Carolyn Castore, "The United States and India: The Use of Food to Apply Economic Pressure—1965–67," in Sidney Weintraub, ed., *Economic Coercion and U.S. Foreign Policy* (Boulder, Colo.: Westview, 1982), pp. 129–153.

47. Jorge I. Dominguez, *Cuba: Order and Revolution* (Cambridge, Mass.: Harvard University Press, 1978), p. 162.

48. More likely, however, the reduction in Soviet grain exports was caused by shipping problems between the two countries and Soviet economic difficulties. See Paul Lewis, "As Shipments of Soviet Grain Lag, Cuba Reduces Daily Bread Ration," *New York Times* (February 7, 1990):5.

49. See "Baltic Lands: 50 Years of Turmoil and Strife," *New York Times* (January 14, 1991):A6.

50. On the concept of blackmail, see Kenneth Oye, "The Domain of Choice," in Kenneth A. Oye, Donald Rothchild, and Robert Lieber, eds., *Eagle Entangled* (New York: Longman, 1979), pp. 15–17.

51. Klaus Knorr, "International Economic Leverage and Its Uses," in Klaus Knorr and Frank Trager, eds., *Economic Issues and National Security* (Lawrence, Kan.: Allen Press, 1977), pp. 99–101.

52. Compliance is often difficult to measure, since the coercing state may have several ill-defined objectives that may change over time. On the difficulties of defining "success" in economic pressure, see Richard Stuart Olson, "Economic Coercion in World Politics, with a Focus on North-South Relations," *World Politics* 31(4) (July 1979):475; and Galtung, "International Economic Sanctions," p. 396.

53. See David A. Baldwin, *Economic Statecraft* (Princeton: Princeton University Press, 1985), pp. 19–24 and 182–183.

54. In all of these cases, however, the importers have not been highly vulnerable because they were not dependent upon the exporters who initiated the embargo.

55. "Soviet Cuts Off Fuel to Britain," *New York Times* (October 30, 1984):A8.

56. See John Eckhouse, "Japan Firms Reportedly Stalled U.S. War Supplies," *San Francisco Chronicle* (April 30, 1991):1.

57. See Keohane and Nye, *Power and Interdependence*, pp. 8–19.

58. Hirschman, *National Power*. Hirschman's study and his treatment of exporter dependence formed the basis for much of the "dependencia" literature of the 1960s and 1970s.

59. This is not true, however, for OPEC countries that have foreign exchange surpluses, like Saudi Arabia, Kuwait, Libya, Abu Dhabi, and the United Arab Emirates. For these countries, the costs of restricting oil supply for a short time would be low. See Stephen D. Krasner, "Petrocurrency Leverage," unpublished ms., March 1982, pp. 11–12.

60. See Paarlberg, "Lessons from the Grain Embargo," p. 148. Paarlberg argues that the 1980 grain embargo did not in fact sharply constrain U.S. grain export opportunities, but that the domestic pressure to lift the sanctions was brought on by the perception that farmers were dependent on the Soviet market. On the role played by domestic interest groups in creating exporter dependence, see Stephen D. Krasner, "Domestic Constraints on International Economic Leverage," in Knorr and Trager, eds., *Economic Issues and National Security*, pp. 160–181.

61. Keohane and Nye, *Power and Interdependence*, p. 15.

62. Judy Shelton, *The Coming Soviet Crash* (New York: Free Press, 1989), p. xvii.

63. This argument is made by Benjamin J. Cohen in "International Debt and Linkage Strategies: Some Foreign-Policy Implications for the United States," *International Organization* 39(4) (Autumn 1985):699–727.

64. Harold Lever, "The Debt Won't Be Paid," *New York Review of Books* (June 28, 1984):3. By the end of 1988 the exposure of the major banks in Latin America had fallen to almost 84 percent of capital reserves. The chairman of the FDIC, William Seidman, argued that with this level of exposure, although still high, the banks would write off all of their outstanding loans and remain solvent. See Jeffrey Sachs, "Making the Brady Plan Work," *Foreign Affairs* (Summer 1989):90.

65. Quoted in Barbara Stallings, "The Debt Crisis: Back to the Dependency Syndrome?," unpublished ms., Yale University, 1985, p. 17.

66. Herbert Feis, *Europe, the World's Banker, 1870–1914* (New York: A. M. Kelley, 1964), p. 201.

67. Peter Gumbel, "Soviets Would Gain by Overhauling Comecon," *Wall Street Journal* (January 2, 1990):A15.

68. Export-Import Bank of the United States, *Report to the U.S. Congress on Export Credit Competition and the Export-Import Bank of the United States*, Washington, D.C., 1983, pp. 3–20.

69. Benjamin J. Cohen, *Banks and the Balance of Payments* (Montclair, N.J.: Allanheld, Osmun, 1981), pp. 3–42.

70. Steve Frazier, "Oil's Lure Led Mexico and Banks into Payment Woes," *Wall Street Journal* (May 15, 1984):34.

71. Lynda Schuster, "Politics Played a Crucial Role in Argentine Lending," *Wall Street Journal* (May 17, 1984):34.

72. Ibid., p. 6.

73. Robert Jervis, *The Illogic of American Nuclear Strategy* (Ithaca: Cornell University Press, 1984), p. 30.

74. Charles Wolf, Jr., "Default versus Deferral of Poland's Debt: Real and Illusory Differences," in *East-West Economic Relations and the Soviet Union's Defense Posture, Report of a RAND Conference*, March 20, 1982 (RAND Note no. N–1877 USDP, September 1982), p. 30.

75. Jervis, *Illogic of American Nuclear Strategy*, p.30.

76. Aggarwal, *International Debt Threat*, pp. 1–6.

77. Of this potential for economic leverage, Stephen Krasner writes that "for a threat to provide political leverage the target must believe that the initiator will carry out the threat, even though implementation would be costly for both the target and the initiator. The target must also believe that the situation is indeed one of high costs for both parties." "Petrocurrency Leverage," p. 18.

78. For a more detailed discussion of these problems in Third World debt negotiations, see Aggarwal, *International Debt Threat*.

79. Cohen, "International Debt and Linkage Strategies," p. 702.

80. See Keith Crane, "The Creditworthiness of Eastern Europe in the 1980s," report prepared for the Office of the Under Secretary of Defense for Policy (Santa Monica, Calif.: Rand Corporation, 1985), p. 138.

81. Sachs, "Making the Brady Plan Work," pp. 93–94.

82. Stallings, "The Debt Crisis," p. 15.

83. Between 1981 and 1988 real per capita income declined in absolute terms in almost every country in South America. In most countries, living standards fell to levels of the 1950s and 1960s. In Mexico, real wages declined by about 50 percent between 1980 and 1988. See Sachs, "Making the Brady Plan Work," p. 91. In February 1989, 300 people died in Venezuelan riots protesting austerity measures instituted in response to the debt crisis.

84. Charles Lipson has argued that these efforts have been largely successful. See "Bankers' Dilemmas: Private Cooperation in Rescheduling Sovereign Debts," in Kenneth A. Oye, ed., *Cooperation Under Anarchy* (Princeton: Princeton University Press, 1986), pp. 200–225. See also Aggarwal, *International Debt Threat*, p. 22.

85. The Brady Plan was announced on March 10, 1989 in a speech by U.S. Treasury Secretary Nicholas Brady. Recognizing that many debtor countries will be unable to pay back their commercial debt in full, even if payment schedules are lengthened, the plan calls on U.S. commercial banks to accept a reduction in the debt of thirty-nine debtor nations and asks the IMF and the World Bank to support the plan by financing guarantees on the remaining portion of the debt.

3. Technology Exodus: The Impact of Imported Innovation on the Soviet Economy

1. Soviet authorities have never published income statistics with much credibility in the West. CIA estimates, assembled over the years from raw Soviet data, have been the most influential. In April 1990, however, the American Enterprise Institute held a conference of American and Soviet experts on the Soviet economy, at which many scholars disputed CIA figures, citing disagreements about the purchasing power of the ruble and uncertainties about the prices and quantities of goods and services produced in the Soviet Union. Most scholars admit that a lack of hard data makes it possible to defend a wide range of estimates.

2. Imogene Edwards, Margaret Hughes, and James Noren, "US and USSR: Comparison of GNP," in U.S. Congress, Joint Economic Committee, *Soviet Economy in a Time of Change—A Compendium of Papers*, 91st Cong., 1st sess., 1979, p. 377.

3. See, for example, Morris Bornstein, *The Transfer of Western Technology to the USSR* (Paris: OECD, 1985), p. 28; Central Intelligence Agency/Defense Intelligence Agency, *Gorbachev's Economic Program: Problems Emerge*, report presented to the Subcommittee on National Security Economics of the Joint Economic Committee, Washington, D.C., April 1988; and John P. Hardt and Richard F. Kaufman, "Gorbachev's Economic Plans: Prospects and Risks," in Joint Economic Committee, *Gorbachev's Economic Plans*, vol. 1 (Washington, D.C.: U.S. Government Printing Office, 1987), pp. 7–10.

4. See Abel Aganbegyan, *The Economic Challenge of Perestroika* (Bloomington: Indiana University Press, 1988), p. 2; Michael Ellman, *Collectivization, Convergence and Capitalism: Political Economy in a Divided World* (London: Academic Press, 1984), pp. 135–146; and Alec Nove, "Has Soviet Growth Ceased?" *Manchester Statistical Society* (November 15, 1983).

5. Soviet estimates cited at the American Enterprise Institute conference on Soviet economic statistics. See Robert Pear, "Soviet Experts Say Their Economy is Worse than US Has Estimated," *New York Times* (April 24, 1990):14; Art Pine, "Soviets Say CIA Overestimates Size of Their Economy," *Los Angeles Times* (April 24, 1990):13; and Peter Passell, "Soviet Economy: Red Storm Ebbs," *New York Times* (April 25, 1990):D2.

6. Richard Perle, "The Eastward Technology Flow: A Plan of Common Action," *Strategic Review* 12(2) (Spring 1984):23, 27.

7. "New Directions in U.S. Trade Policy," San Francisco, January 13, 1982.

8. Quoted in *The Economist* (May 22, 1982):69.

9. "Trade and Security in the 1980s," address before the National Defense Executive Reserve, October 21, 1982.

10. Perle, "The Eastward Technology Flow," p. 26.

11. On Western involvement in the late nineteenth-century czarist economy, see J. McKay, *Pioneers for Profit: Foreign Entrepreneurship and Russian Industrialization: 1885–1913* (Chicago: University of Chicago Press, 1970). The most com-

plete source for a historical view of the role of Western technology in the Soviet economy is Anthony Sutton, *Western Technology and Soviet Economic Development, 1917–1965*, 3 vols. (Stanford: Hoover Institution Press, 1973).

12. See Timothy W. Luke, "Technology and Soviet Foreign Trade: On the Political Economy of an Underdeveloped Superpower," *International Studies Quarterly* 29 (1985):335.

13. In 1990 French President Mitterand and Soviet President Gorbachev signed an agreement by which French holders of czarist Russian bonds would be paid by the Soviet government. See "Redeeming Czarist Bonds," *Wall Street Journal* (October 30, 1990):17.

14. Stalin's goal was to make the Soviet Union independent of the international economy. In the beginning, in order to build a technologically advanced industrial base, he drew heavily on Western technology. For the best discussion of Soviet technology-import policy in the 1920s and 1930s, see Bruce Parrot, *Politics and Technology in the Soviet Union* (Cambridge, Mass.: MIT Press, 1983), chap. 2. In addition to these one-time commercial deals, the Soviet regime focused its industrial goals on the development of military technology, largely with German assistance. See Luke, "Technology and Soviet Foreign Trade," p. 340.

15. Franklyn Holzman, "Foreign Trade Behavior of Centrally Planned Economies," in Morris Bornstein, ed., *Comparative Economic Systems: Models and Cases* (Homewood, Ill.: Richard D. Irwin, 1974), pp. 313–336.

16. Michael Kaser, *COMECOM: Integration Problems of the Planned Economies* (New York: Oxford University Press, 1967), pp. 11–12.

17. See Joseph Berliner, "Prospects for Technological Progress," in U.S. Congress Joint Economic Committee, *Soviet Economy in a New Perspective* (Washington, D.C.: U.S. Government Printing Office, 1976), p. 445.

18. *Pravda* (April 6, 1966):7. Quoted in Philip Hanson, "The Import of Western Technology," in Archie Brown and Michael Kaser, eds., *The Soviet Union Since the Fall of Khrushchev* (New York: Macmillan, 1975), p. 21.

19. Philip Hanson reports that since the 1950s the rate of Soviet commercial acquisition of Western technology has grown faster than most other Soviet activities. For example, between 1955–56 and 1975–76 imports of Western machinery grew at an average annual of 13.9 percent. This rate exceeded that of Soviet domestic output and that of total foreign trade volume. See Philip Hanson, *Trade and Technology in Soviet-Western Relations* (New York: Columbia University Press, 1981), p. 83. See also Roger A. Clarke and Dubravko J. I. Matko, *Soviet Economic Facts, 1917–81* (New York: St. Martin's, 1983), pp. 9, 10, 78–79.

20. John P. Hardt, "The Role of Western Technology in Soviet Economic Plans," paper presented to the NATO Directorate of Economic Affairs Colloquium on East-West Technological Cooperation, Brussels, March 17–19, 1976, p. 3.

21. See U.S. House of Representatives, Committee on International Relations, *Science, Technology and American Diplomacy, An Extended Study of the Interactions of Science and Technology with United States Foreign Policy* (Washington, D.C.: U.S. Government Printing Office, 1977), pp. 544–547. Throughout the 1970s

machine tools and control instruments headed Soviet shopping lists in the West, reflecting a drive to streamline production processes in all industries, with the intention of increasing productivity in all sectors. See U.S. Department of Commerce, "Quantification of Western Exports of High-Technology Products to Communist Countries" (1979). p. 10.

22. U.S. Congress, Joint Economic Committee, *East-West Trade: The Prospects to 1985* (Washington, D.C.: U.S. Government Printing Office, 1982), p. 67 (hereafter cited as *Prospects*).

23. Eugene Zaleski and Helgard Wienert, *Technology Transfer Between East and West* (Paris: OECD, 1980), p. 142.

24. Quoted in Alexander Woroniak, "Economic Aspects of Soviet-American Detente," paper prepared for the Third Atlantic Economic Conference, Washington, D.C., September 12–13, 1975, p. 17.

25. Hanson, *Trade and Technology in Soviet-Western Relations*, pp. 1–19.

26. Business International, *Selling Knowledge and Technology to Eastern Europe: Practices and Problems* (Geneva: Business International, 1978), p. 373.

27. See Philip Hanson, "Western Technology in the Soviet Economy," *Problems of Communism* (November–December 1978):20–25. Estimates of Western technology as a percent of total Soviet investment in capital equipment vary widely. Thane Gustafson estimated that during the ninth Five-Year Plan (1971–1975) 15 percent of Soviet capital equipment was imported from abroad. See *Selling the Russians the Rope? Soviet Technology Policy and U.S. Export Controls* (Santa Monica, Calif.: Rand, 1981). Philip Hanson estimated, however, that Western technology never accounted for more than 6 percent of total Soviet investment in equipment in any one year. See *Trade and Technology in Soviet-Western Relations*, p. 214.

28. Paul Marer and Joseph C. Miller, "U.S. Participation in Industrial Cooperation Agreements," *Journal of International Business Studies* (Fall–Winter 1977):21. A 1977 report by the Economic Commission for Europe indicates that the most frequent form of industrial cooperation before the establishment of joint ventures was coproduction, which accounted for 38.8 percent of the cases studied. The next most frequent form was the supply of plants and equipment (20.5 percent), followed by licensing with buy-back commitments (17.1 percent). Note by the Secretariat, Economic Commission for Europe, "Statistical Outline of Recent Trends in Industrial Cooperation," November 15, 1977, p. 2.

29. Department of Commerce, "Quantification of Western Exports," pp. 7–13.

30. Soviet technology imports from the West totaled $2.33 billion in 1980, down from $2.37 billion in 1979. By 1981 the dollar value of technology imports from the West had dropped to $1.736 billion. Ibid., p. 7.

31. See Michael Borrus, Laura D'Andrea Tyson, and John Zysman, "Creating Advantage: How Government Policies Shape High-Technology Trade," Berkeley Roundtable on the International Economy Working Paper no. 3, University of California, Berkeley, 1984.

32. On the concept of strategic industries, see Richard Nelson, *High-Technol-*

ogy Policies: A Five-National Comparison (Washington, D.C.: American Institute for Public Policy Research, 1984).

33. See Laura Tyson, "Creating Advantage: Strategic Policy for National Competitiveness," Berkeley Roundtable on the International Economy Working Paper no. 23, University of California, Berkeley, 1987; and Nathan Rosenberg, *Technology and the Black Box: Technology and Economics* (New York: Cambridge University Press, 1982).

34. See Office of Technology Assessment, *Technology and East-West Trade*, pp. 228–240.

35. See, for example, Steven Risefielde, "East-West Trade and Postwar Soviet Economic Growth—A Sectoral Production Function Approach: A Report Prepared for the Strategic Studies Center," June 1978; Stanislaw Gomulka and Alec Nove, "Contribution to Eastern Growth—An Econometric Evaluation," in OECD, ed., *East-West Technology Transfer*, Helgard Wienert and John Slater, *East-West Technology Transfer—The Trade and Economic Aspects* (Paris: OECD, 1986).

36. See Gomulka and Nove, "Contribution to Eastern Growth," pp. 13–14.

37. Between 1961 and 1965 Soviet industrial production grew at the rate of 8.6 percent per year. Between 1966 and 1970, with the first real opening of the Soviet economy to Western technology in the postwar period, the annual growth rate of Soviet industrial production dropped slightly to 8.4 percent. The rate of growth declined between 1971 and 1975 to 7.4 percent annually. During that period Western technology imports were at their peak. Between 1976 and 1980 the economic growth rate declined to 5.1 percent. Figures for the years 1961–1970 can be found in A. M. Fallenbuchl, "The Soviet Union and Eastern Europe: Development and Trade, 1971–75," Discussion Paper Series 13, 1973, University of Windsor. For the years 1971–80, see Ernst Kux, "Growing Tensions in Eastern Europe," *Problems of Communism* (March-April 1980):28. See also Hermann Clement, "CMEA Economic Performance in the 1970s: A Balance Sheet of Successes and Failures," NATO Economic Directorate, Brussels, 1982. Conservative estimates claim that the overall economy of the Soviet Union grew by an average of only 3 percent per year between 1976 and 1979, compared with an OECD average of 4 percent. Again, during the same period of expanding technology imports, Soviet economic growth lagged behind both the U.S. and West Germany. See "Spooky Figures on Russia," *The Economist* (January 8, 1983):63.

38. As Joseph Brada has pointed out, "A pervasive thread in the literature on technology transfer is that the international transfer of technology is a 'people' process. That is to say, among the most effective mechanisms for the international transfer of technology are cooperation and exchanges among scientists and engineers from different countries." See Joseph C. Brada, "Soviet-Western Trade and Technology Transfer: An Economic Overview," in Bruce Parrott, ed., *Trade, Technology and Soviet-American Relations* (Bloomington: Indiana University Press, 1985), p. 13. See also Gomulka and Nove, "Contribution to Eastern Growth: An Econometric Evaluation," pp. 12–13.

39. Donald W. Green and Herbert S. Levine, "Macroeconomic Evidence of

the Value of Machinery Imports to the Soviet Union," in John R. Thomas and Ursula M. Cruse-Vaucienne, eds., *Soviet Science and Technology: Domestic and Foreign Perspectives* (Washington, D.C.: George Washington University, 1977), pp. 394–425.

40. Important questions have been raised about the reliability of the Green-Levine estimates. Using the same data, but somewhat different methods, Martin L. Weitzman concluded that the influence of Western machinery had at best an uncertain effect on Soviet productivity, no matter what the level of imports might be. See Martin L. Weitzman, "Technology Transfer to the USSR: An Econometric Analysis," *Journal of Comparative Economics* 3(2) (June 1979):167–177. For a critique of these estimates, see Hanson, *Trade and Technology in Soviet-Western Relations*, pp. 146–153.

41. See, for example, Joseph Berliner, *The Innovation Decision in Soviet Industry* (Cambridge, Mass.: MIT Press, 1976), pp. 158–167; Central Intelligence Agency, *Soviet Chemical Equipment Purchases from the West: Impact on Production and Foreign Trade* (Washington, D.C.: CIA, 1978); and Hanson, *Trade and Technology in Soviet-Western Relations*, chap. 10.

42. Holliday, "Survey of Sectoral Case Studies," pp. 76–81.

43. On the comparison between Western- and Soviet-equipped chemical plants, see CIA, *Soviet Chemical Equipment Purchases*; Holliday, "Survey of Sectoral Case Studies"; and Ronald Amann, "The Chemical Industry: Its Level of Modernity and Technological Sophistication," in Ronald Amann, Julian Cooper, and R. W. Davies, eds., *The Technological Level of Soviet Industry* (New Haven: Yale University Press, 1977), p. 249. On the dismal growth rates of the Soviet chemical industry as a whole in the 1980s, see Richard Seltzer, "Soviet Chemical Industry: Output Falls as Economic Crisis Grows," *Chemical and Engineering News* 68(41) (October 8, 1990):4–5.

44. Hanson, *Trade and Technology in Soviet-Western Relations*, chap. 10.

45. It is, however, difficult to separate out the role of fertilizer shortfalls from other causes of declining productivity, including soil depletion and climatic change. In fact, without the chemical fertilizer produced with Western technology, the productivity decline might possibly have been even greater. Such an interpretation certainly cannot be ruled out.

46. Holliday, "Survey of Sectoral Case Studies," p. 32.

47. Even in the chemical industry, where most progress could be attributed to Western technology, its level remained well below that of the West. Every modern synthetic material in the Soviet Union was introduced into commercial production almost ten years after introduction in the West. Martin Cave estimated that in 1973 the best Soviet computer lagged ten years behind the best U.S. computer. Estimates of the gap in favor of the U.S. in the computer industry vary widely, yet many analysts agree that the Soviets lagged significantly behind in important computing technologies, even those that were no longer state-of-the-art. Despite the fact that the Soviets were credited with leading in software theory, they were behind in the development of large-scale scientific computers, large-capacity magnetic disk stores, microelectronics, ferrite-core

memory (replaced now by semiconductors), and all aspects of software development and use.

48. R. W. Davies, "The Technological Level of Soviet Industry: An Overview," in Amann, Cooper, and Davies, eds., *The Technological Level of Soviet Industry*, p. 66. A good survey of case studies at the microeconomic level of the technological level of Soviet industries can be found in Hanson, *Trade and Technology in Soviet-Western Relations*, p. 46, n. 27.

49. "Introduction," in Ronald Amann and Julian Cooper, eds., *Technical Progress and Soviet Economic Development* (Oxford: Blackwell, 1986), pp. 9–10.

50. A. Kondalev and L. Khomenko, *Pod Znamenem Leninizma* (20) (October 1989), reported in *Interflo* 9(6) (April 1990):18–19.

51. George Holliday's work has explored the "resource-demanding" effects of Western technology on the Soviet economy. See, for example, "The Role of Western Technology in the Soviet Economy," in U.S. Congress Joint Economic Committee, *Issues in East-West Commercial Relations* (Washington, D.C.: U.S. Government Printing Office, 1979). See also Georges Sokoloff, *The Economy of Detente* (Lemington Spa: Berg, 1987), p. 56.

52. Elisabeth Ann Goldstein, "The Impact of Technology Transfer on Production and Productivity in the USSR: The Case of the Ferrous Metals Industry," in Gordon B. Smith, ed., *The Politics of East-West Trade* (Boulder, Colo.: Westview, 1984), p. 86.

53. Franklyn Holzman and Richard Portes, "The Limits of Pressure," *Foreign Policy* 32 (Fall 1978):85. The labor-saving characteristic of imported machinery ran counter to both the ethic of socialism that no worker should suffer as a result of technological progress and the common practice of hoarding labor in Soviet plants. There is no institutional mechanism for transferring workers from one job to another within an industry, and even during slack periods managers tended to keep all of the workers available to provide reserves for periods when the workload increases. This was especially true when foreign machinery was being installed, because managers believed that it was more likely to break down than domestic machinery. They wanted to ensure that they could reach their production targets even if the equipment failed. See Goldstein, "The Impact of Technology Transfer," pp. 76–77.

54. Holliday, "The Role of Western Technology in the Soviet Economy," p. 47.

55. This argument contradicts Anthony Sutton's claim that the Soviets engaged in extensive duplication of Western machinery and equipment. See Sutton, *Western Technology and Soviet Economic Development*, chap. 19. Most of the evidence, however, points to the slow diffusion of technology—whether imported or domestic—in the Soviet economy, and Sutton's examples may indeed be exceptions.

56. The "second economy" encompassed a large range of economic activity not officially sanctioned in the socialist economic system. The most important work on this "second" economy has been done by Gregory Grossman. See, for example, his "The Second Economy in the USSR," *Problems of Communism* 26(5)

(September–October 1977):25–40; "Roots of Gorbachev's Problems: Private Income and Outlay in the late 1970s," in U.S. Congress Joint Economic Committee, *Gorbachev's Economic Plans*, pp. 213–229; and "Sub-Rosa Privatization and Marketization in the USSR," in *Annals of the American Academy of Political and Social Science* 507 (January 1990):44–52.

57. Indeed, the establishment of such a system was an important goal of Gorbachev's reforms. At the Twenty-Seventh Party Congress Gorbachev declared that "wholesale trade with means of production must be developed" and praised the creation of direct links between enterprises. Such reforms, however, threatened Gossnab, and by 1990 Gossnab itself had successfully averted reformist attempts. On the wholesale trade story, see Anders Aslund, *Gorbachev's Struggle for Economic Reform* (Ithaca: Cornell University Press, 1989), pp. 126–128, 144–145.

58. See "The Best of All Monopoly Profits," *The Economist* (August 11, 1990):67.

59. Ed A. Hewett, *Reforming the Soviet Economy* (Washington, D.C.: Brookings Institution, 1988), pp. 172–173.

60. Reported by Richard Parker, "Inside the 'Collapsing' Soviet Economy," *The Atlantic* (June 1990):70.

61. Reported in *ECOTASS* (April 9, 1990):20.

62. Anthony Robinson, "Modest Venture with Revolutionary Results: Foreign Enterprise Helps Bring Change for Soviet Women," *Financial Times* (October 5, 1990):4.

63. G. Alan Petzet, "Soviet Accounting Poses Problems," *Oil and Gas Journal* (April 16, 1990):34.

64. See Berliner, *The Innovation Decision in Soviet Industry*; Ronald Amann and Julian Cooper, eds., *Industrial Innovation in the Soviet Union* (New Haven: Yale University Press, 1982); Gomulka and Nove, "Contribution to Eastern Growth," pp. 35–37. For opposing arguments, see Hanson, *Trade and Technology in Soviet-Western Relations*, p. 215.

65. As the economy continued to decline, however, it became increasingly tempting to argue that these changes were merely cosmetic, initiated only to galvanize domestic political support for Gorbachev himself. Jerry Hough has argued that the key to Gorbachev's political success was his incremental approach to reform. Gradual reforms protect against political instability and are easier to implement. For example, the utility of increased Western imports may have been the provision of consumer goods needed to build political support for Gorbachev's internal economic reforms rather than in the provision of investment goods that would contribute to long-term economic prosperity, but squeeze consumption in the short run. See Jerry F. Hough, *Opening Up the Soviet Economy* (Washington, D.C.: Brookings Institution, 1988). Many former Soviet as well as Western economists argue that the success of real economic reform depends on a minimum cluster of simultaneous institutional changes, or economic "shock therapy," and that foreign technology will not flow into the former USSR until those institutional changes are complete. If old institutions are

not swept away, they will surely block reform and inhibit the growth-enhancing effects of foreign technology. For example, when small private enterprises in the "second economy" were legalized, entrepreneurs were required to obtain licenses from the apporpriate ministry. The granting of these licenses, however, was often delayed or were available only if the entrepreneur could bribe the ministry official. Furthermore, if a license could be obtained, the new legal enterprises had no access to credit or industrial suppliers. Because their costs were high and they had little competition, they charged exorbitant prices, creating further resistance to market innovations. There was thus a central tension between the introduction of new institutions that were necessary for reform but politically exploitative and the retention of old institutions that maintained stability but impeded reform. For excellent overviews and critiques of Gorbachev's economic reforms, see Aslund, *Gorbachev's Struggle for Economic Reform*, and Hewett, *Reforming the Soviet Economy*.

66. A persuasive argument about the withering away of the Soviet state is made by Michael Burawoy and Pavel Krotov, "The Soviet Transition from Socialism to Capitalism: Worker Control and Economic Bargaining in the Wood Industry," *American Sociological Review* 57 (February 1992):16–38.

67. Ibid., p. 34. This same pattern seems to be emerging throughout Eastern Europe as well as throughout the former Soviet Union. See David Stark, "Privatization in Hungary: From Plan to Market or from Plan to Clan?" *East European Politics and Societies* 4 (1990):351–392.

68. Christine Westbrook and Alan B. Sherr, "U.S.-Soviet Joint Ventures and Export Control Policy," Brief Paper no. 3, Brown University Center for Foreign Policy Development, Providence, Rhode Island, March 1990.

69. Michael Todaro, however, argues that, in general, large countries like India, China, and Brazil have a diversified resource base and a large internal demand due to their large populations. These factors enable these countries to exploit economies of scale without the need to penetrate export markets. Smaller countries like Taiwan, South Korea, and Singapore usually have a smaller internal demand and must therefore rely on external demand and foreign markets to stimulate their general economic growth. See Michael P. Todaro, *Economic Development in the Third World* (New York: Longman, 1989), p. 77.

70. Brada, "Soviet-Western Trade and Technology Transfer," p. 17.

71. John Zysman, "Contribution or Crisis: Japanese Foreign Direct Investment in the United States," in Kazo Yamamura, *Japanese Investment in the United States: Should We Be Concerned?* (Seattle: Society of Japanese Studies, 1989), p. 101.

72. Todd Hixon and Ranch Kimball, "How Foreign-Owned Businesses Can Contribute to U.S. Competitiveness," *Harvard Business Review* (January–February 1990):56–57.

73. See Kenneth Gooding, "West Wraps Up Soviet Aluminum Foil Deal," *Financial Times* (October 17, 1990):3.

74. Michael Lev, "Soviet Plant, U.S. Managers: How a Little Known Company Won the Biggest Soviet Computer Contract," *New York Times* (October 1, 1989):C1.

75. Reported in *ECOTASS: The Economic and Commercial Bulletin of the Soviet News Agency TASS* (Oxford: Pergamon Press, November 20, 1989), p. 14.

76. Quentin Peel and Mark Nicholson, "Mac Attack in Pushkin Square," *Financial Times* (January 31, 1990):14. Paul Surovell of *Interflo* estimated that of the more than 200 registered U.S.-Soviet joint ventures, only about 40–60 were actually operational. See *Interflo* 9(9) (July 1990):14. The *New York Times* reported in February 1991 that out of 2,000 joint ventures registered at that time, only 500 were actually operating. See Steven Greenhouse, "Soviet Ventures are Losing Appeal for U.S. Business," *New York Times* (February 4, 1991):C6.

77. "Potemkin's Ghost: Soviet Free Enterprise," *The Economist* (January 6, 1990):68.

78. This complaint was voiced in *Rabochaya Tribuna* (May 10, 1990) and reported in *Interflo* 9(9) (July 1990):15.

79. John Wyles, "West Slow to Join in Reforming Soviet Industry: Foreign Investment is Not Having an Impact on Manufacturing," *Financial Times* (January 11, 1990):3.

80. "Potemkin's Ghost," p. 68.

81. Luca Ciferri, "Fiat, Soviets Join Forces in $1 Billion Auto Venture," *Automotive News* (December 4, 1989):1; and John Wyles, "Moscow to Widen Links with Fiat by Building Panda Car," *Financial Times* (May 30, 1990):4.

82. I conducted interviews with officials from nine firms selling technology within Russia in August 1990, of which seven were large multinational corporations. The chief industries in which these firms engage are: telecommunications and electronics, medical instruments, computers, peripheral equipment and software, office business machines, precision instruments, agricultural machinery, and chemicals.

83. The Netherlands Foreign Trade Agency Deputy Director V. Maarse Nenas stated that "the term *joint venture* is sought after in the Soviet Union as a 'last straw.'" See "Trade Expert Comments on Lithuania's Economy," LD 1101142090 Vilnius TIESA (in Lithuanian), November 11, 1989, p. 5; in *FBIS SOV* (January 12, 1990):63.

84. U.S.-USSR Trade and Economic Council, Finance and Legal Committee, January 1990.

85. Business International, *Selling Knowledge and Technology to the Soviet Union and Eastern Europe* (Geneva: Business International, 1978).

86. Rose Brady and Rosemarie Boyle, "Combustion Engineering's Dislocated Joint Venture," *Business Week* (October 22, 1990):49–50.

87. "Hyundai Likely to Build Factory in USSR," *FBIS EAS* (December 19, 1989):17.

88. The sale of entire production systems was especially pronounced in the

automotive and chemical industries. See CIA, *Soviet Chemical Equipment Purchases*; and U.S. Central Intelligence Agency, National Foreign Assessment Center, *USSR: Role of Foreign Technology in the Development of the Motor Vehicle Industry* (Washington, D.C.: Central Intelligence Agency, 1979). These two studies suggest that productivity is enhanced by the import of entirely new systems of production in industries that have a high level of expertise among engineers rather than by implanting new pieces of equipment in an old production system—even in industries where the level of expertise is relatively high.

89. See Stephen Haggard and Chung-in Moon, "The South Korean State in the International Economy: Liberal, Dependent, or Mercantile?" in John G. Ruggie, ed., *The Antinomies of Interdependence* (New York: Columbia University Press, 1983), pp. 150–152.

90. See Thomas B. Gold, "Entrepreneurs, Multinationals, and the State," in Edwin A. Winckler and Susan Greenhalgh, eds., *Contending Approaches to the Political Economy of Taiwan* (New York: M. E. Sharpe, 1988), pp. 175–205.

91. See Burawoy and Krotov, "The Soviet Transition," p. 36.

92. Luke, "Technology and Soviet Foreign Trade," p. 336. Luke notes that in 1913 agricultural products comprised 73.8 percent of all exports. Russian factories produced only 2.2 percent of all mechanically powered units in world industry, agriculture, and transport. Russia produced 6 percent of world output of iron ore and 5.8 percent of world production in cast iron. The average annual output per industrial worker in Russia was the world's lowest.

4. Western Technology and Soviet Military Power

1. The resolution of this conflict in March 1992 is discussed in chapter 1.

2. For a review of these claims, see Gary K. Bertsch and John R. McIntyre, eds., *National Security and Technology Transfer* (Boulder, Colo.: Westview, 1983), p. 98.

3. See David Holloway, "Innovation in the Defense Sector: Battle Tanks and ICBMs," in Amann and Cooper, eds., *Industrial Innovation in the Soviet Union*, pp. 368–414.

4. CIA, *Soviet Acquisition of Western Technology: An Update* (Washington, D.C.: Central Intelligence Agency), p. 1.

5. The most important English-language source for this historical account is Julian Cooper, "Western Technology and the Soviet Defense Industry," in Parrott, ed., *Trade, Technology, and Soviet-American Relations*, pp. 169–202.

6. For a detailed discussion of the development of Soviet nuclear weaponry, see David Holloway, *The Soviet Union and the Arms Race* (New Haven: Yale University Press, 1983).

7. Cooper, "Western Technology and the Soviet Defense Industry," p. 185.

8. On this case, see CIA, *Soviet Acquisition of Western Technology*; Cooper, "Western Technology and the Soviet Defense Industry," pp. 183–184; and Gustafson, *Selling the Russians the Rope?*, p. 10.

9. U.S. Department of Defense, "The Technology Security Program," a report to the 99th Congress, pp. 5–6.

10. CIA, *Soviet Acquisition of Western Technology*, p. 1.

11. Ibid. The Soviet Military Industrial Commission (VPK), through both intelligence and legal channels, seeks one-of-a-kind military and dual-use hardware, blueprints, product samples, and test equipment to improve the technical levels and performance of Soviet weapons, military equipment, and defense manufacturing equipment. In the late 1970s alone, about $1.4 billion each year was used to purchase one-of-a-kind Western hardware and documents. See United States Central Intelligence Agency, *Soviet Acquisition of Western Technology: An Update* (Washington, D.C.: U.S. Government Printing Office, 1985), pp. 2–6.

12. Panel on the Impact of National Security Controls on International Technology Transfer, Committee on Science, Engineering and Public Policy, National Academy of Sciences, National Academy of Engineering, and Institute of Medicine, *Balancing the National Interest: U.S. National Security Export Controls and Global Economic Competition* (Washington, D.C.: National Academy Press, 1987), p. 41.

13. United States Department of Defense, *Soviet Military Power: An Assessment of the Threat, 1989* (Washington, D.C.: Department of Defense, 1989), p. 142.

14. See CIA, *Soviet Acquisition of Western Technology Update*, p. 1.

15. CIA, *Soviet Acquisition of Western Technology*, p. 4; and CIA, *Soviet Acquisition of Western Technology Update*, p. 7.

16. United States Department of Defense, *Soviet Military Power: 1987* (Washington, D.C.: U.S. Government Printing Office, 1987), pp. 111–118.

17. Department of Defense, *Soviet Military Power: 1988*, p. 140.

18. Ibid., pp. 143–149.

19. Department of Defense, *Critical Technologies Plan 1989*, p. 10.

20. U.S. Department of Defense, *Critical Technologies Plan for the Committee on Armed Services, U.S. Congress* (Washington, D.C.: U.S. Government Printing Office, March 15, 1990), p. A127.

21. Department of Defense, *Soviet Military Power 1988*, p. 149.

22. Statement by the Hon. Richard E. Delauer in U.S. House of Representatives, "The FY 1983 Department of Defense Program for Research, Development, and Acquisition," 97th Congres, 2d sess. (Washington, D.C.: U.S. Government Printing Office, 1982), pp. 11–22.

23. U.S. Department of Defense, *Soviet Military Power 1981* (Washington, D.C.: U.S. Government Printing Office, 1982), p. 75.

24. CIA, *Soviet Acquisition of Western Technology*, pp. 7–8; and CIA, *Soviet Acquisition of Western Technology Update*, p. 13.

25. Department of Defense, *Soviet Military Power 1987*, pp. 115–116.

26. Department of Defense, *Soviet Military Power 1988*, p. 146.

27. NAS, *Balancing the National Interest*, p. 49.

28. CIA, *Soviet Acquisition of Western Technology Update*, p. 29.

29. Ibid., p. 6.

30. Between 1960 and 1975 trade between Council for Mutual Economic Assistance (CMEA) and OECD countries showed a ninefold increase. The value of machinery imports (a measure of technology imports) from OECD to CMEA countries jumped from $1.0 billion in 1965 to $10.2 billion in 1977. During 1974 CMEA machinery imports from the West increased by 35 percent from 1973 levels, and in 1975 the increase was 55 percent. The 1970s also saw an explosion of industrial cooperation agreements. While virtually no agreements were signed in the 1960s, 600 had been signed by 1973, and 1,000 had been signed by 1975. The majority of these agreements had been signed with Western European firms and subsidiaries of U.S. firms located in Europe. See Zaleski and Wienart, *Technology Transfer Between East and West*, p. 66.

31. *The Military Critical Technology List* (Washington, D.C.: Department of Defense, Office of the Undersecretary of Defense, Defense Research and Engineering, October 1984). The approach makes a distinction between a military system and a weapons system. For example, radar is not usually considered a weapon, but it can be used in a military system. Also, a nonmilitary system could be improved or changed with high-technology components for use as a military system. Thus, an existing radar system for an airport may not be sophisticated enough to be used by the military, but could be upgraded. See Martin McGough, "Technology Assessment of Military Critical High Technology," unpublished ms., p. 4.

32. This view was expressed repeatedly in interviews with Western European officials and firms engaging in trade with the Soviet Union, May–June 1983. See also Susan Rasky, "What is Good for Security May be Bad for Business," *New York Times* (October 18, 1987):5.

33. For a comprehensive discussion of COCOM's problems in the 1970s, see Michael Mastanduno, "The Management of Alliance Export Control Policy: American Leadership and the Politics of COCOM," in Bertsch, ed., *Controlling East-West Trade*, pp. 257–266.

34. See, for example, Karatsu Hajime, "Dead Letters on the COCOM List," *Japan Echo* (November 1987):22.

35. U.S. Department of Defense, *The Technology Transfer Control Program: A Report to the 98th Congress* (Washington, D.C.: U.S. Department of Defense, 1984), pp. 11–14.

36. David Buchan, "Western Security and Economic Strategy Toward the East," *Adelphi Papers* no. 192 (London: International Institute for Strategic Studies, 1984), p. 24.

37. Richard Perle, "The Eastward Technology Flow: A Plan of Common Action," *Strategic Review* 12(2) (Spring 1984):23.

38. See Department of Defense Directive 5230.25, "Withholding of Unclassified Technical Data from Public Disclosure," November 6, 1984; Directive 5230.24, "Distribution Statements on Technical Documents," November 20, 1984; "New Regulations on Export of Computers, Software and Communica-

tions Switching" (*Federal Register*, December 31, 1984). All are reprinted in Department of Defense, *The Technology Security Program: A Report to the 99th Congress* (Washington, D.C.: U.S. Department of Defense, February 1985), appendix.

39. Department of Defense Directive 2040.2, "International Transfers of Technology, Goods, Services, and Munitions," January 17, 1984, Section D.

40. See Buchan, "Western Security and Economic Strategy"; Gary K. Bertsch, *East-West Trade, COCOM, and the Atlantic Alliance* (Paris: Atlantic Institute for International Affairs, 1983); Tom Donnelly, "Pentagon Seen Stemming High-Tech Flow to East," *Air Force Times* (July 22, 1985):1; Jonathan Kapstein and Boyd France, "The West's Crackdown on High-Tech Smuggling Starts to Pay Off," *Business Week* (July 29, 1985):46–48.

41. Office of the Undersecretary of Defense for Policy, *Assessing the Effect of Technology Transfer on U.S./Western Security: A Defense Perspective* (Washington, D.C.: U.S. Government Printing Office, 1985), pp. E1–E8.

42. U.S. Senate Committee on Banking, Housing, and Urban Affairs, *Hearings: Toshiba-Kongsberg Technology Diversion Case*, June 17–July 14, 1987, 100th Congress, 1st sess. (hereafter cited as *Toshiba-Kongsberg Hearings*), p. 31.

43. Damon Darlin, "Japanese Firms' Push to Sell to Soviets Led to Security Breaches," *Wall Street Journal* (August 4, 1987):15.

44. *Japan Company Handbook* (Tokyo: Toyo Keizai Shinposa, 1986), p. 600.

45. Propeller noise is caused by turbulence and by cavitation, a process of bubble formation in turbulent fluid flows. Regions of low pressure form in water near a rapidly spinning propeller. In the low-pressure regions, water and air expand to form bubbles, which pop. If the amount of cavitation is severe, passive sonar equipment listening on other ships, aircraft, or sonar buoys can hear the submarines many miles away, and at a much longer distance than they can hear the submarine's other noises. Large propellers are inherently quieter than small ones. To produce the equivalent thrust, a large propeller will turn more slowly than a small propeller. Cavitation and turbulence noise increase with the speed of the propeller blades; since a large propeller's blades move more slowly, it is quieter. See Steve Homer, "National Security and the Toshiba Case," unpublished ms., 1987.

46. See Karl Lautenschlaeger, "The Submarine in Naval Warfare, 1901–20001," in Steven E. Miller and Stephen van Evera, eds., *Naval Strategy and National Security* (Princeton: Princeton University Press, 1988), p. 243.

47. It had a maximum of forty officials engaged in full-time screening of 200,000 annual export applications. This was especially small when compared with the U.S. government's export control bureaucracy of 620 officials screening over 114,000 applications in 1986. See U.S. Department of Commerce, Bureau of Export Control, *Export Administration Annual Report*, FY 1986 (December 1987), p. 14.

48. The eight deception techniques were: 1) the submission of a formal but false contract to the trade and finance ministries and banks, and a secret contract with the Soviet customers; 2) the construction of false instrument panels to

conceal an embargoed item; 3) concealment of embargoed technology in hand-carried baggage not inspected by customs agents; 4) the concealment of embargoed items in diplomatic cargo; 5) the division of a plant into parts shipped separately as "spare parts"; 6) the choice of small customs houses where inspectors are less sophisticated; 7) the use of third countries as middlemen to reroute sensitive goods to Soviet buyers; and 8) indefinite loan of restricted items to Soviet laboratories. (MITI allows companies to ship banned items to the Soviet Union for public relations purposes.) The text of Kumagai's letter is printed in *Japan High Technology*, September 1987, pp. 3–4.

49. C. Itoh and Co., the contractor in the sale, was ordered to suspend machine-tool exports to the Communist bloc for the next three months. Itoh was given a lighter sentence than Toshiba because MITI said it didn't have enough evidence that the trading house intentionally violated export regulations.

50. Before this action, the companies had been able to ship a large variety of products under single permits called distribution licenses. Without such bulk license rights, they would have to obtain individual licenses for every product of strategic value that they import from the U.S. This would lead to additional paperwork that could hamper their competitiveness.

51. Actually, five different pieces were proposed in Congress after the Toshiba revelations. S. 1420, known as the Multilateral Export Control Sanctions Act of 1987, amends the Export Administration Act of 1979 and the Export Administration Amendments Act of 1985. The import ban against Toshiba products was contained in amendment no. 59, authored by Senator Garn of Utah. Exemptions would be allowed for goods essential to the national defense, for component or spare parts, and for goods under contract by May 1, 1987. The bill placed retroactive import restrictions on other firms whose past violations of export control agreements might come to light, and would apply to future violations as well. The Senate voted to incorporate the text of S. 1420 within the text of the omnibus trade bill.

52. *Japan Company Handbook*, p. 600.

53. In April President Reagan ordered the first trade sanctions against Japan since World War II—a 100 percent tariff against $300 million worth of Japanese exports containing computer chips—in retaliation for Japan's violation of a 1986 semiconductor agreement. The sanctions were lifted on November 4, 1987 after the Commerce Department determined that Japan was no longer dumping chips on the world market.

54. Statement of Representative Duncan Hunter in *Toshiba-Kongsberg Hearings*, July 14, 1987, pp. 5–11.

55. Quoted in *Aviation Week and Space Technology*, July 6, 1987, p. 2.

56. Andrew Pollack, "Toshiba Warns on Jobs in U.S.," *New York Times* (July 2, 1987):27.

57. There was debate over the extent of decline. Lt. P. Kevin Pette argued that "the U.S. submarine force no longer holds any significant acoustic advan-

tage over a growing number of frontline Soviet nuclear-powered attack sub-marines," while Thomas Stefanick argued that the Akula-class submarines were still ten times noisier than the newest U.S. Los Angeles-class attack submarines. See Lt. P. Kevin Pette, "Acoustic Showdown for the SSNs," *U.S. Naval Institute Proceedings* (July 1987):33; and Thomas Stefanick, *Strategic Antisubmarine Warfare and Naval Strategy* (Lexington: Lexington Books, 1987), p. 73.

58. Vice-Admiral Bruce DeMars, U.S. Deputy Chief of Naval Operations for Submarine Warfare, interview recorded in *U.S. Naval Institute Proceedings* (October 1987):48.

59. *Jane's Fighting Ships, 1985–1986* (New York: Jane's, 1985), p. 522.

60. See "Chronology of Events in the Toshiba/Kongsberg Propeller Milling Technology Diversion Case," in *Toshiba/Kongsberg Hearings*, July 14, 1987, p. 23; and Stephanie Hafner and Robert Carroll, "The Propeller Project: U.S. Submarine Superiority Takes a Dive," *Defense Electronics* (November 1987):115–125.

61. Statement of Representative Duncan Hunter in *Toshiba-Kongsberg Hearings*, July 14, 1987, pp. 5–11.

62. Quoted in Susan Chira, "Nakasone Asserts Toshiba Betrayed Japan with Sales," *New York Times* (July 15, 1987):1. See also Daniel Sneider, "Japan Disputes U.S. View of Damage Done by Toshiba Sale," *Christian Science Monitor* (July 20, 1987):7.

63. See "Toshiba vs. the U.S.: A Japanese View," *World Press Review* (August 1987):18; Yozo Hasegawa, "Exporters Fear Extra Controls Harming Trade with Eastern Bloc," *Japan Economic Journal* (August 8, 1987):1.

64. Personal communication, December 7, 1987. See also Hasegawa, "Exporters Fear Extra Controls," p. 1.

65. See White House Statement, September 18, 1987, "Strategic Technology Export Controls," *U.S. Department of State Bulletin* (November 1987):33.

66. George R. Packard, "The Coming U.S.-Japan Crisis," *Foreign Affairs* 66 (Winter 1987–88):353.

67. Eduardo Lachica, "Toshiba Sanctions Could Be Eased if Japan Produces Tough Export Control Law by September," *Wall Street Journal* (August 28, 1987):1.

68. An amendment to Japan's foreign exchange and foreign trade control law increased the maximum jail sentence for violators, increased the statute of limitations on violations from three years to five, and allowed MITI to extend a ban on exports from companies violating the law to three years from one. Furthermore, the law recognized even attempted violations as a crime. Previously, Tokyo authorities could not penalize exporters who falsified shipping documents unless the goods were actually shipped. In addition to the amendment, the government established committees to review potentially sensitive exports, expanded export control staff in MITI from none to eighty people, and initiated on-site inspections of high-technology manufacturers. Also, MITI accepted a U.S. offer of technical assistance to improve its own export-screening system. In Norway, police reported that they were reviewing more than 100 transactions by

Kongsberg to see if COCOM rules were violated. Customs inspections would be tightened and the statute of limitations would be extended to ten years from two.

69. Tim Carrington, "Japan to Take Part in SDI: Toshiba Barred for a While," *Wall Street Journal* (July 22, 1987):5.

70. Eduardo Lachica, "U.S. and Japan Near Signing of SDI Pact," *Wall Street Journal* (July 7, 1987):23.

71. See Mayo Issobe, "Defense Agency Picks F-16 as Model for Japan's FSX," *Japan Times Weekly* (November 7, 1987);2; and Packard, "The Coming U.S.-Japan Crisis," pp. 356–357.

72. In addition to stiffer export controls, the U.S. wanted the allies to lift laws that block the extradition of persons charged with export violations. See Eduardo Lachic, "U.S. Asks Allies to Curb Exports to Soviet Union," *Wall Street Journal* (June 22, 1987):22.

73. Steven Greenhouse, "French Linked to Soviet Sale," *New York Times* (October 17, 1987):29.

74. Susan F. Rasky, "U.S. to Seek Tighter Controls," *New York Times* (October 17, 1987):29.

75. Susan Fenton, "Europe Respects, Doesn't Share Anger in U.S. Toward Toshiba," *Japan Economic Journal* (July 25, 1987):3.

76. See Francis Clines, "Russia to Fight Private Sell-Offs by Ex-Officials," *New York Times* (February 29, 1992):4.

77. See Eric Schmitt, "U.S. Worries about Spread of Arms from Soviet Sales," *New York Times* (November 16, 1991):5.

78. The European Community and Russia also promised to assist in financing. See Thomas Friedman, "Baker and Yeltsin Agree on U.S. Aid in Scrapping Arms," *New York Times* (February 18, 1992):1.

79. Opponents claimed that the acquisition of Moscow's best technology could save Washington and American industry many billions of dollars in development costs, ease Russia's economic woes, discourage the spread of Russian scientists to the Third World, and help the U.S. compete with foreign rivals. See William Broad, "U.S. Moves to Bar Americans Buying Soviet Technology," *New York Times* (March 1, 1992):1. In response to both of these moves, a panel of 120 scientists and engineers from the National Academy of Sciences recommended that the U.S. provide $150 million to support Russia's scientific elite. The panel also called on the U.S. to open its markets to ex-Soviet high technology in order to create more revenue in the former Soviet Union and discourage the exodus of Russian scientists. See William Broad, "Panel Calls for Wider Help for Ex-Soviet Arms Experts," *New York Times* (March 14, 1992):3.

80. On the Imhausen-Chemie sale to Libya, see Steven Engelberg with Michael Gordon, "Germans Accused of Helping Libya Build Nerve Gas Plant," *New York Times* (January 1, 1989):1; Gary Milhollin, "Bonn's Proliferation Policy," *New York Times* (January 4, 1989):21; Elaine Sciolino, "U.S. Criticizes Bonn on Response to Charges on Chemical Company," *New York Times* (January 6, 1989):11; Serge Schmemann, "Bonn Clears Company of Libyan Role," *New York*

Times (January 6, 1989):11; Serge Schmemann, "Bonn Asks U.S. for Evidence of Libya Connection," *New York Times* (January 7, 1989):4; Serge Schmemann, "Bonn Will Tighten Curb on Exports of Deadly Goods," *New York Times* (January 11, 1989):1; Serge Schmemann, "Belgian Charged in Illicit Shipment for Libyan Plant," *New York Times* (January 13, 1989):1; Serge Schmemann, "Bonn Says It Knew of a German Role in a Libyan Plant," *New York Times* (January 14, 1989):1; Serge Schmemann, "Angst and Anger in Bonn," *New York Times* (January 16, 1989):1; Serge Schmemann, "Bonn Discloses 9 Years of Warnings on Libyan Gas," *New York Times* (February 16, 1989):3.

5. Resource Dependence and Natural Gas Trade Between the Former Soviet Union and Europe

1. This account is taken from Crawford and Lenway, "Decision Modes and International Regime Change," pp. 395–399. See also Jentleson, *Pipeline Politics*.

2. "Proposed Trans-Siberian Natural Gas Pipeline," *Hearing before the Committee on Banking, Housing, and Urban Affairs, United States Senate, November 12, 1981* (Washington, D.C.: U.S. Government Printing Office, 1982), p. 116 (hereafter cited as "Hearings").

3. "New Directions in U.S. Trade Policy," speech before the International Trade Committee, National Association of Manufacturers, San Francisco, January 13, 1982, pp. 9, 11.

4. "Hearings," p. 116.

5. Ibid., p. 5.

6. Ibid., p. 164.

7. From *Pipeline and Gas Journal* (April 1990):27.

8. Daniel Yergin, "Crisis and Adjustment: An Overview," in Daniel Yergin and Martin Hillenbrand, eds., *Global Insecurity* (New York: Penguin, 1983), p. 25.

9. Figures calculated from Robert Stobaugh, "World Energy to the Year 2000," in Yergin and Hillenbrand, eds., *Global Insecurity*, pp. 52–53.

10. Vienna Institute for Comparative Economic Studies, *COMECON Data 1989* (Westport, Conn.: Greenwood Press, 1990), p. 402.

11. *Current International Gas Trades and Prices*, Energy Series paper (Washington, D.C.: IBRD, 1988), p. 5.

12. "Statistical Aspects of the Natural Gas Economy in 1989," in *Rapid Reports: Energy and Industry*, Statistical Office of the European Community, 1990, p. 2.

13. The estimate for 1983 is from the *Financial Times Energy Economist* 17 (March 1983):7. The estimates for 1990 are taken from General Accounting Office, "European Alternatives to Importing Soviet Natural Gas," a report to Senator Lloyd M. Bentsen (Washington, D.C.: GAO, May 16, 1983), appendix II, p. 20. See also European Community, *The European Community and the Energy Problem* (Luxembourg: European Community, 1983), p. 42.

14. "Statistical Aspects 1989," p. 2.

15. Statistics for the former DDR are calculated from the Vienna Institute,

COMECON Data 1989, Table V/2.3, p. 400. Statistics for West Germany are calculated from the Statistical Office of the European Community, *Energy Monthly Statistics* (October 1990):65.

16. These percentages are calculated from the Vienna Institute, *COMECON Data 1989*, Table V/2.7, p. 402.

17. These accounts are taken from Jonathan Stern, *Soviet Oil and Gas Exports to the West: Commercial Transaction or Security Threat?* (Brookfield, Vt.: Gower, 1986), pp. 48–60.

18. Office of Technology Assessment, *Technology and Soviet Energy Availability* (Washington, D.C.: Office of Technology Assessment, 1983), p. 75.

19. Stern, *Soviet Oil and Gas Exports to the West*, p. 32.

20. United States Central Intelligence Agency, *Soviet Energy Data Resource Handbook: A Reference Aid* (Washington, D.C.: Central Intelligence Agency, Directorate of Intelligence Documents Expediting [DOCEX] Project, May 1990), p. 25.

21. See Peter Odell, "The West European Gas Market," *Energy Policy* (October 1988):485–486.

22. Since 1983, however, much of Algeria's export increase to Western Europe can be accounted for by transport through the forty-eight-inch Trans-Mediterranean Pipeline. Nevertheless, price disputes hindered Algerian sales to its Western European customers in the latter half of the 1980s. See IBRD, *Current International Gas Trades and Prices, 1988*, p. 5.

23. General Accounting Office, *European Alternatives to Importing Soviet Natural Gas* (Washington, D.C.: U.S. Government Printing Office, 1983), pp. 8–11. For a more detailed examination of problems faced by Norway and the Netherlands as alternative suppliers, see Robert S. Price, Jr., "The Gas Market in Western Europe into the Twenty-First Century," paper presented to the Hydrocarbons '83 International Conference, Great Yarmouth, England, March 1, 1983, pp. 20–24.

24. Odell, "The West European Gas Market," p. 486.

25. IBRD, *Current International Gas Trades and Prices, 1988*, p. 5.

26. Ed A. Hewett, *Energy, Economics, and Foreign Policy in the Soviet Union* (Washington, D.C.: Brookings Institution, 1984), p. 217, n. 30.

27. Ibid., p. 158.

28. Henry S. Rowen and Vladimir G. Treml, "As Oil Prices Fall, Moscow's Woes Rise," *Wall Street Journal* (March 6, 1985):22.

29. "Hearings," p. 111.

30. Bundesverband der deutschen Gas und Wasserwirtschaft, *Gasstatistik 82* (Frankfurt am Main: ZfGW Verlag, 1983), p. 11. Cited in Stefanie Lenway and Eric Paul Thompson, "Trading with the Adversary: Managed Interdependence in East-West Energy Trade," paper presented at the annual convention of the American Political Science Association, Washington, D.C., August 30–September 2, 1984, p. 11.

31. The region votes overwhelmingly Christian Socialist Union (CSU), the most conservative, anti-Soviet political party in West Germany. In 1983, for

example, the CSU received 60 percent of the Bavarian vote. See *Das Parliament,* no. 10 (Bonn: Bundeszentrale für Politische Bildung, March 12, 1983), p. 3. On the anti-Soviet politics of the CSU, see Kendall L. Baker, Russell J. Daltan, and Kai Hildebrandt, *Germany Transformed* (Cambridge, Mass.: Harvard University Press, 1981), pp. 124–128.

32. Consumers in general constitute a large, "latent" interest group that have great difficulty organizing as a political pressure group because the benefits are diffuse but the costs would fall disproportionately on a few. They are conspicuously absent in the political process. See Manchur Olson, *The Logic of Collective Action: Public Goods and the Theory of Groups* (Cambridge, Mass.: Harvard University Press, 1975), especially p. 50. For a good survey of the literature that supports this argument with empirical case studies, see Stefanie Ann Lenway, *The Politics of U.S. International Trade: Protection, Expansion, and Escape* (Boston: Pitman, 1985), chap. 2. See also Andrew Schonfield, *Modern Capitalism* (New York: Oxford University Press, 1965), pp. 239–264. Presently, no German political party program, even that of the Green party, deals with consumer issues.

33. *Gasstatistik 82*, p. 11.

34. Stern, *Soviet Oil and Gas Export to the West,* p. 32.

35. Hewett, *Energy, Economics, and Foreign Policy,* p. 177.

36. See Philip Hanson, "Soviet Foreign Trade and Europe in the Late 1980s," *World Today* 24(8–9) (August/September 1986):144.

37. Philip Hanson, *Soviet Foreign Trade Policies in the 1980s* (Cologne: Bundesinstitüt für Ostwissenschaftliche und Internationale Studien, 1986), p. 49.

38. Ed A. Hewett, "Near-Term Prospects for the Soviet Natural Gas Industry and the Implications for East-West Trade," in U.S. Congress Joint Economic Committee, *Soviet Economy in the 1980s,* p. 6.

39. Wilfried Czerniejewicz, "The Soviet Natural Gas Project in Western Europe," paper presented at the Energy Conference, Harvard University, Cambridge, Mass., November 8, 1982.

40. Jonathan Stern, "Spectors and Pipe Dreams," *Foreign Policy* 48 (Fall 1982):21–36.

41. Hewett, *Energy, Economics, and Foreign Policy,* p. 193. In 1992 all of the states of the former Soviet Union became net oil importers except Russia, and Russian production fell dramatically, causing Russia to curtail its exports to other former Soviet republics with the warning that exports would only be delivered to those that could pay hard currency. See Werner Gumpel, "GUS-Erdoelwirtschaft droht der Kollaps," *Süddeutsche Zeitung* (March 26, 1992):34.

42. OTA, *Technology and Soviet Energy Availability,* pp. 356–358.

43. Jonathan Stern, *Soviet Natural Gas Development to 1990* (Washington, D.C.: Heath, 1980), p. 99; and Hewett, *Energy, Economics, and Foreign Policy,* p. 158.

44. Ibid., p. 217.

45. Angela E. Stent, *Soviet Energy and Western Europe* (New York: Praeger, 1982), p. 32.

46. *Gasstastik 82*, p. 38, cited in Lenway and Thompson, "Trading with the Adversary," p. 12, and Stent, *Soviet Energy and Western Europe,* pp. 93–94.

47. Stent, *Soviet Energy and Western Europe*, p. 93.

48. Czerniejewicz, "The Soviet Natural Gas Project," p. 6.

49. Gas imported from the former Soviet Union, however, has a higher heating capacity than gas produced in Europe. This means that domestic customers in the former Soviet Union have appliances that are adjusted for burning higher-BTU gas. This requires special installation, which in turn requires lead time for preparations. See Lenway and Thompson, "Trading with the Adversary," pp. 22–23.

50. Stent, *Soviet Energy and Western Europe*, p. 32.

51. Lenway and Thompson, "Trading with the Adversary," p. 16.

52. GAO, "European Alternatives," p. 20.

6. Financial Instability and Debtor Leverage in East-West Economic Relations

1. "Hearings" p. 117.

2. For a detailed account of U.S. policy toward financing trade with the Soviet Union since 1917, see Beverly Crawford, "How Regimes Matter: Western Control of East-West Trade Finance," *Millennium: Journal of International Studies* 16(3) (Winter 1987):431–452.

3. Herbert Hoover, letter to Senator Joseph I. France, February 10, 1923; letter to C. V. Hibbad, March 23, 1923; and statement at press conference, April 13, 1926. Box 11, Herbert Hoover Collection, Archives of the Hoover Institution.

4. In 1977 CMEA commercial debt stood at $40.2 billion and LDC commercial debt was $127.7 billion. By 1982 CMEA commercial debt was almost $64 billion; at the end of the year, however, it had been reduced to $63 billion. LDC commercial debt, on the other hand, had grown to $362.7 billion. See Richard S. Dale and Richard P. Mattione, *Managing Global Debt* (Washington, D.C.: Brookings Institution, 1983), p. 11.

5. See David D. Driscoll, "Sovereign Debt: The Polish Example," (Washington D.C.: Congressional Research Service, January 1982), p. 9.

6. Thomas A. Wolf, "East-West Trade Credit Policy: A Comparative Analysis," in Paul Marer, ed., *U.S. Financing of East-West Trade* (Bloomington, Ind.: International Development Research Center, 1975), p. 171.

7. The Soviet Union began the 1970s with a clear preference for official credit. In 1970 77 percent of the gross debt was covered by official credit guarantees. Beginning in 1975, however, the Soviets began to borrow on the Eurocurrency markets to finance escalating imports. By 1980, government credits covered only 43 percent of the debt. Other CMEA countries followed suit. Although they relied less heavily on official credit in the early 1970s, 41 percent of both Bulgaria's and Czechoslovakia's debt was owed to Western governments; by 1980 official credits represented only 6 percent of the Bulgarian debt and 12 percent of the Czech debt. Hungary, too, demonstrated a preference for borrowing on commercial markets. It began the decade of the 1970s with only 10

percent of its debt owed to Western governments, and half of the rest was owed to the IMF. By 1980 official credits, both bilateral and multilateral, accounted for only 30 percent of the total gross debt. These percentages were claculated from figures in *Prospects*, pp. 41, 94, 154, 173, 227, 264, and 308.

8. Nicholas Cumming-Bruce, "Jan Woloszyn's Struggle for Poland," *Euromoney* (October 1980):100–102, cited in J. Andrew Spindler, *The Politics of International Credit* (Washington, D.C.: Brookings Institution, 1984), p. 86.

9. Poland asked 500 creditor banks to delay the repayment of $2.4 billion in principal, which was to come due in 1981, until December 1985. The banks agreed, the condition for agreement being that Poland pay 5 percent of the principal during 1982 and that it pay the $500 million in interest accrued between March and December 1981 by the end of that year. The interest rate on the rescheduled principal was high: 1.75 percentage points over the LIBOR, which was 15 1/16 percent. See David D. Driscoll, "East European Hard Currency Debt to the West" (Washington, D.C.: Congressional Research Service, 1982), p. 5.

10. Benjamin J. Cohen, "International Debt and Linkage Strategies: Some Foreign-Policy Implications for the United States," *International Organization* 39(4) (Autumn 1985):707–708.

11. Personal communications, Department of State officials, Washington, D.C., May 11–12, 1985. See also John Hardt and Donna L. Gold, "Soviet Gas Pipeline: U.S. Options," (Washington, D.C.: Congressional Research Service, 1983), p. 4, and *New York Times* (February 6, 1982):38.

12. Driscoll, "Sovereign Debt: The Polish Example," p. 7.

13. Cohen, "International Debt and Linkage Strategies," p. 707.

14. Personal communications, U.S. Treasury and State Departments, May 11–12, 1985. See also Karen Lissakers, "Dateline Wall Street: Faustian Finance," *Foreign Policy* 51 (1983):27. Cohen contends that the Reagan administration backed down primarily because of domestic constraints and arguments made by domestic forces. He cites fears of financial disruption, political disruption in the alliance, and fear of losing an instrument of leverage over Poland. See Cohen, "International Debt and Linkage Strategies," pp. 711–712.

15. W. Allen Wallis, Undersecretary of State for Economic Affairs, "East-West Economic Issues, Sanctions Policy, and the Formulation of International Economic Policy," *Hearings before the House Committee on Foreign Affairs*, March 29, 1984 (Washington, D.C.: U.S. Government Printing Office, 1984), pp. 5–6, 17.

16. Personal communications with U.S. and European Community "Consensus" officials at the European Commission in Brussels, June 14–15, 1983.

17. Driscoll, "East European Hard-Currency Debt," pp. 7–8. Only one bank, the Bank of Boston International in New York, accepted payment from the CCC, for $154,000.

18. See Driscoll, "Sovereign Debt," pp. 18–28.

19. See Peter Truell, "Poland and Banks Near Agreement on Rescheduling," *Wall Street Journal* (April 26, 1984):33.

20. Padriac Fallon and David Sharreff, "The Betrayal of Eastern Europe," *Euromoney* (September 1982):19–27.

21. During the thick of the Polish crisis, the DDR negotiated special credits with West German banks guaranteed by the government of the West Germany. This was reportedly in exchange for a more liberal emigration policy. And in 1984, the DDR arranged for $500 million of new credit with U.S. and Japanese banks with no political strings attached and on excellent terms for the DDR: 7/8 percentage points over the LIBOR, to be repaid in seven years with a three-year grace period. See Frederick Kempe, "East Germans Benefit from U.S. Bank Credits that Don't Call for Human Rights Concessions," *Wall Street Journal* (March 19, 1985):36.

22. See also Lawrence J. Brainard, "Overview of East Europe's Debt: The Evolution of Creditworthiness in the 1980s," *Business Economics* (October 1990):10–16.

23. See Daniel Chirot, "What Happened in Eastern Europe in 1989?" in Daniel Chirot, ed., *The Crisis of Leninism and the Decline of the Left: The Revolutions of 1989* (Seattle: University of Washington Press, 1990), pp. 3–32.

24. See Elie Abel, *The Shattered Bloc* (Boston: Houghton-Mifflin, 1990), p. 152.

25. See Deutsche Bank Economics Department, *Rebuilding Eastern Europe* (Frankfurt: Deutsche Bank, 1991), pp.40–44.

26. OECD, "The International Financial Situation of the Central and Eastern European Countries," in *Financial Market Trends*, no. 48 (Paris: OECD, 1991), p. 19.

27. "Debt Relief for Poland," *Financial Times* (February 8, 1991):14.

28. Ibid.

29. Andrew Fisher, "Banker Tells of Fears over Soviet Debt," *Financial Times* (April 25, 1991).

30. OECD, "The International Financial Situation of the Central and Eastern European Countries," in *Financial Market Trends*, vol. 48 (Paris: OECD, February 1991).

31. A Western embassy economist stated at the time that "it is the culmination of Serbian attempts to undermine the federal government and keep alive a dying economy by pumping unearned new money into it to pay off loss-making enterprises, pensions, and farmer subsidies." "Yugoslav Government Dismay at Secret Loan," *Financial Times* (January 9, 1991):5.

32. See, for example, Stephen Fidler, "Banks Lend Less to Eastern Bloc," *Financial Times* (January 8, 1991):3.

33. Throughout the Cold War period, the Soviet Union was rated by U.S. investors as an "A" credit risk—it was subsequently downgraded to a low double "B," similar to Mexico and Venezuela. See Anthony Robinson, "Rescheduling of Bank Debt Likely," *Financial Times* (May 30, 1991):2.

34. OECD, "The International Financial Situation."

35. "Polish GDP Falls 12 Percent," *Financial Times* (January 30, 1991):7.

36. Peter Riddell, "Row in G7 over Scale of Polish Debt Write-off," *Financial Times* (February 4, 1991):20.

37. Peter Riddell, "U.S. Believes Deal Near on Polish Debt Cuts," *Financial Times* (March 6, 1991):4.

38. David Goodhart, "Polish Debt Write-off May Benefit Bonn Finances," *Financial Times* (March 19, 1991):2.

39. Until the Polish deal, the Paris Club had given debtor countries a maximum of 33 percent writeoff.

40. Stephen Fidler, "Poland Secures Deal to Cancel Half Its Debt," *Financial Times* (March 16, 1991):2.

41. Stefan Wagetyl, "Japan Halts $500 M Loan to Poland," *Financial Times* (April 16, 1991):2.

42. "Banks Will Lose Money if Sofia is Pressed on Debt," *Financial Times* (April 15, 1991):2.

7. Interdependence, Vulnerability, and the Consolidation of Market Control

1. This lack of attention can be explained by the fact that much of the security debate was focused on the Cold War, and interdependence among adversaries was low. There were, however, a few pioneering studies that make this connection. See, of course, Hirschman, *National Power*, pp. 4–5. See also Knorr, *Power and Wealth*; and Knorr and Trager, eds., *Economic Issues and National Security*. At the Cold War's end, more scholars have turned their attention to this connection in terms of the relations among allies and between industrialized capitalist countries and the Third World. See, for example, Theodore Moran, "The Globalization of America's Defense Industries," *International Security* 15(1) (Summer 1990):57–99; Theodore Moran, "International Economics and National Security," *Foreign Affairs* 69(5) (Winter 1990–91):74–90; Michael Borrus, Wayne Sandholtz, Jay Stowsky, Steven Vogel, and John Zysman, *The Highest Stakes: Technology, Economy and Security Policy* (New York: Oxford University Press, 1992); and Ethan Kapstein and Raymond Vernon, eds., "Searching for Security in a Global Economy," *Daedalus* 120(4) (Fall 1991).

2. See Stephen M. Walt, "The Renaissance of Security Studies," *International Studies Quarterly* 35(2) (June 1991):211–239; and Joseph S. Nye and Sean Lynn-Jones, "International Security Studies: A Report of a Conference on the State of the Field," *International Security* 12(4):5–27.

3. "Global Transactions and the Consolidation of Sovereignty," in Ernst-Otto Czempiel and James N. Rosenau, eds., *Global Changes and Theoretical Challenges* (New York: Lexington, 1989).

4. Barry Buzan, *People, States, and Fear*, 2d ed. (Boulder, Colo.: Lynne Reiner, 1991), pp. 124–131.

5. Raymond Vernon and Ethan Kapstein, "National Needs, Global Resources," *Daedalus* 120(4) (Fall 1991):4.

6. Moran, "The Globalization of America's Defense Industries," p. 82.

7. Michael Borrus and John Zysman, "The Highest Stakes: Industrial Competitiveness and National Security," in Borrus et al. *The Highest Stakes.*

8. Keohane and Nye, *Power and Interdependence,* p. 11.

9. "Global Transactions and the Consolidation of Sovereignty," in Robert J. Art and Robert Jervis, eds., *International Politics* (New York: HarperCollins, 1992), pp. 310–330.

10. See Robert Kupperman and Tamara Kupperman, "The Politics of Pan Am 103," *New York Times* (November 16, 1991):15.

11. See Robert E. Sullivan and Nancy E. Bader, "The Application of Export Control Laws to Scientific Research at Universities," *Journal of College and University Law* 9(4) (1982–83):451–467; "Science and the Citizen," editorial, *Scientific American* (July 1984):66; and Gary Putka, "U.S. Blocks Access of Foreign Scientists to High Technology," *Wall Street Journal* (January 25, 1985):1; National Academy of Sciences, *Scientific Communication and National Security* (Washington, D.C.: National Academy of Sciences Press, September 1982).

12. See also Michael Mastanduno's argument at the conclusion of his essay, "The United States Defiant: Export Controls in the Postwar Era," *Daedalus* 120(4) (Fall 1991):91–110.

13. Kenneth N. Waltz, "The Stability of a Bipolar World," *Daedalus* 93(3) (Summer 1964).

14. See, for example, John Prados, *The Soviet Estimate* (New York: Dial, 1982).

15. "Reagan and the Americans: American Policy Toward the Soviet Union" in Oye, Lieber, and Rothchild, eds., *Eagle Resurgent?.* See also Fred Halliday, *The Making of the Second Cold War* (London: Verso, 1983), pp. 105–133; and Coral Bell, *The Reagan Paradox* (Worcester, England: Billing and Sons, 1989).

16. See Halliday, *The Making of the Second Cold War,* pp. 46–80.

17. Stephen van Evera, "The Cult of the Offensive and the Origins of the First World War," *International Security* 9(1) (Summer 1984).

18. Stephen van Evera and Barry R. Posen, "Defense Policy and the Reagan Administration: Departure from Containment," *International Security* 8(1) (Summer 1983).

19. The term *essentialist* comes from Lapidus and Dallin, "Reagan and the Americans." See also Strobe Talbott, *The Masters of the Game* (New York: Knopf, 1988), *Deadly Gambit: The Reagan Administration and the Stalemate in Nuclear Arms Control* (New York: Knopf, 1984) and *The Russians and Reagan* (New York: Vintage, 1984). More extreme views in this school of thought related specifically to the Reagan administration can be found in F. H. Knelman, *Reagan, God, and the Bomb: From Myth to Policy in the Nuclear Arms Race* (Buffalo, N.Y.: Prometheus Press, 1985); Robert Scheer, *With Enough Shovels* (New York: Random House, 1982); Michael Rogin, *Ronald Reagan: The Movie* (Berkeley: University of California Press, 1987).

20. See Jerry Sanders, *The Peddlers of Crisis: The Committee on the Present Danger and the Politics of Containment* (Boston: South End Press, 1983); and Garry Wills, *Reagan's America: Innocents at Home* (Garden City, N.Y.: Doubleday, 1987).

21. Prados, *The Soviet Estimate.*

22. Stephen van Evera, "Why States Believe Foolish Ideas: Non-Self-Evaluation by Government and Society," unpublished manuscript, 1988.

23. See Robert Jervis, *Perception and Misperception in International Politics* (Princeton: Princeton University Press, 1976).

24. See *FBIS* SOV 90–229 November 28, 1990, pp. 33–34 for the text of Maslyukov's report to the USSR Supreme Soviet on the state plan for 1991, from "Maslyukov, Pavlov report to Deputies," *Izvestiya* (November 26, 1990).

25. Text of this speech, which appeared in *Izvestiya* (March 25, 1990), is translated in *FBIS* SOV 90–060, March 28, 1990, p. 3.

26. See Eric Schmitt, "U.S. Worries about Spread of Arms from Soviet Sales," *New York Times* (November 16, 1991):5.

27. Matthew L. Wald, "Russians Ban Some Oil Exports," *New York Times* (November 16, 1991):17.

28. See, for example, Graham Allison and Grigory Yavlinsky, "Window of Opportunity: Joint Program for Western Cooperation in the Soviet Transformation to Democracy and the Market Economy," Harvard University, John F. Kennedy School of Government, Strengthening Democratic Institutions Project, June 1991.

29. This argument is made by Mitchel B. Wallerstein, "Controlling Dual-Use Technologies in the New World Order," *Issues in Science and Technology* (Summer 1991):70–77.

30. In March 1992, the U.S. began to purchase space equipment from the Russians, including a nuclear reactor, hull thrusters, which provide a means for using electric current to propel objects in space, and plutonium. See James Gerstenzang, "U.S. Purchases Space Equipment from Russians, *Los Angeles Times* (March 28, 1992):1. This policy reversed an earlier policy that had banned the purchase of such equipment in the United States. See William Broad, "U.S. Moves to Bar Americans Buying Soviet Technology." *New York Times* (March 1, 1992).

31. "Curb Deadly High-Tech Trade," *New York Times* (April 12, 1991):A28.

32. "Three More Ex-Soviet Warheads Missing," *San Francisco Examiner* (March 29, 1992):A4.

33. National Academy of Sciences, National Academy of Engineering, and Institute of Medicine, *Finding Common Ground: U.S. Export Controls in a Changed Global Environment* (Washington, D.C.: National Academy Press, 1991).

34. For assessments of these vulnerability claims see, for example, Kenneth Waltz, "Another Gap?" in Robert E. Osgood, *Containment, Soviet Behavior, and Grand Strategy* (Berkeley: Institute of International Studies, 1981), pp. 74–86; and Barry Posen "The Defense Resource Riddle," in Beverly Crawford and Peter W. Schulze, eds., *The New Europe Asserts Itself* (Berkeley: International and Area Studies, 1990), pp. 33–44.

Index